D1592141

Andrew Peterson and the Scandia Story

Andrew Peterson and the Scandia Story

A historical account about a Minnesota pioneer whose diaries have been "reborn as a piece of world literature" through Vilhelm Moberg and his writings

By Josephine Mihelich

Copublished by the author and
Ford Johnson Graphics
Minneapolis, MN., 1984

This edition is a first issue limited to
1000 copies. Each book has been individually
numbered and initialed by the author.

No. 767 JM

Library of Congress Catalog Card Number: 84-080917
ISBN: 0-917907-00-0

To the citizens of Minnesota

CONTENTS

FOREWORD

Andrew Peterson was an extraordinary person, and yet he never lost the humanity that often marks people of national or even statewide fame and unites them with their contemporaries. The consistency with which he kept his diary for more than forty-four years is not the mark of an ordinary person. In the everyday affairs of that pioneer community of Scandia, he was a respected leader who never lost the common touch.

Steeped in the work ethic, comforted and guided by his religion, and irresistibly moved to contribute to his community, he exemplified the best in the pioneer spirit of his day. In his pioneer work of establishing apple orchards in Minnesota is revealed many of the qualities that marked this man. Persistently and patiently he sought out, tested, and evaluated apple varieties for cold hardiness and fruit quality. He acquired plant breeding skills, developed new varieties, and actively promoted and disseminated plants to others. He accepted well-deserved accolades with humility and was quick to give others their share of the credit. The apple industry in Minnesota is in part a legacy of Peterson's early efforts.

The message in this accounting of Peterson's life, aside from the historical aspects, is that in quiet ways common men and women do make significant contributions to help build a better society. I commend the author for undertaking this task and for revealing the life of a man whose contributions are woven into the fabric of Minnesota history.

Francis de Vos
Director, Minnesota Landscape Arboretum
December 30, 1983

PREFACE

In many communities throughout the United States, citizens prepared for the nation's bicentennial in 1976 by sifting through records and papers for information about their past. History buffs compiled and printed pamphlets and books and promoted exhibits, tours, and other memorable events. Carver County was no exception. As local historians delved into stories about the past, a significant amount of information began to surface about Andrew Peterson, Swedish pioneer farmer, horticulturist, Baptist, and diarist. Peterson lived with his wife and family in a settlement that was known as Scandia, located near the present city of Waconia in Laketown Township, about thirty-two miles west of Minneapolis.

In his own time, Peterson had become one of the area's leading horticulturists and had won recognition from fruit growers, experimental station staff members, and the Minnesota Horticultural Society. But fifty years after his death, he began to win even greater acclaim from a wider segment of the population. His fame came about as a result of the diaries he faithfully kept from the earliest days of his settlement in Minnesota in 1855 until shortly before his death in 1898.

Peterson and his journals began achieving prominence when the noted Swedish author and historian, Vilhelm Moberg, revealed that he had used the diaries to help write his famous novels (1951-1961) about Swedish emigration to the United States—*The Emigrants, Unto a Good Land, The Settlers,* and the *Last Letter Home.* Two movies were later made from these books, *The Emigrants* and *The New Land*.

Moberg discovered the diaries at the Minnesota Historical Society Archives in St. Paul. They had been deposited there in 1939 by the three surviving Peterson children, Emma, Charles, and Oscar, through the courtesy of Joseph H. Ball, then of St. Paul (who in 1940 would become a United States senator) and William H. Alderman, former head of the Department of Horticulture at the University of Minnesota. Moberg, who spent five years researching his books in both Sweden and the United States, called the Peterson journals the most important discovery he made.

There is a total of ten ledger books (including bookkeeping), plus one small book. Outwardly drab in appearance, some with two-toned marbleized covers, they measure 8 by 11 inches. The small journal, whose existence was almost unknown until fairly recently, is approximately 3 by 3¾ inches in size and dates from May 18, 1850, when Peterson started his trip from Sweden, through July 30, 1850, the same day he arrived in Burlington, Iowa. The diary came into the possession of the Reverend Carl Tideman, then pastor of the Scandia Baptist Church where the Petersons were members, probably in 1930. After Tideman's death, the booklet was passed on to his son Philip, now retired, but then professor of geography at St. Cloud State University. Roger McKnight, associate professor of Swedish and chairman of Scandinavian studies at Gustavus Adolphus College in St. Peter, translated this first diary. Philip Tideman later donated it to the Minnesota Historical Society, and it is now among the collection of Peterson's journals and papers.

It was McKnight's translated version of Peterson's ocean voyage and information about his fami-

Courtesy of Swedish Information Service

ly from early Swedish church records researched by Swedish journalist Anne-Marie Johansson, as well as passenger information from studies by Nils William Olsson, that provided the necessary building blocks used in this story.

The main body of the Peterson diaries dates from January 1, 1855, to March 29, 1898, two days before Peterson's death. The journals include over 14,000 entries. They were written in ink, over a period of forty-three years, and were translated by (Emma) Margareta Ahlquist in the 1930s. (She was associated with Peterson's family through the Reverend Carl Tideman and Dr. Jonas Ahlquist, who was a missionary in Assam, India.)

Vilhelm Moberg noted that the diaries are written in the colorful old Swedish peasant language and are often difficult to read. Peterson's writings include out-of-the ordinary and out-of-style colloquial expressions; some of the terms were used by Moberg's grandmother. Moberg was familiar with Peterson's use of the language because he also was born in southern Sweden, not far from Peterson's home province of Östergötland.

In addition to the outmoded language, Peterson often spelled English words as he would have in Swedish. He also spelled phonetically, and used expressions he heard from other immigrants (notably German and French) while he was still learning his new language, English. One section of loose pages, dated June 23, 1854, to January 1, 1855, remains untranslated because it is so difficult to read.

Four sets of transcripts were made from the translation. One copy is in the Minnesota Historical Society's Division of Archives and Manuscripts, along with the original handwritten manuscript. One transcript of two volumes remained with Peterson's children, while another was sent to the family of Peterson's sister, Gustava Johnson, in Illinois. Another set, given to the University of Minnesota College of Agriculture, is now in the Andersen Horticultural Library, University of Minnesota Landscape Arboretum in Carver County (fittingly only a short distance from where Peterson carried on his horticultural experiments). The university's Wilson Library also has a microfilm copy.

Besides telling about his family through writings which are often terse, unadorned, and generally unemotional, Peterson reveals their daily routine. He provides a wealth of information about the community, the crops, his horticultural work, and their church life. The diaries also provide a first-hand description of the rhythms of seasonal work on the frontier, set in the context of social, political, economic, and religious life.

By incorporating factual information from the diaries, Moberg brought to life his fictional characters – Karl Oskar Nilsson, his wife Kristina, and his brother Robert. Moberg wrote of his debt to the diaries; indeed, parallels between the real life of Peterson and the fictional life of Karl Oskar can be found, although many differences exist. One important difference is the setting in America, for Moberg chose to locate his settlers in Chisago County in Minnesota, where the percentage of Swedes was higher than anywhere else in the world outside of Scandinavia. It is still known as "Swedeland, U.S.A."

Carlton C. Qualey, professor emeritus at Carleton College and research fellow at the Minnesota Historical Society, wrote that "the character Karl Oskar in the Moberg novels is said to have been modeled after Peterson." Gunnar Eidevall, in another article, maintained that Karl Oskar had too little in common with Peterson for the latter to have served as a model. Karl Oskar, Kristina, and Robert, wrote Eidevall, all sprang instead from Moberg's inner self. His characters and their lives were meshed with real-life events and conditions of ordinary people, as well as the more well-known historical persons, particularly some of the religious leaders of the day.

Perhaps more important than how closely Moberg hewed to his real-life models is that the diaries provide a background against which the novelist set his actors and let them work out their destinies. His creations represent a vast segment of Swedish immigrant society in the United States. Not surprisingly, then, the distinguished Swedish sculptor Axel Olsson chose to embody the immigrant movement in his representations of Karl Oskar and Kristina, the original of which stands at the port city of Karlshamn in Sweden. One copy of the statue has been featured at the Emigrant Institute in Växjö, Sweden, and another impressive replica stands in Lindstrom, Chisago County, Minnesota. Of the latter, one reporter wrote: "Each year, the Swedes come by the busload to see the area immortalized in Vilhelm Moberg's novels. The first stop is usually in front of the statue of Karl Oskar and Kristina."

Even before Peterson and his diaries aroused so much international interest, well-known Minnesota historian and writer Grace Lee Nute defined their significance in an article written in 1945. She also described Peterson's farm and lands, which still looked much as they had fifty years earlier, at the time of Peterson's death. Nute wrote:

> The grove of maples was still there, and so were his apple trees and his grape vines, so lovingly planted and scientifically experimented with. The great vat for boiling maple sap into syrup and sugar was in plain evidence in the farmyard. In one of his buildings were quantities of his wooden, hand-hewn sap buckets. In one place, I saw his tools and implements for grafting. In his house I saw his psalmonica, a unique musical instrument. At that time I urged this pioneer farm to be made into an historical monument like the ones I had seen in Skansen openair museum in Stockholm.

In the mid-1970s, the first steps toward the goal Nute had envisioned thirty years earlier were taken. In 1975, I was asked to complete a survey in an attempt to place Coney Island of the West on the National Register of Historic Places. This interesting isle in Waconia Lake has always held a particular fascination for me because it was one of the first tourist attractions in Minnesota in the 1880s. One visitor, a French wine importer named Emile Amblard, visited the island in 1894 and noted three hotels and numerous cottages there. He was so impressed with the surroundings that he subsequently purchased property in Waconia and built a large complex of four buildings in town, one of which he called the Auto Club. Amblard also secured the southwest corner of the island and proceeded to build three villas there. The Auto Club (now known as the Wishing Well Apartments) is the only building he designed that survives, and it is also one of the best-preserved landmarks associated with the city's resort history. It was nominated by the State Review Board to the National Register of Historic Places and accepted by the United States Department of Interior in 1978.

Although pleased that the island was placed on the register, I was surprised by the fact that only a single site had been so recognized in Carver County prior to 1976. (The farm of Wendelin Grimm received National Register status in 1974 following the attention Grimm received as the developer of the world's first strain of alfalfa as a winter-hardy forage crop.) Knowledge of the decaying historic resources in Carver County prompted me to accept leadership on behalf of the Waconia Bicentennial Commission, as well as the Carver County Bicentennial Committee (later called the Heritage Committee), to organize an open forum to provide an opportunity for citizens to discuss this issue. This event called attention to land-use alternatives and was partially funded by the Minnesota Humanities Commission. It was held June 9, 1976, at the Carver County Courthouse Annex in Waconia.

Individuals from throughout the county identified over eighty landmarks worthy of historic recognition. Out of this meeting came completed survey papers for the Andrew Peterson Farm, Waconia; the Henry Gerdsen Farm, Victoria; the Johann Schimelpfenig Farm, Norwood; the Beyrer Brewery, Chaska; the Zoar Moravian Church, Creek Road, between Chaska and Waconia; and the Lake Auburn Moravian Church in Victoria.

Of these, all but the Gerdsen farm were placed on the Register in 1978, along with numerous other places the surveys of which had also been prepared by the Minnesota Historical Society as part of a pilot program—the beginning of a statewide survey of existing landmarks in Minnesota.

As time went on, stories about Andrew Peterson, his wife Elsa, his nine children, and others who had been living in the vicinity became increasingly interesting to me. The residential development in which my husband and I live, Rolling Meadows, is located within the boundaries of the former settlement known as Scandia, only a short distance from Peterson's homestead. When we moved to Waconia in 1962, we became acquainted with some of the older residents of the community—men and women who are or were directly related to families mentioned in Peterson's diaries. After examining some of the journal transcripts, the full impact of my neighborly association with William Peltz, then an elderly widower and farmer who had lived his entire life on his grandparents' farm (the John Zieman homestead), came home to me. Bill's conversations while seated at our dinner table, and discussions about families and life in the early days, suddenly took on a new meaning for me. His reminiscences became sources of confirmation and elaboration about facts and comments recorded in the Peterson diaries.

Peterson, who, as mentioned, had a writing style that was brief and even brusque, rarely identified the people he mentioned. As time went on, my direction became quite clear. I was inspired to compile information, lore, legends, extant photographs, and identifications of people in the diaries before they were lost forever.

The story in these pages progressed through the use not only of the Peterson diaries, but other papers now in the Minnesota Historical Society Division of Archives and Manuscripts in St. Paul. Also of use were Scandia Baptist Church records, Scandia school records, Laketown Township Board records, published reports from the Minnesota Horticultural Society, minutes of other organizations, newspaper accounts, and collections in private hands such as Helen Booth Wettstein's "Our Linnéa Story" and the "Saga of Sunny Hill Farm," compiled by Rhoda Lundsten.

Perhaps most valuable of all were the recollections of Bill Peltz and several other second- and third-generation residents of what is now Waconia, who passed along the stories and traditions of the community. These accounts and memories of the men and women who witnessed the end of the pioneer era brought this history to life.

An attempt has been made to provide a context for daily events, a brief background of the life unfolding around Peterson, his family, friends, and neighbors relating to agriculture, politics, religion, war, and education, so that other readers—particularly those in Sweden—will better understand our beginnings. And—in order to follow the emigrant movement that was taking place, especially during the earliest years within the settlement—code numbers have been printed after the first mention of property owner names as they appear in the text as well as index pages. They correspond to specific locations established on the map on page 20. This was the historic setting reviewed by Vilhelm Moberg as he developed the world of Karl Oskar, Kristina, and Robert.

I want to express my sincere appreciation to Sarah Peterson for use of the translated diaries which she had inherited. I am also indebted to all of those other families and friends of the "Scandia Generation" who helped me along the way, as well as those newer acquaintances, Anna Anderson and Helen Weberg, in the Maynard and Leenthrop areas. I wish to thank the employees of the Carver County Register of Deeds Office, the county librarians, and the Heritage Committee members Lucie Hartley, Kathy Perschmann, and Susanna Thilquist. I am particularly indebted to Susanna for her translation of materials from Swedish and for her loan of private copies of articles and publications.

And there were others. Tage Pousette, Swedish Consul General in Minneapolis, and his staff helped me to obtain information from Sweden, as did Retired Colonel Axel Friman of Gothenburg, Sweden, who helped by sending a Swedish book of maps to me. Carlisle Madson, Carver County surveyor, donated an early wall map of the county, and Taimi Anderson skillfully prepared the contemporary maps for this book. June Rogier, librarian, Andersen Horticultural Library, University of Minnesota, lent her special skills and reviewed the manuscript, particularly the chapter related to horticulture. The late June D. Holmquist, assistant director, publications and research, Minnesota Historical Society, provided direction and encouragement. Elisabeth Weller helped me conclude an otherwise tedious job—that of proofreading and indexing. Virginia L. Martin, formerly an editor at the Minnesota Historical Society and now with Control Data Corporation, was the book's editor.

I am especially grateful to June Rogier, Elisabeth Weller, and Virginia Martin for their kindness to me, and here I must also mention Dr. Rodney C. Loehr, history professor emeritus, University of Minnesota. His examination of an early draft of this book and his recommendations were of tremendous help after this undertaking grew beyond the scope of projected funding thought necessary to complete the work. In 1978, the Minnesota Historical Society provided a grant of $2,500, matching a cash contribution of $1,250 from Ward and Georgene Holasek, the current owners of the Peterson farm. Well over $1,250 donated "in kind" (time and money) was also contributed in behalf of this project.

Additional funds were also raised by the Carver County Heritage Committee through a successful fund-raising campaign in 1981. Although several Scandia families and other friends made generous contributions, a large amount of financial support to assist this effort was provided by the Waconia Chamber of Commerce and the Vasa Order of America-Park Association, Paul Steiner of Steiner and Koppelman, and Curtis L. Carlson of Carlson Companies, all from Minneapolis.

Boyer H. Palmer was a major contributor. Still a lad when he left Småland, Sweden, with his mother and sister in 1924, he is today one of Minnetonka's industrial developers as well as president of the drywall construction firm known as Taping, Inc. Palmer, a resident of Plymouth, Minnesota, is a world traveler as well as goodwill ambassador, and has received honors in Minnesota. He was recognized as Minnesota's Swedish Immigrant of the Year for 1982.

A celebrated song and its connection to this story captured Palmer's imagination and interest, and led him to support this effort. The song is "Röd Lyser Stugan" ("Red Shines the Cabin") also known as "The Song of Småland." The music was written for the 1912 Olympics by Ivar Widéen, the composer, and Linnéa Widéen Andrén, the lyricist, who were Andrew Peterson's grandnephew and grandniece. In 1961, on the song's fiftieth anniversary, the composers were honored and an article about Ivar and Linnéa was published in the *Vetlanda Posten,* April 1, 1961. A copy of the newspaper eventually found its way to the United States and into the hands of Helen Booth Wettstein—another grandniece of Andrew Peterson. The article identified the Widéens as the grandchildren of Johannes Rydell, Andrew Peterson's brother, who had remained in Sweden to pursue a musical career. For the first time, relatives of this family, on opposite sides of the Atlantic, learned of each others' existence quite by accident as a result of the publicity generated by the song. (This stirring story is told in more detail in Chapter 24.)

Boyer Palmer's interest in the preservation of Swedish culture and facts relating to Andrew Peterson's relationship to the renowned musicians from Småland prompted him to make this book possible through his contribution. Thus "The Song of Småland" has linked past and present, Swedes and Swedish-Americans, as well as a dream to its reality—this book.

Josephine Mihelich
Heritage Committee, Chair
October, 1976-January, 1979
Carver County Historical Society

ÖSTERGÖTLAND
Forsnäs
Sjöarp
Västra Ryd
Svinhult
Helgesfall
Eksjö
SMÅLAND
Lake Solgen
Bellö
Krakshult
Mellby
Värne
JÄMTLAND
ÅNGERMANLAND
Umeå
MEDELPAD
HÄRJE DALEN
HÄLSINGLAND
GULF OF BOTHNIA
FINLAND
GÄSTRIKLAND
NORWAY
DALARNA
Oslo
UPPLAND
Uppsala
VÄSTMANLAND
VÄRMLAND
Arboga
Lake Mälaren
Stockholm
NÄRKE
SÖDERMAN-LAND
DALSLAND
BOHUSLÄN
Varnhem
Skara
ÖSTER-GÖTLAND
Kisa
VÄSTER-GÖTLAND
Gränna
Gothenburg (Göteborg)
JÖNKÖPINGS LÄN
Eksjö
Västervik
Vimmerby
Nässjö
Vetlanda
Värnamo
HALLAND
SMÅLAND
GOTLAND
DENMARK
Växjö
Kalmar
Halmstad
Laholm
ÖLAND
Karlshamn
KRISTIANSTADS LÄN
SKÅNE
BLEKINGE
BALTIC SEA
Copenhagen
Malmö

CHAPTER 1

The King's Realm

Andrew Peterson was born Anders Petterson on October 20, 1818, the eldest of eight children of Petter Jonasson and Ingrid Samuelsdotter. Andrew (he later Americanized his name) led a fairly typical peasant existence for the first thirty years of his life; then, in 1850, while still single, he joined the first wave of emigrants to leave Sweden in one of the greatest mass emigrations in history. Between 1860 and 1930, more than one million Swedes – nearly 20 percent of the population – left their homeland to settle in America. Their reasons for doing so were probably much like those that impelled Andrew Peterson to leave.

From the earliest years of Andrew's life until he was twenty, Petter and Ingrid had been tenant farmers living on a *prästlönehemman*, property belonging to the state Lutheran church.[1] As renters of church-owned land, Andrew's parents helped pay the local minister's salary. Their home was small and fairly typical – a heavily timbered cottage, with low roof of bark and sod. It was situated in a clearing surrounded by thickets of dense underbrush, deciduous trees, and spindly pines at a place called Sjöarp. This village was in Västra Ryd, a parish in the province of Östergötland.

The lives of Andrew and his younger brothers and sisters most likely included responsibilities similar to those of most peasant children of that generation who were obliged to work for the landholder as well as their parents. They assumed the care of livestock and a fair share of the work in the fields, and they also took charge of younger family members. Following Andrew's birth, Johannes, Maria Christina ("Maja Stina"), baby Anna, who died while in infancy, Gustava, Samuel, Anna Charlotta, and Carl were born to Ingrid and Petter.

H. Arnold Barton, in an anthology called *Letters from the Promised Land* (1975), quotes some of the emigrants who left Sweden because of harsh conditions. One woman from Värmland, who explained that her only wages were the food she was served while caring for children at the manor, was probably luckier than most, considering existing reports of hunger and starvation throughout the kingdom. She wrote:

> I had to go out and earn my bread already at the age of eight. Most of what I did was to look after children. Had to get up at four o'clock in the morning with the others....I got rotten herring and potatoes, served out in small amounts so that I would not have the chance to eat myself sick.

At the age of fourteen – marked by confirmation in the state church – the children of tenant farmers could expect payment while working for the land-

1. Susanna Thilquist, student of the Swedish language and translator of material used in this book explained Swedish pronunciation as follows:

a. Although some dialects might pronounce å like in *small*, this long vowel sound resembles *eau* as in *beau* or like *Smo land*.

b. The letter with umlaut over the ö is pronounced like *ea* as in *earned*.

c. The umlaut over the ä is similar to the letter *a* in *adding*.

d. The letter j is pronounced like *y*.

e. The slash mark over the letter *e* as in Widéen places the emphasis on that particular letter.

owner or they could seek work elsewhere. However, the alternatives were not always so appealing. One woman, who struggled until she was eighteen before she was allowed to hire out, finally received her first wages, but exclaimed, "And what work! No hope of saving anything in case of illness, but rather I could see the poorhouse waiting for me in the distance."

A third correspondent—a farmhand whose writings were also included in Barton's collection—wrote that the crofter for whom he worked fed him "herring five times a day and [I] had to be at the manor at four o'clock in the mornings and quit at eight-thirty in the evenings, and then go a mile and half home to get a little oatmeal and milk and four hours' sleep."

Although food shortages were common, other conditions for Andrew and his siblings were probably not quite as bleak as those Barton's correspondents painted. For one thing, there is evidence that the family of Petter and Ingrid was exposed to reading, writing, and music even before compulsory education laws took effect in 1842. Before the enactment of those laws, it was the responsibility of priests to see to it that all members of their parishes acquired sufficient skill to read the Bible.[2]

Since few men could even sign their names before the law in 1842, and even fewer women could write at all, one might conclude that Andrew's and his brother Johannes's above-average schooling—as well as interest in music, experimental agricultural techniques, and scientific farming—had been promoted by the clergy. As property owners, priests would have had a special interest in furthering agricultural development, and their library shelves may well have held a collection of books on the subject.

Throughout Andrew's time in Sjöarp, as elsewhere throughout the realm, the king's subjects struggled for survival. The population in Sweden doubled between 1810 and 1910, despite the emigration loss. Part of this gain was caused by the development of a vaccine against smallpox, which had been the most deadly epidemic disease, and the introduction of the potato in Sweden in the late eighteenth century, which provided a cheap and plentiful source of nutrition.

Industrialization did not absorb very much of the population increase at first, and the result was heavy pressure on the land. For many of the poorer classes, life was hard under the best of circumstances, and in years of poor harvest or low agricultural prices, there was widespread distress. When grain prices were low, the grain was made into liquor called *brännvin*, which provided a supplemental source of income, but the clergy were often among the largest beneficiaries. The *Riksdag* had set limits on the size of the still each landowner could have, based on the amount of land owned. Since the clergy owned some of the largest tracts of land, they often owned some of the largest stills. Potatoes were also converted into liquor, and there was widespread abuse of alcohol throughout Sweden.

Apart from seasonal work on the farms, laborers found limited employment working on harbors and canals, dredging waterways, ditching swamps, and repairing roads. From time immemorial, these families who tilled the soil tried to sustain themselves in other ways. In addition to planting and harvesting their own crops, they raised cattle, tanned skins and hides, and spun cloth from flax and wool. Although there were some professional tailors and shoemakers, most of the peasant classes used the coarse, hairy wool called *wadmal* for outer clothing they made themselves; and they fashioned their own shoes out of wood.

As far back as 1435, Sweden was governed by the *Riksdag* composed of the nobility, clergy, burghers, and peasantry; but only the *bonder* or independent landowners were represented in the latter class—a tiny fraction of the total. It was a system of privilege and class distinction that gave rise to much jealousy and anger at the establishment.

Another component of the establishment that caused widespread dissension was the state Lutheran church, which held a virtual monopoly over religious practices. Under the infamous *Konventikelplakatet* or Conventicle Decree of 1726, unauthorized religious gatherings were prohibited under pain of fine, imprisonment, or exile. Although it is well-known that the early colonists

2. Although the *Riksdag* or parliament passed the landmark act of 1842, and required each parish to establish a common school, it took many years before universal education became a reality in Sweden. When it did come, it was through the efforts of Thorsten Rudenschöld and P. A. Siljeström.

An earlier ordinance by the king in 1807 followed the influence of the Moravian Brethren for formal education. The king established a professorship in education at Uppsala. According to the August, 1978, issue of *Life in Early America*, "The Moravians at Bethlehem" by Vernon H. Nelson, the Moravian educational practices have been attributed to the work of John Amos Comenius who died in 1670. He was the bishop of the Moravian Church and one of the greatest educators of all time.

who settled in the United States in the seventeenth century had fled England, Holland, and other countries to seek religious freedom, it is less well-known that two centuries later some Scandinavians left their native countries for similar reasons.

Nevertheless, from about 1830 on, some lay religious leaders risked punishment to lead movements for reform of the church, or to begin new sects altogether. The "Awakening," as it was called, was a reaction to the dry formalism and overintellectualism of the state church. One such group was called the Åkians after its founder, Åke Swensson. Other insurgents were Carl Olav Rosenius and Hans Jacob Lundborg, who preached Methodism, and Lars Levi Laestadius, a botanist who underwent a personal religious experience that led him to preach that salvation resulted not from baptism but from public confession of sin and acknowledgement of Christ as savior.

Perhaps the most radical of these was Erik Jansson, a self-styled prophet who relentlessly attacked the church and burned books and tracts printed by the state church. He was arrested for violating the Conventicle Decree, but escaped from prison and fled to the United States in 1845. He was joined by 1,200 of his followers who founded the Christian commune of Bishop Hill in Illinois. They built an impressive community, and it flourished through pooling of resources and talents in a communal way of life. This settlement was enlarged by continual new arrivals, but was also the starting point for other settlements since, as disaffected members left Bishop Hill, they moved outward and set up other Swedish colonies. Thus, writes Barton in *Letters from the Promised Land*, Bishop Hill "became the focal point for early Swedish immigration...the basic 'mother colony' of Swedish America." The community itself gradually died out after Jansson was murdered under somewhat mysterious circumstances in 1850.

Yet another religious leader was Frederick Olaus Nilsson. The orphaned son of an impoverished alcoholic landowner, he became a shoemaker's apprentice and then, at the age of eighteen, a seaman. He was converted at Baptist Mariners' Church in New York City; later he himself was baptized by a minister from Denmark. He organized the first Baptist church in Sweden at a small rural retreat called Vallersvik. In 1849, it had grown to fifty-two members. Nilsson soon came to the attention of the authorities, and he was persecuted, imprisoned, and in 1850 banished from Sweden. He first went to Denmark and several years later to the United States, where his life became entwined with that of Andrew Peterson, first in Iowa, then in Minnesota.

If there were negative influences or "push" factors that resulted in vast numbers of families leaving Sweden, there were also "pull" factors drawing them to North America. The economic opportunities, religious freedom, and lack of class distinctions were all important elements favoring emigration to America. Liberal ideas began to be promoted widely in Sweden in spite of government opposition. One such promoter was Carl Gustaf Sundius, a pharmacist, who spent some time in Copenhagen before returning to Sweden to open an apothecary shop in Kisa Parish in Östergötland. Another was Peter Cassel, a miller who lived just outside of Kisa and who joined with Sundius in calling for improved social conditions and for emigration to America.

Carl Friman and his sons, who established a claim in what is now Racine County in southeastern Wisconsin, also played an important role in the emigrant movement. They wrote back to relatives in Varnhem, Västergötland, as early as 1838, and their news reached parish families, local papers, and C.L. Herta, the editor of the Stockholm newspaper *Aftonbladet*. Herta publicized the opportunities available in the New World as did the short-lived Emigration Society, founded in 1840 by liberal elements in Stockholm.

The Frimans were thought to have been the first Swedes to settle in what became Wisconsin. Although failing health forced the elder Friman (also known as Freeman) to return to Sweden in 1839, his ten-year-old son Herman (who accompanied his father) rejoined his brothers Carl Johan, Wilhelm, Otto, and Adolph in America three years later. Often-misunderstood correspondence by Carl and his sons caused the eldest son, Carl Johan, to write home: "Father, you must not send our letters to the newspapers, because when the Swedes come here and do not find the conditions as ideal as they had expected them to be, they say that it is our correspondence which has lured them to come."

Gustaf Unonius, another important promoter of emigration, called himself the "first emigrant," and based his authority upon the fact he was the first to leave Sweden after the ban on emigration had been lifted in 1841. Until then, it was necessary to apply for special permission from the king. He settled in Pine Lake, Wisconsin.

One year after Unonius' departure, Polycarpus von Schneidau, a captain in an elite Swedish regiment, and his wife, a Jew, both ostracized from society as a result of their marriage, joined Unonius and his followers at the Pine Lake settlement. They came with a number of upperclass men and women from Uppsala. Polycarpus von Schneidau's letters to his father, a retired military man living at Kisa, probably captured Peter Cassel's attention at the time he advocated emigration to America, and he followed through with plans for his own dream – better social conditions for his children. Cassel finally left Kisa in 1845 with twenty-one people. Although Pine Lake had been their intended destination, the group abandoned the idea shortly after arriving in America. They settled instead in Jefferson County, near Burlington, Iowa, in a community they called New Sweden.

All of these settlements and their leaders were influential in promoting more emigration. News of these communities spread back to the homeland through "America letters" like von Schneidau's – letters containing information that down-played existing hardships and difficulties. Also important were newspaper accounts and books. Travelers such as Charles Dickens, Alexis de Tocqueville, and, perhaps most important for the Swedish emigration, the famous writer Fredrika Bremer, were influential in persuading others to go to the New World. Emigrant guides, some of them translations of works by Germans and Norwegians who had begun emigrating earlier than the Swedes, described America and gave advice to prospective settlers.

In 1838, when Andrew Peterson was twenty years old, his parents moved from the church-owned property where they lived as tenant farmers and joined the shifting tide of the proletariat who migrated to other parishes within Sweden. They settled at Helgesfalls (South Farm) in Östergötland. From church records in the provincial archives at Vadstena, it appears Andrew accompanied the family and probably worked with his father, or as a hired hand, until he was twenty-seven. Then he found employment at the lumbermill in Forsnäs at Sunds Parish, where he lived for less than a year, until he was notified of the death of his father. As the eldest son, Andrew was apparently called back to take care of his mother, and they returned to Sjöarp.

As in the case of most young people of that generation, it seems natural Andrew would have chafed under existing restrictions and the lack of opportunity he and his peers encountered. As an intelligent, imaginative man exposed to reports from neighbors in Östergötland about unlimited opportunities in North America, it is not surprising he made plans to leave Sweden.

Andrew's situation prior to his departure was not as encumbered as that of Moberg's characters, Karl Oskar and Kristina Nilsson. For one thing, Andrew was a bachelor. He was not burdened with the seemingly insurmountable problems confronting Karl Oskar, who, as the eldest son of a land-owning peasant family, had the burden of his legacy, his parents' property. Along with the responsibility of caring for his aging parents and finding the wherewithal to make the mortgage payments, Karl Oskar was also in debt to other family members for their share of the family inheritance.

Finally in 1850, four years after his father's death, Andrew Peterson and his sister Gustava (known to all as Gustava Petersdotter), lured by economic opportunity, political and religious freedom, and adventure, decided it would be to their advantage to leave for America with several others from their parish. They requested and received church papers and the required endorsements certifying their standing in the community from the local bailiff. They obtained their passports and in May, 1850, set out for Gothenburg, the seaport city from which they would depart for Boston on the other side of the Atlantic.

They left behind their mother Ingrid and brothers Johannes and Samuel. Samuel, then nineteen, probably took over Andrew's role as head of the household and caretaker of his mother. He never married. By then, thirty-year-old Johannes was a father, musician, and church organist, married to a woman named Anna Carin. The couple had a three-year-old daughter named Anna Lovisa. Also left behind for now were sisters Maria Christina, twenty-four; Anna Charlotta, sixteen; and brother Carl, thirteen. But these latter three members of this family would follow in their brother's wake eventually.*

***Note:** references to sources used for each chapter start on page 188 under the title, "Sources, Comments, and Related Reading."

CHAPTER 2

Voyagers from Västra Ryd

Andrew Peterson was thirty-two years old when he and his sister Gustava started out on the first leg of their journey to America in the beginning weeks of May, 1850. They were accompanied by several others from the parish of Västra Ryd in the province of Östergötland, Sweden.

Among them were their neighbors, from Sjörap, Gustaf Larsson, his wife Catharina Pehrsdotter, and their four children. Those from Helgesfall where Anders once lived were Johan Peter Jonsson, his wife Anna Stina Andersdotter, and their two children. Anders Samuelsson and his spouse Anna Catharina Johannesdotter were also in the group, as well as two single people, Christina Catharina Jaensdotter, a thirty-four-year-old shoemaker's daughter, and Erik Magnus Anderson, a twenty-four-year-old servant.

If the Larsson or Jonsson children had reminisced about that journey in later life, their tales about the preparations and farewells would probably parallel this graphic description written by an 1849 emigrant from Östergötland:

> As soon as it became a fixed fact that the old home should be left, hundreds of things came up to be thought about and to be seen to; clothes to be made; chests to be procured to carry clothing and provisions in; money to be collected and paid out; personal property to be disposed of...the Rector's certificate of good character and the King's passport to be procured. The first was obtained by weaving the cloth at home, and then calling in the parish tailor, who, with his apprentices, worked away two or three weeks to make each of us, both male and female, two suits apiece, while the men folks have an extra suit, consisting of sheepskin coat and pants of reindeer skin. Boots and shoes were made by the parish shoemaker....The chests were made by carpenters versed in the art, and ironbound by my father who was a blacksmith, and then a painter was called in to put the finishing touches on the work, and when done the chests looked large and strong enough to cross the Atlantic in....
>
> And then this most weighty document [the church document and that from the Bailiff of the district] had to be presented to the Governor of the province in order to receive a passport from that august personage and to do this was a serious affair as a person heard nothing but jeers and insults from the time one entered the anteroom and gave his name and business to the liveried flunky, until one had safely got outside again of the executive mansion. After having presented the credentials from Rector and Bailiff, the Governor with all the eloquence at his command tried to dissuade one from so foolish and fatal a step (as in the Governor's belief) one is about to take....Having received authority from everyone concerned to migrate, it was our next duty to get away as soon as possible. Accordingly our chests were packed with clothing, provisions, and a few such articles as we did not wish to sell, or thought would be necessary on our arrival to this country. Teams were hired to convey us to the nearest station on the canal running between Stockholm and Gothenburg.

Andrew and his party had to travel a similar long journey to get to Gothenburg. These travelers moved by caravan from Östergötland, where they met others from their province. Among the seventy-five known voyagers on board the ship, the *Minona,* Andrew and Gustava were two of ten adults and six children from the parish of Västra Ryd in Östergötland. On that spring day, May 19, 1850, when they had completed the inland journey and were setting sail from Gothenburg, Andrew began recording daily happenings in a journal, a habit he would continue almost to the day of his death.

After sailing beyond Jutland and its churches, Andrew noted, "In the evening most of the passengers were stricken by seasickness, to the extent there was terrible vomiting along the railings." He thought his neighbors from Västra Ryd were exempt from this suffering because they had been exposed to the pitching of the boat earlier while traveling on Lake Mälaren.

Many of the emigrants who steadied themselves on deck probably were moved to tears as they watched the billowing sails propel their ship through Skagerrak, then Farsund's Point in Norway, where they were positioned for their last glimpse of Scandinavia. The seasickness finally subsided after they passed the Orkney Islands of Scotland, the Shetlands, and the smaller islands of Sule Skerry and Rona.

The wind was from the northwest on May 26, and the brig reversed its course, or tacked, the whole time. Andrew concluded his diary entry for that day with this facetious remark: "The captain does not say prayers with us, but we have been doing so ourselves. The crew itself has also been saying prayers. The captain needs no god, since he is god himself."

Andrew did not record reminders about others from Östergötland, any of the other passengers, nor say anything of general living conditions on board this vessel.

Vilhelm Moberg describes shipboard conditions for the emigrés who sailed in these normally freight-laden boats. Dividers of canvas were used to separate the families, the single men, and the single women. All were assigned to single or double bunks, and families had fenced-in areas called bed pens.

The hold of the ship was dark and smelly. The passengers received their only source of light and air through small openings in the lid of the hatch. During storms, when the cover was closed, it was suffocating. Kerosene lamps were generally forbidden, and there was little or no privacy. Boxes or chests served as makeshift tables. The weekly allotment of the ship's ration of food (which eventually became riddled with vermin) was kept with private belongings, and each family waited its turn to cook in the galley.

Jons Larsson was one of the emigrants on board the *Minona* seeking refuge from unpleasant personal situations. He had recently been called before the Nykil Parish church council, which had warned him about the disharmony in his marriage. Now he was on board this vessel, having deserted his wife and children. Other passengers included an unmarried woman who was traveling alone with her illegitimate child, and Isak Petersson, who had been branded by the church council as a disturber of the peace and a person of loose morals. Perhaps few knew the circumstances of Otto Pehrsson or that of the woman and her two children he was escorting. She was the wife of his former employer (Dahl's Tannery in the parish of Loneberga), who had abandoned her.

Andrew wrote primarily of weather conditions and more general matters. He wrote on May 30 of a huge squall line: "It was so bad that the water blew onto the deck, and we had to wade in water over our knees."

On June 2, he said, "The wind was the same as yesterday, and we had beautiful weather. Late in the evening a big storm came up. Among other big waves came one so huge that it broke over the deck, filling most of the people on board with a terrible fear."

Later in the month, he wrote, "Wind so westerly and so light that the brig is making little time—a mast has also been blown off, so there is quite a mess on board." Then, although five single men with journeymen carpenter credentials were on that same voyage, he wrote: "We are working on a new mast. The carpenter and I have been working all night." He also recorded that "Some of the people have seen huge ocean fish today. We have located them by a bellowing sound that they make. Appearing as big as a ship, they have lain off the starboard side."

Without mention of any illness on board (after the initial seasickness subsided), his entries for June 20 and 21 were: "Calm weather, and the brig is rolling considerably. Gustaf's youngest daughter from Sjöarp died today at six o'clock in the morning at the age of one year and five months. The body was wrapped in a sheet, then it was wound about with a sail, with a sinker around the feet. Next it was carried up on deck and laid on a plank that was placed on the railing. Then the captain read the funeral service over it, and it was lowered down into its deep grave, about thirty-four fathoms deep, approximately in the middle of Newfoundland's Grand Bank."

On June 22-23 he said: "A good southwest wind. The brig is following its proper course. It is such beautiful weather today, Midsummer Day, that all the passengers are on deck—but there are no leafy forests to stroll through." That pensive mood of quiet melancholy may have been brought about by reminders of the summer solstice. At home during this longest day of the year, Sweden was bathed throughout the night with an eerie light. Cottages were scrubbed clean and decorated with branches and garlands. There were festivities, maypole dances, and floral decorations everywhere.

On July 2, he said: "Early in the morning we caught sight of Boston's lighthouses with the signal lights burning, but they were on the islands and islets far out at sea. They are for the aid of sailors when it is dark. Later in the day a steamboat arrived and [the guide] asked if the captain wanted his brig to be pulled into the harbor, but we had such a good wind that it was not necessary. A little later the pilot arrived in his big, bright-colored sloop and jumped on board our ship. He acted as captain all the way into the harbor. A short while after the pilot's arrival, the quarantine inspector came aboard to see if everyone was healthy, which we all were. In the evening we docked the ship and went out to view the big city of Boston."

Subsequent brief entries trace a four-week journey to the center of the continent that began with a steamboat trip from Boston to Albany. Andrew said on July 6, 1850, that "The boat was delayed because the canal was out of order, and we had to stay there for five days and nights."

When they resumed their journey, they saw fifteen to twenty towns every day. At Buffalo, the travelers exchanged a horse-drawn canal boat for a lake steamer that took them across Lake Erie, through the straits at Detroit to Lake Huron, and across Lake Michigan to Chicago, where once more they boarded a canal boat. Not until they reached Peru, Illinois, did they leave the water at last and travel on land.

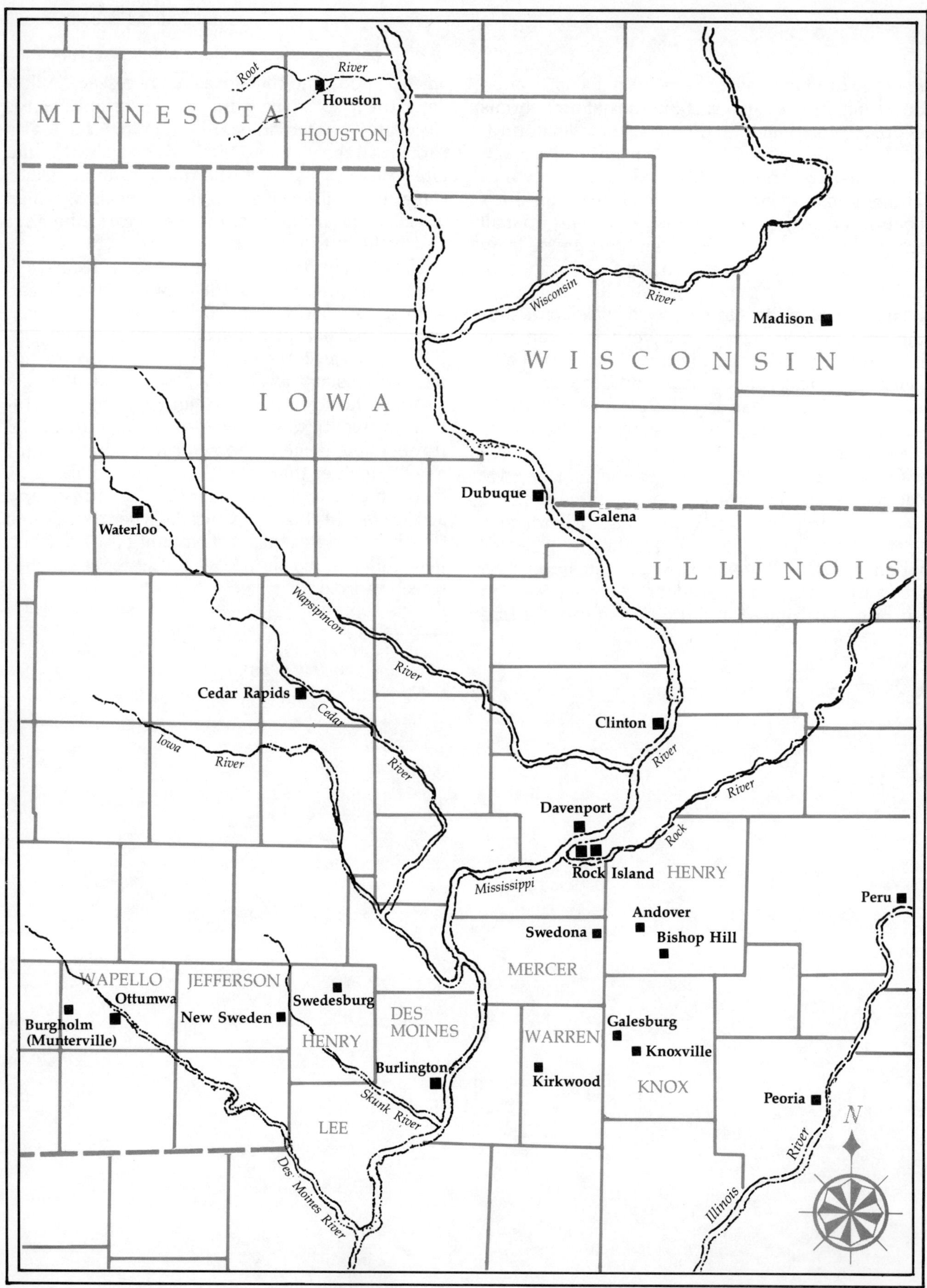
MINNESOTA
Root River
Houston
HOUSTON
WISCONSIN
Wisconsin River
Madison
IOWA
Dubuque
Galena
ILLINOIS
Waterloo
Wapsipincon River
Cedar Rapids
Cedar River
Iowa River
Clinton
River
Davenport
Rock River
Rock Island
HENRY
Mississippi
Peru
Andover
Swedona
Bishop Hill
MERCER
WAPELLO
JEFFERSON
Ottumwa
Swedesburg
Burgholm
(Munterville)
New Sweden
DES MOINES
HENRY
WARREN
Galesburg
Knoxville
Burlington
Kirkwood
KNOX
Peoria
Skunk River
LEE
N
Des Moines River
Illinois River

CHAPTER 3

Sojourn in Iowa

Gustava and Andrew Peterson, together with eight other adults and six children, arrived in Illinois in midsummer after a trip that had begun with a horse-drawn wagon in Sjöarp in May, 1850. Now some were going separate ways. Gustaf Larsson, his wife Catharina, and their children, Amanda, Mathilda Carolina, and Christina Charlotte (their fourth daughter, Gustava, was the infant who had died at sea), left their companions, to settle in Swedona in Mercer County, Illinois. There they were joining 300 emigrants who had left Sweden the year before. These earlier arrivals had planned to go to New Sweden, Iowa, but changed their plans after observing the current in the mighty Mississippi and settled in Illinois instead.

Gustaf Larsson, wanting to join these countrymen, directed his wagon to Swedona while Andrew and Gustava continued on to Iowa. Gustava probably found domestic employment in Burlington while Andrew earned his keep working for a farm owner in the vicinity of a settlement called Village Creek. This was close to the area where Peter Cassel, the former Swedish miller and reform politician, had settled in 1845 with twenty-one followers. Upon his arrival in America, Cassel had experienced a slight change in direction. He had expected to join Gustaf Unonius and Polycarpus von Schneidau in Pine Lake, Wisconsin.[1]

1. The settlement begun in Pine Lake, Wisconsin, by Unonius and his followers turned out to be an unrealized dream. This group tried to put into practice a life of "pastoral simplicity and republican virtue," but it failed, partly as a result of the lack of practical experience on the part of its primarily upperclass citizens.

But when Cassel arrived in New York City, he met a former sea captain, Pehr Dahlberg, who told him he chose a place for his family in Iowa because the farmland was better. Having been convinced the most fertile acreage in Wisconsin had already been taken, Cassel and his followers traveled to Iowa instead. They established their colony northwest of Burlington in Lockridge Township, Jefferson County. This place, the village of New Sweden, became the first lasting Swedish settlement in the United States. Peter Cassel's dream of freedom for his children and countrymen had far-reaching results. Both directly and indirectly he contributed to Swedish emigration and Swedish colonization in the United States. He was not only responsible for the Swedish settlement at New Sweden, but his work contributed to the settlements at Village Creek, Swedes Point, (now called Madrid near Des Moines), Bergholm (now Munterville) in Wapello County, and Swedesburg in Henry County, Iowa.

The spiritual needs of the New Sweden pioneers were attended to at first by Magnus Frederik Håkansson, a shoemaker and Lutheran lay preacher, who also took care of a small congregation in Burlington. But most of the parishioners, including Cassels and Johan Danielsson and their families, were converted to the Methodist church in 1850. Partly this conversion came about through the persistence of a visiting Methodist preacher from Victoria, Illinois, Jonas Hedstrom. Apparently one of the reasons for this change in loyalties was that the Methodists were temperance advocates. Drinking had already become a widespread social problem in New Sweden (as it had been in the

Old World) and a source of concern for Cassel, Danielsson, and others. Settlers made their own brew, and when it ran out they hauled in alcohol from Burlington.

Unonius made a visit to Burlington in the mid-1850s and later wrote that most of the area surrounding this town had already been settled.[2] Immigrants who wanted to live there had to pay ten to fifteen dollars an acre for an uncultivated piece of ground—a high cost for land at that time. To buy eighty acres to start farming seemed to involve a princely sum, especially since the trip to the United States had cost so much. And after buying land, the settlers still had to build houses and barns, and invest in seed and livestock.

The scarcity and high cost of land no doubt prompted Andrew Peterson to look elsewhere. Possibly about this time, too, a letter to some of the immigrants in Burlington arrived from a countryman named Andrew Bergquist, who told about the rich land available in Minnesota Territory. In 1853, Peterson and John Anderson made a trip to Minnesota Territory where they established preemption claims, and then returned to Burlington where they would stay for two more years, working and completing arrangements for their final move to Minnesota.

Meanwhile, Frederick Olaus Nilsson, the religious leader, and his wife Soffia Ulrika, had fled the Gothenburg area in Sweden with twenty-two fellow Baptists and had traveled to the United States. They arrived in New York on June 23, 1853, where Nilsson boarded a freight train, traveled by boat to Chicago, and finally by horseback to Rock Island, Illinois. There, in 1852, Gustaf Palmquist, a former Stockholm schoolteacher, had organized the first Baptist church in the United States. (Palmquist's brothers were also active in the free church and temperance movements.) At the same time, Anders Wiberg and Nilsson were beginning to lay the foundations of the Swedish Baptist churches in America.[3]

Nilsson and Palmquist learned that a small Swedish congregation near Burlington (thought to be Village Creek) lacked a minister, and they immediately set out to help. They were Baptists; the congregation was Lutheran. The worshipers heard the two missionaries, and the result was that, in 1854, another group of Swedes broke away from the Lutheran church. Among them, baptized on January 21, were Andrew Peterson, his sister Maria Christina (who by that time was in America and also married), and her husband John Anderson. Alexander and Sara Karin Johnson and Jonas Peter and Greta Johnson—all of whom would leave Iowa with Peterson—joined the Baptist church in that year.

When Charles Carlsson and Olaf Pettersson of New Sweden also joined the Baptists, an issue revolving around the church property became explosive since these two men held the deed to the land on which the Lutheran church had been built. They were on a collision course with other Lutheran families, who had helped to make construction of the chapel possible through donated time and material. Moreover, the congregation had built the meeting house with a sizeable cash contribution from the famous Swedish singer, Jenny Lind. When the issue was resolved on July 19, 1854, the Baptists built their own church and established their own cemetery, not far from the Lutheran church.[4] These and the third church in town—the Methodist—provided spiritual guidance for the villagers living in New Sweden, as well as

2. After Unonius left the Pine Lake settlement, he entered the Episcopalian Seminary at Nashotah, Wisconsin, and was ordained in 1845. He served several churches before he became the first minister at the St. Ansgarius Scandinavian Episcopal Church in Chicago. After nine years he resigned and returned to Sweden in 1858, but was not accepted as a Lutheran priest. He found employment by following in his father's footsteps and becoming a collector of customs (imposing duties on imported and exported merchandise) at the seaport town of Grisslehamn. He is remembered for his published work entitled *Minnen från en sjuttonårig vistelse i nordvestra America (A Pioneer in Northwest America 1841-1858,* translated by Jonas Oscar Backland for the Swedish Pioneer Historical Society).

Polycarpus von Schneidau left Pine Lake and became a professional photographer in Chicago and was active in the Episcopalian church there.

3. Dr. Norris Magnuson, librarian and professor of history at Bethel Seminary, states in his article, "Our Unsung Heroines," in the May 15, 1977, issue of *The Standard* that Anders Wiberg was a devout and popular Lutheran pastor in Sweden for nearly a decade. He had come to admire the godly lives of the Baptists with whom he had come in contact, but he did not admire their theology, and had determined to write a book refuting their views on baptism. After his conversion and subsequent baptism by Nilsson in Denmark, he wrote books and pamphlets in cooperation with the Baptist Publication society in Philadelphia. He married Caroline Lintemuth, the daughter of a prominent Philadelphia family. Wiberg is said to have been the true founder of Baptist work in Sweden. He was also the contributing factor in the beginnings and early development of the Baptist General Conference.

4. According to Iowa statutes, houses of worship belonged to the dominant party if an unincorporated congregation became divided.

others living in the surrounding area.

Artisans and tradespeople in New Sweden farmed and in addition exchanged their services and skills on a barter basis. The community had masons, carpenters, cabinetmakers, blacksmiths, tailors, shoemakers, and bakers. It even had a pipe organ builder, and a snuffmaker who made up special blends for each of his customers.

Meanwhile, Ingrid Petterson, mother of Andrew and Gustava, died in Sweden on April 25, 1853. Apparently after her death, two more children—Carl and Maria Christina—followed their two siblings and came to the United States to settle near Andrew and Gustava in Burlington. Two brothers, Samuel and Johannes, and a sister, Anna Charlotta, remained in Sweden. Samuel worked as a hired farmhand, and Johannes followed his musical career as an organist. For professional reasons, Johannes adopted the surname of Rydell, which he took from the name of his birthplace, Västra Ryd. Anna Charlotta married a man named Peder Norman.

It was at this time, while in Burlington, that Andrew anglicized his own name.[5] He would no longer be known as Anders Petterson, but as Andrew Peterson.

Of Andrew's siblings in America, Maria Christina married Johannes Anderson (he changed his name to John Anderson), the son of Anders Andersson and Anna-Stina Carlsdotter from Västra Ryd. Johannes had settled in Burlington with his older brother Per Daniel and younger sister Louise.

Gustava later married Louis Peter Johnson, and the couple eventually moved across the Mississippi River and settled in western Illinois. Maria Christina's sister-in-law Louise Anderson (John's sister) married a man named Schots or Schultz and they continued to live in Iowa. Carl served in the Civil War and after his discharge pushed farther west to Colorado.

Andrew Peterson probably continued to record his daily experiences in a journal between the period of his arrival in Iowa and the time (Emma) Margareta Ahlquist actually started to decipher his notes. The worn sheets of information prior to 1855 suggest these loose pages were part of a diary that may have been lost. The missing book or pages might have helped fill in the details about the farmer and nursery operator named Nealley (or Neally) for whom Andrew worked. Peterson's probable employer, based on the 1850 census (particularly the pages recorded October 6 and 29) for Des Moines County, was G.C. Neally, who in that year was sixty-two years old and the most prosperous of the three Neallys listed.[6] Neally, who had a wife Sally, daughter Mahalia, and son Joseph (ages sixty-one, twenty-four, and twenty-eight, respectively) had real estate valued at $5,000. Most convincing is that their business employed, along with one other laborer, a man named Andrew whose last name in the census records is not legible. His age was given as thirty-four, but Neally was probably guessing, since Peterson was then thirty-two.

After the aforementioned gap in the journal pages, Andrew's diary begins again on January 1, 1855, while he was living on a farm near Burlington and working for Neally. From then on, his diary described a variety of farm responsibilities, carpentry, and nursery work. He told, for example, of working on "gates" for several days, finishing a table, building a shaving box, and sharpening scissors. He installed shelves in a dining room, scoured boxes, washed sacks, and made a grafting table.

Here are some typical entries. On January 13, 1855, he wrote: "For Nealley. Made some clamps for the grafting table. Bought candles for 25 cents, also some snuff 10 cents." Later, he wrote, "Hammered in the shop and grafting room," a comment repeated for several days, but he did not give any more detailed description of his work.

In addition to his duties as a hired man, Peterson also farmed independently. On January 19, he wrote: "During the forenoon Alexander [Johnson] and I hauled oatstraw for me. Old man Anders has husked corn for me for $1.20. This I have paid. After dinner I went to town and mailed a letter to F.B. in Rock Island. Bought letter stamps for $.15."

Peterson also mentioned working for Neally on a day-to-day basis. He shoveled snow, grafted, worked in the shop, set and sharpened saws, and

5. Except in instances where names appear in quoted material, the most common or Americanized version has been used throughout this story.

6. According to genealogy charts prepared by Clyde C. Waters (husband of Oma Johnson, the Reverend John and Maria Christina Anderson's granddaughter), Senator William B. Allison owned the nursery where Peterson and others in his family worked. It is doubtful the senator had a working interest in horticulture, unless he and his second wife Mary Nealley (spelled ey) inherited partial ownership. His wife was one of two cousins—both named Mary. They were mere children (ages one and five) during the time Andrew Peterson worked in Iowa.

made a railing for a bookshelf. During his combined work report for January 26 and 27, he wrote: "For Nealley. Finished the bookshelf. Began on a clock. Finished the clock, fixed a table and made a chair for the church."

During February, 1855, he made a kitchen table and worked in the shop on a variety of projects which were not explained. He made apple ladders and noted his trip to town as well as his purchases—cloth for trousers, $2.90; shaving knife, $.95; ink, paper, envelope, $.15; and snuff, $.10. He also worked on successive days on the bunkhouse, and spent one evening in Burlington where he picked up clothing tailored for him by Jonas Peter Johnson. He made bench drawers and mentioned receiving a Bible from his brother-in-law, John Anderson.

During March and most of April, he experienced spells of fever for several days, for which he bought wine and quinine and recorded a payment of $.50 for two visits to the doctor. On successive days, he made a hayrack, mended the drag and the sled, sewed blinds on the harness, and repaired the door between the dining room and sitting room (presumably in Neally's home). He made doors for a pigsty and grafted roots as well as apple trees. He simply made ditto marks for subsequent records of his nursery work.

After he "made up accounts with Nealley and received $38" at the end of April, he paid $.40 for transportation to Burlington the following day.

Without any previous information about making a decision to leave Iowa (or his earlier journey to Minnesota), on May 4, 1855, Andrew, the Reverend Frederick Olaus Nilsson and Soffia, John and Maria Christina, and several others of the Baptist group set out on the riverboat journey to Minnesota.

Of the various locations near the place where Andrew lived in Iowa, a few are still in existence. Village Creek cannot be found on existing maps, but the general area of New Sweden can be located by the two Swedish churches still standing in the township of Lockridge in Jefferson County, Iowa. Four Corners, a rural crossroads, was the first center; then the village of Lockridge became the postal address for the community. Although the log dwellings have been replaced with modern buildings and the roads improved, the countryside remains much the same as it must have appeared to the founding father, Peter Cassel, and his group of emigrants from the parish of Kisa.

According to the historical documentary called "Peter Cassel's America" (by Lilly Setterdahl), the location of the Swedish Baptist Church (demolished in 1893) is marked by a commemorative stone. The Methodist Church (built of logs in 1856 but rebuilt in 1872) has undergone recent improvements and is currently in use. For the Swedish Lutheran Church (built in 1851 but rebuilt in 1860), time has stood still. Although the congregation incorporated its services with those of another church, the Stukstedt bell in the tower still calls people to a special service on the first Sunday in June. This chapel has been placed on the National Register of Historic Places.

While the cemeteries of these churchyards mark the resting place for many of the first immigrants (from as many as 300 families), visitors will notice few descendants are left in the area. Most migrated to other settlements mentioned earlier, as well as to Minnesota, Kansas, Nebraska, and Colorado.

CHAPTER 4

The Settlers

The trip Peterson and his brother-in-law John Anderson made to explore Minnesota Territory in 1853 had been in response to a letter sent by Andrew Bergquist. A fellow countryman, Bergquist told acquaintances in Illinois and Iowa that homesteads were available in the "Big Woods" of Minnesota. (These woods were in the central and southern parts of the state—a region one hundred miles long and forty miles wide, of hardwood, mainly oak, maple, basswood, and ironwood.)

Bergquist, a former trumpeter in the Swedish army, and his wife Nilla Eliasdotter, were from the province of Kristianstad. He had been born on July 29, 1814, in Ubbalt, Vittsjö Parish, the son of Nils Quist and Ingar Svensdotter. Nilla was born in Röshult, Hörja Parish, the daughter of Elias Svensson and Nilla Nilsdotter. Passport papers show they were accompanied on their journey to North America by their children Nilla, Ingrid, and Henrik, and by Nilla's brother Pehr Eliasson. Frank (Franz or Francis), a son who was nine years old, remained in Sweden.

A few German settlers had preceded Bergquist to what is now Carver County, but none had established claims adjacent to this particular sizeable body of inland water admired by him. This lake and surrounding countryside would later be designated Laketown Township. During Bergquist's brief stay, he explored the entire lakeshore and met a few friendly Indians along the way.

From the moment he saw the glistening lake surface located in the midst of a vast expanse of timber, his thoughts apparently turned to his fellow immigrants. It is not clear how he managed to send word to his Swedish friends, but at least one of the letters he wrote reached the Baptist group in Burlington.

Bergquist was not exaggerating when he explained that the soil was unbelievably rich and fertile. The clarity of water, surging in gentle swells against its sandy shore, suggested that the lake was springfed. The beauty of this shimmering expanse of blue and emerald isle appealed to something fundamental in his nature. He singled out 160 acres on a hill on its eastern shore. He named the body of water Clearwater Lake, but in later years the Indian name of Wa-ko-ni-ya Mde or Waconia Lake, meaning lake of the fountain or lake of the spring, was restored and officially adopted.[1]

1. During the visit of Chief David W. La Framboise (Blue Eagle) to Waconia (see *Waconia Patriot*, September 13, 1912, p. 1.), he explained that Waconia meant "Boiling of Vapor Springs." The vapor is apparent on cold days when the space above the springs (between the island and the peninsula) remains open and the rest of the lake has frozen over.

Another interpretation of the words *Mde Wa-ko-ni-ya* is "lake" and "from out of the earth comes life." This version is based on studies carried on by Arlo Hasse, a longtime friend and Indian benefactor from Carver County. He defines the latter word as radiant energy or the reflection of heat waves.

A noteworthy comment regarding the name of the lake was made by Carlisle Madson: "Ten or so years ago I made an inquiry of the Minnesota Geographic Board regarding the proper name of our favorite lake. The board responded that Clearwater Lake and Lake Waconia are both misnomers. The correct name is Waconia Lake. Old John Brunius [surveyor] must have been aware of that back in 1872 because that is the way he referred to the lake in his field note." *Waconia Patriot*, July 17, 1975, p. 2.

Although property dimensions and family names changed throughout the years, the code on this map establishes the physical locations of sites related to Andrew and Elsa Peterson—their homestead, church, school, neighbors' houses, farms, and the like. While this information does not give exact dates of claims or land purchases, it does establish general facts (from Index Book "A," Carver County Courthouse) about these transactions.

1. George W. King, May 5, 1857; Roswell P. Russell, November 3, 1857.
2. Peter Swenson, 1857; Kathrina Lingenfelser, 1868; Adolph Burandt, 1873.
3. Swan Johnson, 1861; Borrow Swanberg, 1874; Swan Johnson, 1875.
4. Robert Mueller, 1876; Josephine Hassenstab, 1881.
5. John Behrenfeld, 1860; John Grieshammer, 1861.
6. Frederick Moy, 1860; August Held, 1887; Rudolph Hilk, 1899.
7. John Scheuble, 1861; Christian Hauter, 1875.
8. Joseph Frey, September 29, 1860; Christ Becht, October 6, 1860; Christian Shilling, 1871; Emma Brauche, 1873; Olaf Anderson, January 2, 1874; John Nelson, March 23, 1874; Olaf Anderson, April 2, 1874; subdivided by Charles Emmert, 1881; now Pillsbury or Camp Manakiki.
9. Christian Shilling, 1860; District 42 or the Nelson School, 1870.
10. Joseph Frey, 1860; Emma Brauche, 1873; Olaf Anderson, January, 1874; John Nelson, March, 1874.
11. John A. Peterson, 1861; Axel Jorgenson, 1878; Andrew and Ellen Swanson, 1883. (A stream which is still called Peterson's Creek flows from Goose Lake and beyond through John Peterson's claim. The Department of Natural Resources maintains the carp trap located at the inlet into Waconia Lake.)
12. Olaf Anderson, 1860; John Johnson, 1874; the Coney Island or Great Northern Railroad Depot (also known as the Minnesota Valley Railroad as well as the St. Paul, Pacific, and Sioux City Railroad).
13. Magnus Peterson, 1860; Carl Biersdorf, 1866.
14. Michael Reichenberger, 1860; John Reichenberger, 1920.
15. Great Northern Railroad, 1864; John Robline, 1881.
16. Michael Groos, April, 1857; Cyrus Stauffer, June, 1857; Ellen Barlow, August, 1857; John and George Neunzinger, January, 1863; George Green, April 1863.
17. John Neunzinger, 1857; Wendelin Grimm*, 1859.
18. John Peltz, May 18, 1857; John Heinson, May 20, 1857; Frederick Maas, December 24, 1867; Wendelin Grimm, December 29, 1867; Frank Grimm, 1879.
19. John Luedhart, 1860.
20. Franz Schoener, May 18, 1857; John G. Heinson, May 19, 1857; Theodore Hoehn, 1868; Michael Hall, 1870.
21. John Peltz, 1857 (also 25 and 26).
22. Peter Nilsson, 1866; George Brethorst, 1867; August Pofahl, 1871; Edward Pofahl, 1915.
23. Andrew Mattson, 1858 and 1860; Mons Janson, June 24, 1859; Andrew (Swenson) Swanson, August 11, 1859; August, Frederick and William Ziemer, 1876.
24. Fred B. Ludwig, 1860; Ferdinand Krienke, 1863.
25. John Peltz, May 18, 1857; John Heinson, May 19, 1857; Walter and Frederick Maas, 1867.
26. John Peltz, 1857; Walter, Frederick and Martin Maas, 1867 and 1901.
27. John Walter, 1866; Henry Sohns, 1900.
28. Frederick Zoerb, 1874.
29. John Holtmeier, 1860; Lake Auburn Moravian Church* (Church of the Brethren), 1863.
30. Henry Gerdsen, 1860; and 1866.
31. Hubert Wey, 1861; Jacob Hedke, 1862; F.W. Klatt, 1863; District 16 or the Gerdsen School.
32. John Toban, February 22, 1859; Catherina and Charles Warner, March 1, 1859; Franz Tefler, 1861; Catherina and Charles Warner, 1862; Nils Mortenson, 1867; Ferdinand and Julius Buelow, 1868.
33. John Erickson, 1860; August Pofahl, 1867; George Brethorst, 1871.
34. Alexander Johnson (the entire NE¼ of Section 8), 1860; John Zieman, 1863; Simon Peltz, 1888.
35. Alfred Johnson, October 8, 1860; Per Daniel Anderson, December 11, 1860; Fritchof Anderson, inheritance; William Goethke, 1919.
36. Alfred Johnson, 1860; Taylor August Johnson, 1861; Karl Vieglahn, 1866; Frederick Schwichtenberg, 1871; Herman Schwichtenberg, 1888.
37. John (Johannes) Anderson, 1860; Jacob Jenni, 1863; August Pofahl, 1877; Paul Pofahl, 1886.
38. John (Johannes) Anderson, September 27, 1860; Swen Bengston, September 27, 1860; Gottfried Lobitz, 1866; Herman Lobitz, 1878.
39. Louis Fisher, 1866; Nils Malmberg, 1875; District 17 or the Scandia School, 1873; Adolph Lindenberg, 1873.
40. Peter Fisher, 1861; Johanna and Louis Fisher, 1866; Adam Fisher, 1876.
41. The Reverend F. O. Nilsson, 1857; Andrew Hakanson, 1861; Peter J. Freed, 1874; John Peltz, 1886.
42. John Lundsten, 1858; Frank Lundsten, inheritance.
43. John Lundsten, 1858; Andrew Nilson, 1863; G. B. Nilson, 1872; John Lundsten, 1876 ($55 for ten acres); John Kaufhold, 1896.
44. John Lundsten, 1858; Andrew Nilson, 1863; G. B. Nilson, 1878; John Kaufhold, 1896.
45. Jonas P. Johnson, 1858; John Lundsten, May 14, 1863; Swan Halling, May 14, 1863; Hans Hanson, 1864; Thomas Johnson, 1868; Henry Rietz, 1869; Henry Peterman, 1888; Otto Peterman, inheritance.
46. Andrew Peterson*, October 8, 1860.
47. The Reverend F. O. Nilsson, 1857; Nicholas Swenson, 1861; Charles Klatt, 1904.
47A. The Reverend F. O. Nilsson, 1857; the log school in Scandia District 17, 1860.
48. George Mattson, 1857; John Suntheim, 1863; Frank Peterson, 1904; Selby Peterson, 1918.
49. George Mattson, 1857; the Scandia Baptist Church, 1859.
50. Andrew Bergquist, the Scandia Post Office, 1857; Frank Bergquist, 1866; Peter Swenson, 1868; Peter Magnus Johnson and Charles Jorgenson, 1874; Enoch Broberg, 1886; James Holmquist, 1898; Andrew Anderson, March 27, 1902; August Nelson, March 27, 1902. (See Nelson, no. 62.)
51. Andrew Bergquist, 1857; and the Scandia Baptist Cemetery, 1859.
52. John Johnson, 1860; Andrew Bergquist, 1861; Peter Swenson, 1865; Charles Lundgren, 1874; Peter M. Johnson, 1875; and the Scandia Baptist Cemetery, 1882; Enoch Broberg, 1886.
53. Located by Stieger Lake—Leonard Breher, 1882; Gustaf Holmberg, 1893; Ted Nordberg, 1913.
54. The Victoria or Minneapolis and St. Louis ("M. & St. L.") Railroad Depot.
55. John Salter, 1863.
56. Herbert Wey, November 1, 1866; Henry Rietz, November 3, 1866; Henry Rietz Jr., 1876; Elmer Rietz, 1929.
57. John G. Maetzold, July 19, 1867; Heinrich (Henry) Peterman, July 20, 1867.
58. John Rauen, 1860; Engen Zahler, 1875.
59. Hubert Lohmar, 1865; Hubert Lohmar, Jr., 1904.
60. The Coney Island or Minneapolis and St. Louis ("M. & St. L.") Railroad Depot. (See Coney Island*, Waconia Lake.)
61. Michael Bloetzer, January 24, 1873; John (Johnson) Broberg, December 4, 1873; Theodore and Elwell Broberg, inheritances.
62. August Nelson, 1902.
63. Henry Schraan, 1860; Andrew Schraan, 1870.
64. Catherine Frazee, April 6, 1858; Clara Muchleberg, May 15, 1858; William Behmer, 1859; Axel Jorgenson, 1867; Sebastian Allman, 1875; Henry Rietz, 1879.
65. Swan Swanson, 1879; John Swanson, 1912; Anna Louise (Anderson) Larson, inheritance.
66. Joseph Hartman, 1867; Peter, Andrew, Theodore, and John William Broberg, 1873, 1880, 1896, and 1898 respectively; Martin Litfin, 1900.
67. Tobias Ottinger (located in Section 22; close to Pierson's Lake), 1861.
68. Zoar Moravian Church (built in 1863)*.

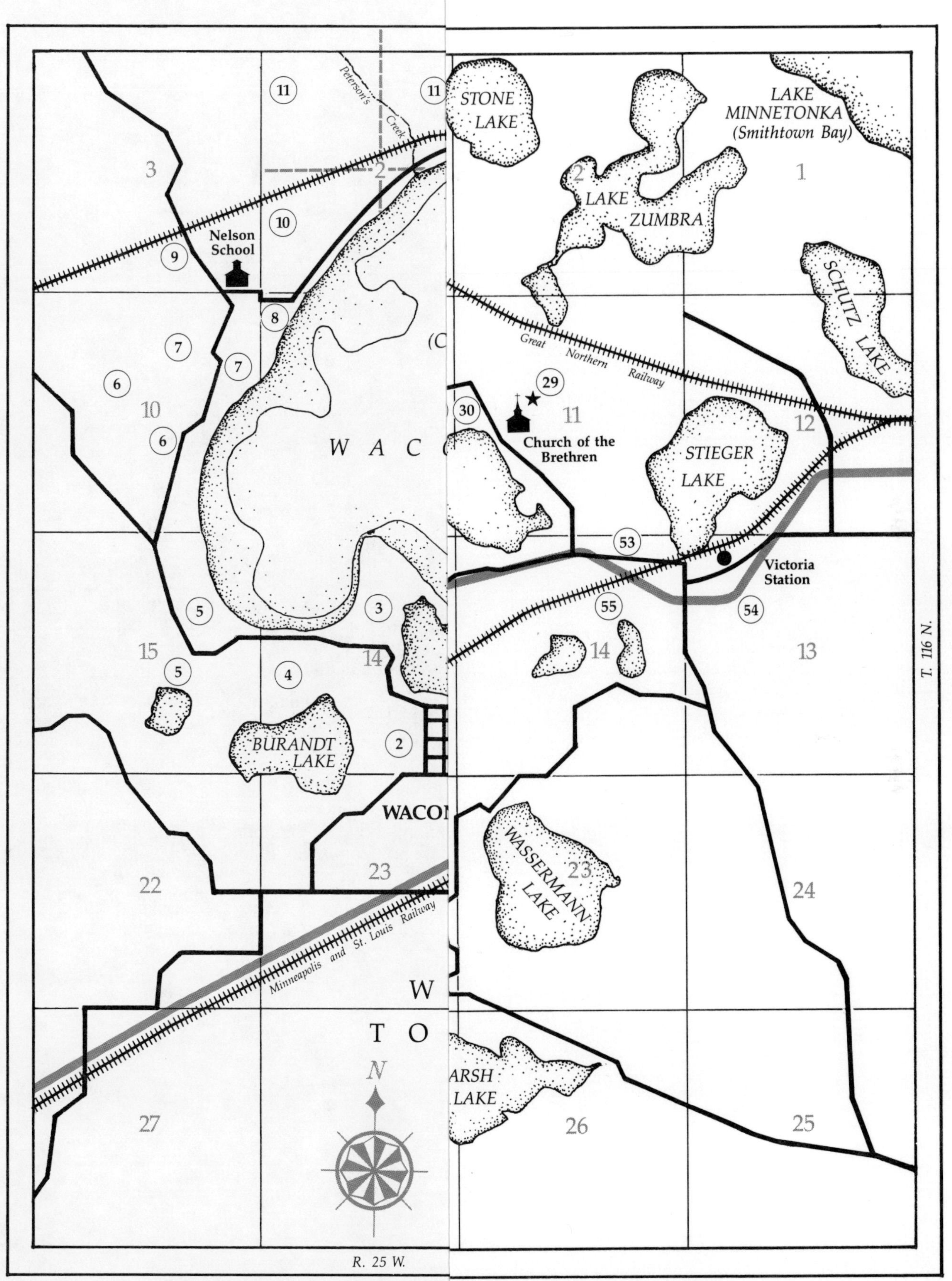

★ National Register of Historic Places

Although the environment appeared tranquil, its serenity had been rudely interrupted prior to Bergquist's arrival. The Dakota (also called Sioux) and Ojibway (or Chippewa) nations had been engaged in a death struggle on the opposite or northwest shore of the lake. This battle, fought September 7, 1852, had been a contest for the supremacy and control of land—the favorite hunting ground of both the Dakota and the Ojibway.[2]

Even after signing the treaties of Traverse des Sioux and Mendota in 1851, it was several years before the Indians left the surrounding area. When they finally moved, however, these people continued to wander back to the places they preferred to be during the summer months. Perhaps some of the bands did not understand they were violating agreements stating they would confine themselves to the property designated by the government—at the Upper and Lower Indian agencies or the reservations at Redwood and Granite Falls. (Both sites can be located in the upper regions of the Minnesota River—see map, page 46 for boundary.)

Peterson and his brother-in-law John Anderson arrived at the wharf along the Minnesota River in 1853 and tramped twelve miles through the dense forest. They found Bergquist living alone on a claim *(map 50, 51)* he had staked out as his homestead. He lived in an improvised shelter made from a covering of blankets spread over tree branches. Having established preemption claims of 160 acres each, Peterson *(map 46)* and John Anderson *(map 37, 38)* probably traveled with Bergquist part of the way on their return trip to Iowa.

According to an undated newspaper clipping belonging to the Bergquist family, Bergquist returned to Knoxville, Illinois, after choosing his claim on the shore of Waconia Lake. When he arrived, he found his children were motherless. His wife and eldest daughter had died during an epidemic of cholera. After his second marriage (the date is not known) to Ellen, a thirty-two-year-old widow, he returned to his claim in 1855. He was accompained by his children as well as Ellen and her offspring. It is not known when Frank left Sweden or joined his father and stepmother in Minnesota. It is known that he taught school in the first session of public school in Scandia in 1858. At that time, the household consisted of Nathaniel, Henrietta, and Kate (ages unknown), as well as Ingrid, ten; Stina, five; Mary, three; and Nelly, one.[3]

It was that same year, 1855, that Peterson squared his account with his employer and set out on May 4 on the riverboat journey to Minnesota Territory. He was accompanied by the families of his sister Maria Christina, the minister F. O. Nilsson, and the Johnsons. After a five-day-trip on board the *Sir Campbell*, the *Alhambra*, and the *Lady Franklin* in succession, they disembarked at St. Paul. There, John Anderson and Alexander and Jonas Peter Johnson (two men whose exact relationship is unknown) and their families boarded the steamship *Black Hawk* and proceeded up the Minnesota River.

Peterson was too ill to go on, and remained in St. Paul from May 9 until May 22. He was most likely in the company of Per Daniel Anderson (John Anderson's brother) who had arrived earlier from Iowa. The Nilssons were also in St. Paul until several days before Peterson's departure.

An unprecedented flood of immigrants poured into Minnesota in 1855 when navigation opened on April 17. People had to camp on the streets because the hotels were completely filled. Although Peterson did not say where he stayed during his convalescence, he included a payment of $.75 to "Swansons for board" in his financial account. He listed the cost of provisions he carried from Iowa, payments made for pie purchased

2. The *Waconia Patriot* on September 13, 1912, wrote about this 1852 battle and also about Chief Blue Eagle (also known as Chief La Framboise). The son of a French fur trader and a Dakota woman, Chief Blue Eagle was educated at the Indian school in Pennsylvania. He was the nephew of Chief Other Day (a friendly Indian who was credited with saving a number of lives during the Sioux Uprising in 1862). According to Chief Blue Eagle, his visit to the island in Waconia Lake and subsequent decision to permit diggings into the burial mounds (one of which was said to be a common grave for at least fifty braves) confirmed the tracings on a stone he carried whose etchings provided a guide to the Dakota Indians and their wanderings from the Minnesota River to Big Stone Lake, Mendota, Fort Snelling, Waconia, and Minnetonka. The island mounds, as well as another common grave located at the place now known as Manakiki or Pillsbury Camp *(map 8)* on the northwest shore of the lake, are the burial places of Wild Buffalo, Chief Chaska, and Chaska's grandmother. Although it was said the Dakota losses were slight (the women and children had been confined on the island), Chief Chaska and his grandmother both died during this battle.

3. By June 12, 1860, those still living at home in the combined post office and dwelling of Andrew and Ellen Bergquist were Ingrid, fifteen; Stina, ten; Mary, eight; Nelly, six; Clara, four; and Emma, two. The name of the Reverend John A. Peterson, twenty-five, also appeared as a member of the Bergquist household, according to the United States Census. By 1861, however, the Reverend Peterson was engaged in farming at his own homestead on the north shore of the lake *(map 11)*.

in Rock Island and Galena, food in St. Paul, as well as $2.45 for medication. Medicines included quinine, port wine, castor oil, a bottle of stoop beer, white sugar, brandy, and two bottles of "Power and Result."

He purchased carpentry tools, some on his own and some in common with the other immigrants. He left St. Paul May 22, and the following day he wrote, "In the evening I arrived at the wharf, San Francisco," which was a small hamlet at Carver Rapids two and one-half miles upstream from the village of Carver. It was at that time the county seat of the newly organized Carver County. The place no longer exists.

He listed as his costs for the journey as follows: deck passage from Burlington to St. Paul, $5.00; belongings, $2.43; carriage of "things" from the river in St. Paul, $.10; chest to the river in Burlington, $.10; the chest to the river in St. Paul, $.10; and freight for the chest on the Black Hawk, $.50. This totaled $8.23.

After Peterson's arrival at the San Francisco wharf, there is a gap in his record. According to the biographical reports which were printed in the *Compendium of History and Biography of Carver and Hennepin Counties, Minnesota*, Peterson returned to his claim on the quarter-section he had staked out in 1853. While at his chosen site "a claimant for his land appeared and Mr. Peterson was compelled to pay him twenty dollars, his entire capital at that time, to induce the man to leave him in undisputed possession."[4]

Peterson's reaction seems to suggest he thought the problem was an honest mistake. His payment illustrates his peaceful nature and reflects concern over future relations with this settler—a neighbor who had technically jumped his claim.

In the entry of June 18, Peterson states cryptically: "Today I bought a claim from the German for $25.00." Although he did not elaborate on that statement, it was Peter Fisher who received this payment. Fisher remained in the settlement *(map 40)* with his wife and children, and is mentioned frequently in the diaries as exchanging labor with Peterson.[5]

The early years in Scandia were ones of backbreaking labor, not the least of which were felling trees and grubbing stumps. Even before their shelters were complete, the settlers began clearing the land and, as soon as a field was tillable, planting crops.

Peterson wielded a grub hoe and planted potatoes on his claim with help from John Anderson and Alexander *(map 34)* as well as Jonas Peter Johnson *(map 45)*.

During the next several weeks in June and July, Peterson built his shanty and helped others with theirs. (The word "shanty" is used in the translated diaries, but refers to log cabins).

John Anderson's dwelling was the first one finished, and his family moved in July 11. Peterson reported that his was the next to reach the completion stage, on August 3, 1855: "In the morning I borrowed Swan's *[map 3]* oxen and moved my things to the shanty[,] including my trunks. In the afternoon I split some timber and hewed it into shape for a table." The reference to Swan Johnson indicates that other Scandinavians had established themselves around the lake during the time Bergquist, Anderson, and Peterson returned to Illinois and Iowa to make arrangements for the return trip with their families. Subsequent entries in the diary suggest that Peterson moved his possessions to the shelter, but it took several months before he occupied it. It is possible that the Reverend Nilsson and his wife Soffia moved in with John and Maria Christina Anderson after their arrival on July 20, 1855. Peterson worked on Nilsson's dwelling *(map 41, 47, 47A)* at the same time he was finishing work on his own cabin and that of Alexander Johnson—one of the men who traveled with him from Burlington. Soffia Nilsson moved into her cabin even before Peterson had finished the work on it.

4. Regarding information about Peterson's earlier journey to Minnesota in 1853, it is presumed this biographical material had been submitted by Peterson's children before the book was published in 1915. Although numerous Carver County names appear in this volume, significant numbers of pioneers did not receive similar tribute. This might have been the result of a lack of interest on the part of the pioneer. More likely he or his family did not want to pay the fee the publisher of these local compendiums asked for publication of these sketches.

5. Neither Peterson nor the biographical report in the *Compendium* actually mentioned the name of the neighbor who received payment for the land Peterson had previously claimed. Local residents were familiar with stories about this incident, which took place while squatters changed property titles through unofficial business transactions. This event occurred during a period in history when similar problems were often resolved through violence.

Although government surveyors eventually prepared individual legal descriptions and Peterson tells that his "entree" was made in 1856, the mattter was not recorded in the book at the Register of Deeds Office at the Carver County Courthouse until October 8, 1860. His certificate, or *patent*, which was issued by the United States government, finally became a matter of record on July 1, 1861.

Nilsson also kept a journal. His diary, 260 pages long, starts in 1855 and provides a comparable account of life in nineteenth-century America. Along with interesting information about the early colony, Nilsson reveals his personal conflict with the Swedish state church and his reasons for emigrating to America.

Nilsson was not the faithful correspondent that Andrew Peterson was, however, and Professor Roger McKnight writes: "One can only regret that he did not resume his writings after returning to Minnesota in 1868; we would then have had an even more thoroughgoing account of the social life in pioneer Minnesota to complement Peterson's detailed journal of farm life."

On July 20, 1855, the day of his arrival at Scandia, Nilsson wrote in his journal: "Purchased a claim, one quarter section of land. Brother Anders [Andrew Peterson] has begun to build a little house for us. Arranged for two Swedes, Sven and Magnus, to help with the work on the house." The following month, Nilsson's diary revealed he traveled to St. Paul where he purchased a cow and a calf for $39. After his arrival at Scandia from a second journey to St. Paul (to purchase flour, pork, sugar, salt, and a live pig) he said, "Upon my return the house was so near completion that my wife had moved into it. Paid Sven 6 dollars 75 cents, and Magnus 7 dollars 19. Bought window frames in St. Paul, cost 2 dollars."

Shortly after settling in Scandia, Peterson mentioned Nilsson's brief visit in Iowa. However, Nilsson found himself occupied with activities in Minnesota while his home was being built and the Scandia church was being established.

Several years passed before Nilsson's journal revealed that he had returned to Iowa where he attended church meetings. It is likely he ministered to those families who had recently established the Baptist church in New Sweden, the settlement that Peter Cassel had founded.

Prior to Nilsson's return, Peterson had already disclosed on-going relations with friends in Iowa. On August 28, 1856, he wrote: "Shillenstrom [Schillerstrom] from New Sweden has come here."[6]

On August 31, 1855, Peterson wrote, "Swan and I have finished up odds and ends at Nilsson's shanty and helped them move in. Johannes [Peterson's brother-in-law] arrived today from St. Paul with Nilsson's cow."

On September 1, he said, "I have put in the window in Nilsson's shanty, put up some shelves, dug a well and covered it."

Among the details of building that Peterson mentioned were stripping bark, clearing the land where the cabin was to stand, cutting timber, hauling logs, and chopping out rafters and shingles. He hewed out planks, stripped timbers, joined the foundation, installed rafters, and covered the roof. From the time his own cabin was "three rows high," four men worked several days to complete the walls. After the roof was on, the women helped daub mud in the chinks between the logs. When the roof and side walls were in place, the holes were chopped for windows, planks were hewed for the floor, and boards were made for the door. The windows, putty, glass, and nails were brought from St. Paul by Per Daniel Anderson. Per Daniel, John Anderson's brother, had also left Burlington. He established his own claim *(map 35)* near that of his brother, then returned to work in St. Paul.

Even though some of the pioneers had fireplaces in their dwellings, others who could afford them purchased stoves instead and had them shipped from St. Paul to Carver by steamboat, where they were picked up by ox team and wagon.

Household furnishings consisted of puncheon tables and benches made of split logs held up with legs driven into the rounded sides. After Andrew Peterson made a carpenter's bench, he made chairs, too. He carved legs and wove seats of cane during the winter of 1856.

Chests filled with belongings from Sweden served as extra tables. Bedsteads were usually frames which were fitted and fastened into the corner of the room and held in place with a single leg. The cornhusk mattresses rested on wood slats or cords tied to pegs or holes in the frame. The beds were usually built high off the floor to push the cradle, trundle bed, or other essentials under them when these furnishings were not in use. Peterson said he stored several containers filled with grain under two beds he had made.

According to Ardith K. Melloh's description of household utensils and available sources of food, pioneer women worked with whisks made from willow twigs and brooms made from a single block of wood. Assorted-size gourds served as dippers

6. The families of Gustav Schillerstrom and Peter Cassel settled in New Sweden, Iowa, in 1846. Schillerstrom's grandson and great-granddaughter still live in New Sweden and Fairfield, Iowa. Ardith K. Melloh, "Life in Early New Sweden, Iowa," in *The Swedish Pioneer Historical Quarterly*, 32:141 (April, 1981).

and containers while woodland sprouts provided nourishing ingredients for soups. Nettles, rose hips, lambs-quarters, chicory, sorrel, hops, and other wild plants were used. Melloh also quoted a member of that generation of Swedish pioneers, who compared their household duties with those of today. She explained:

> If one is being taught how to make a loaf of bread today, you first go to the market and buy the yeast, but my Mother had to plant a hop vine and when I helped her pick the hops to make the yeast for the bread, I not only learned the nature of the hop plant, but its beauty...the blossoms looked like green cones with petals folded over one another like the scales of a fish. It was these blossoms that were used in making the yeast. If we were going to make soap, we first had to make the lye[,] which was accomplished by putting the wood ashes from the kitchen stove into the big wooden hopper made for that purpose. It was quite wide at the top and narrow at the bottom. Mother knew just the right amount of water to pour over the ashes to make the lye strong enough and it drained out of a small spout at the bottom. Then came the great day for making the soap. A fire was built in the back yard; the big iron kettle with the lye in it was hung over the blaze and hot coals, and when it began to boil, the fats were dropped in and we stirred it with long wooden paddles.

Containers of water were kept close by so that female workers could dip the edges of their woolen skirts into the pails. In that way, sparks simply smoldered on their wet garments while they moved around the open fire.

On October 18, 1855, Peterson "was at the German, Fisher, for a house raising bee." A few days later, the surveyors established section and property lines in the township. On October 31, 1855, Andrew wrote: "First I went with the surveyor and measured out Johannes claim. Then the surveyor and May [Mathias Falk's wife] went over mine and Nilsson's claims, putting out markers. Nilsson got his legal description from the surveyor with a payment of $5.50. My brother-in-law got his for housing and boarding the surveyor, and I paid $5.00 and am owing $.50."

Peterson and the Reverend Nilsson entered into a gentlemen's agreement about an exchange of land even before the licensed surveyor arrived in Scandia. The November 20, 1855, entry which said, "Nilsson paid me $15.00 for my claim," substantiates the story told by John Peltz, the tenant farmer who farmed the Peterson property in later years. Peterson had originally chosen the high ground in the southeast quarter of Section 8, *(map 41, 46, 47)*, and Nilsson had a large meadow in his northeast quarter of Section 17 *(map 46, 47, 47A)*. After a cash consideration, each traded off half of his respective properties so each farm became long and narrow instead of square. Peterson received meadowland for hay, Nilsson received land covered with timber.

Frequent references in the diaries describe "cutting hay on the island." Peterson was referring to a portion of swampland he had received in the land exchange (located near the railroad tracks on the map). During the late summer, the center or higher elevation of the bog dried and became an "island."

In subsequent entries during 1855, Peterson tells of working on housing details such as doors and windows. On November 15, he wrote, "We moved into my shanty. Did a bit of everything." He does not say who moved in with him. Then, on November 29, he arranged to board with Mrs. Nilsson, but with "no decision as to price."

The Reverend Nilsson's wife Soffia was large of stature, in robust health, and well-educated for that day. Soffia was also known as a peaceful, godly woman who was hospitable in the best tradition of the frontier—always sharing freely of meager resources with neighbors as well as with needy strangers.

Family stories (from those surviving in the Anderson families) confirm that at least three families were living with John and Maria Christina Anderson for a time. Perhaps several of the men moved to Peterson's cabin when his was finally completed.

The lakes and streams provided an easily accessible source of food, and the settlers' dependence on fish was recorded in a number of instances. In May, 20, 1857, he wrote, "After dinner we went fishing with the seine, and we got a splendid lot." When Andrew bought a calf from John Peterson *(map 11)* in 1860, he received a gift of eighteen pounds of fish in addition to his purchase.

During those beginning months especially, the settlers used their animals and tools cooperatively because it was essential for survival. Peterson kept a strict account of the work exchanged. In fact, this bartering of services and breeding dates for his animals seemed to be one important reason for writing in his diary. His reminders included such unusually long entries as that of November 28, 1856, in which he describes work exchanges with "Alfred," an otherwise unidentified man whom Nilsson had recently brought with him from St. Paul. Peterson wrote in the following meticulous detail:

> Borrowed Jonas Broberg's oxen to haul logs for the fence on the other side of the maple. Alfred was also here with his oxen and hauled logs. He owed me 2½ days work, one day I counted off for the oxen and the half day I counted off for the sinkers he made for the seine and the mending of the net. In the evening Nilsson and I made up our account for the last period of boarding and the 6½ days work, I had done during that time, also for the five days of work I had done and the boards I had given that should count off when I built his cow shed because of the board I had had when I built mine.

Even between relatives who were very close emotionally and spiritually, favors and exchanges of labor became a matter of record. On December 15, 1857, Peterson wrote, "Johannes [Peterson's brother-in-law], took 5 bushels of corn down to Carver for me. He got $.60 a bushel but had to take planks instead of cash." On May 12 to 14, 1858, the entry read: "Was at Johannes and helped him clear a field to pay for plowing and harrowing my wheat field."

Up until 1862, settlers could stake out markers on 160 acres of land. They were obligated to make improvements while they lived there for a specified period of time. When these "squatters" traveled to the United States Land Office in Minneapolis, many of them had scarcely enough gold or silver to pay $1.50 an acre, which was the land office charge to secure the deed to the land.

On December 6, 1856, Peterson made a trip with Nilsson to Minneapolis, where he visited the United States Land Office to "prove up" his claim. That is, he demonstrated that he had made the improvements on his claim required by law and had paid for the land. He wrote the single diary entry about his journey after his return and recorded nothing more until March 18, 1857, at which time he indicated that "Nilsson and I went to Minneapolis and Nilsson paid for his claim."

During the gap of weeks in Peterson's diary, the boundaries of a proposed town of Scandia were outlined in a document drawn up on February 14, 1857, by John Oswald Brunius. Brunius described himself in the declaration as the surveyor of the town and the proprietor of the timber area within the boundaries of Scandia *(map outline)*. The plat of the proposed town exists in a book of plats which had been prepared on behalf of several persons calling themselves proprietors of the town.[7] Besides Brunius, the landowners included Josiah Talbot, John W. Stevens, Artimas Stevens, Simon Stevens, and Cathrina Freeze, none of whom are mentioned in the Peterson diaries.

Since the proposed town was never actually incorporated, the plat is not a part of the Carver County records and it is difficult to determine the exact boundary lines of the town from Brunius's proposal. The approximate site of the town of Scandia can be described as 310 acres of land lying east of the present city of Waconia and southwest of the farms owned by Peterson, Nilsson, and the Baptists of this story. The present-day sanctuary and school of the Trinity Lutheran Church, built in 1969, lies on the edge of the proposed site.

Glowing reports by local residents and the proprietors platting the town of Scandia may have promoted speculation on the part of one Roswell P. Russell. Russell, an aggressive businessman and owner of a store in St. Anthony (later Minneapolis), was also engaged in lumbering and flour milling. From 1854 to 1857, he was associated with the United States District Land Office, and he became interested in a site west of the proposed town of Scandia because of its potential as a future resort area. With this in mind, he purchased land on the shore of Clearwater Lake *(map 1)* and hired G.W. King to survey and plat the resort. King arrived in Carver County sometime during March, 1857.

While Russell promoted land sales in the resort village of Waconia, many of the early arrivals spent brief periods of time in the actual settlement of Scandia. Some of the homeless pioneers stayed with friends or relatives in crude dwellings where they slept in lofts or on packed earth floors. Others lived in abandoned shelters. During the day they

7. The plat book description (see Sources) for the Town of Scandia stated: "That the town is located on the North (½) of the North East (¼) of Section (24) and the East half of the South East fractional quarter of Section (13) in Township (116) North Range (25) West of the Fifth Principal Meridian and on the N.W. fractional (¼) of the N.W. (¼) of Section (19) and the S.W. fractional (¼) of the S.W. (¼) of Section (18) and on fractional Lot No. (3) in Section (18). Township (116) North Range (24) West of Fifth Principal Meridian containing (310) Acres more or less."

Warren Upham says in his book, *Minnesota Geographic Names: Their Origin and Historical Significance* (St. Paul, 2nd ed., 1969), 83, that the name "Scandia" is a derivation from an ancient Roman name. Upham also said the village of Waconia was given its name by Roswell Russell after the original Indian name of the lake.

worked as hired hands or traveled to nearby settlements to search for places of their own.

On the day Minnesota became a state, May 11, 1858, each township organized and elected its first officers. Andrew Bergquist was elected clerk of the township during a meeting held in the home of Merritt Green. Other elected officers were John Groetsch, Henry Wetzig, and Fred (Henry) Rietz, supervisors; John G. Maetzold, collector; Charles Kauffman, assessor; John Groetsch and Joseph Schaaf, justices of the peace; Henry Schwartz, constable; and Henry Wetzig, overseer of the poor.

After the first assembly and election, other citizens of the township expressed dissatisfaction. They complained that the meeting had been poorly attended and was not fairly representative of the population. They also felt the township name, "St. Valentine," which was the first selection, was not suitable.[8]

Andrew Bergquist was sworn in as clerk of the township at a special meeting called on June 12 to reconsider the results of the May 11 meeting. The election of officers during the May 11 meeting was unanimously approved. John A. Salter, a German who had arrived in the early 1850s, made a motion to change the name of the township. Because he could see five lakes from the elevation of his cabin *(map 55)*, he proposed that the name be Laketown. His motion carried.

The meeting also established mandatory fencing laws to keep farm animals from wandering at large. Specific rules defined the height of fences, amount of space allowed between the rails, the capture and holding of strays, and compensation for damage and animal care.

The pioneers were plagued with "identity problems" after one of the first post offices in Laketown Township had been established in the home of Andrew Bergquist. There was and still is the picturesque community called Scandia, in Washington County, as well as the village of this story, no longer in existence, called Scandia in Carver County. Although many of the settlers eventually changed their own names because so many were similar, the Nelsons, Johnsons, and Petersons were among those experiencing problems as to the exact destination of correspondence being mailed to the states from Sweden as well as elsewhere.

Andrew Bergquist wrote about the new settlement in the September 8, 1858, issue of the *Hemlandet* (Homeland), a well-known Swedish periodical published in Chicago:

> This settlement is in my opinion the best and most beautiful in Carver County. It is situated on one of the most beautiful—if not the most beautiful—lakes in the whole state. This is also the consensus of opinion of all travelers who have visited it. The lake is twelve [?] square miles, surrounded by a rich growth of sugar maple, and the soil is extremely fertile. The Swedes own most of the land contingent on the lake, and fourteen lakes border [within several miles] on its shore. The price of land at present is $6 an acre. The Swedes who have settled here came from different provinces of Sweden, and most of them have embraced the Baptist faith. They have already erected a meeting house. In 1855 only seven families had settled at Scandia, but the numbers soon increased to twenty-two. Some of them came from Galesburg, Illinois; others from Burlington, Iowa, led by Baptist preacher, Rev. Fr. O. Nilson *[sic]*. Some Swedish Lutheran families that had settled here did not like to mingle with the Baptists, and thereupon they sold their lands to the Germans, who bought also large tracts of land south of the lake.

Fall work for the new settlers included cutting and husking corn, digging potatoes, and threshing—an activity which was shared by all. The people in the community moved from farm to farm until the threshing was done. They cut, cradled, stacked, and threshed grain together. During the first year or two of the settlement, wheat harvesting was done by hand with a sickle and flail. Whenever it became necessary to take wheat to the mill for grinding, or prepare it for use as seed, the wheat was fanned. It was a simple process. Wheat was poured into a winnowing basket which was swirled so that the wind caught the lighter chaff and carried it off, leaving the kernels behind.

One of the first threshing machines in the vicinity was owned by Wendelin Grimm, who is famous for perfecting a winter-hardy strain of alfalfa. Grimm's machine was propelled by the continuous circling motion of four horses. Peterson referred to such a machine in a detailed account of wheat and rye yield on October 26, 1858, and it is quite probable that he was referring to Grimm's thresher, because the latter's farm was at the northern border of Scandia.

On April 15, 1858, Grimm moved his family to the log cabin and homestead he had purchased

8. Although several sources give Liberty as the first name given the township, records confirm the name was St. Valentine. Since there is no real order to the pages in Laketown Record Book "A," where this documented evidence exists, the number 19.8 was marked for identification purposes at the lower left corner of this particular page.

Andrew and Ellen Bergquist

from John Neunzinger *(map 17)*. He also enlarged his tract *(map 18)* as property became available or as he could afford it. The success of the dairy industry in Carver County was due largely to the continued efforts of this Laketown Township pioneer who, starting with seed brought from Germany, patiently replanted seeds from plants that survived the cold Minnesota winters. In 1859, and every season thereafter, Grimm sowed the "ewiger klee" or seeds from surviving stock even though, according to Theodore C. Blegen, he did not understand the "practical or scientific importance of his experiment in acclimatization."

Another time-consuming and laborious task was the hewing out of rails for fences. For many days the brief entry "making rails" was repeated. Finally, Peterson recorded that he had completed 2,000 rails and was ready to put up fences.

As the small settlement grew, Peterson recorded work exchanges with an increasing number of people. After laboring in the vicinity of Parley Lake on December 27, 1858, he wrote, "In the morning I was over at Peter Nilsson and chopped runners for the sled." He joined Nilsson's foundation to his home and was repaid with matching hours of field work. He later mentions the burial of Peter Nilsson's son in 1862. When Nilsson's wife, too, passed away on December 5, 1864, Nilsson apparently lost his incentive to stay and left the settlement, selling his place *(map 22)* to George Brethorst.

Peterson's use of oxen was also typical of Scandia's early days. Oxen were preferred to horses because they were less expensive to buy and just as strong, while they required only half as much food and were less temperamental. When they could no longer be used as draft animals, they could be slaughtered for food. Unlike horses, they did not need an expensive leather harness. A primitive wooden yoke with homemade traces was all that was necessary.

While John Anderson, one of the original settlers, worked his farm, he studied to prepare himself to become a minister. In September of 1860, he sold 20 of his 160 acres *(map 38)* to Swen Bengston. That same year, on December 12, 1860, Peterson mentioned the death of his nephew—John and Maria Christina Anderson's son. "Then I made a casket for Johannes' boy Ludwik."

Three years later, Anderson received $925 for the remainder of his homestead. He sold out to Jacob Jenni after he accepted the call for his services from the Vasa Baptist congregation in Goodhue County in the vicinity of Red Wing. The Reverend Anderson also served parishes at Eggleston, Minneapolis, and finally, the church at Leenthrop, a rural town close to Maynard and Montevideo in Chippewa County.

As time went on, the farms in the vicinity of Parley and Clearwater lakes defined a growing settlement. Scandia itself included the Scandia Baptist Church (also called the meeting house), the cemetery or final resting place of the pioneers ("God's Acre"), the post office and school, cleared fields, animal shelters, and primitive dwellings.

Although the proposed town of Scandia remained rural within the thousands of acres forming the boundaries of the township, the adjacent villiage which Russell had envisioned grew as planned. With its growth, Clearwater Lake, the name given by Bergquist, gradually faded in popularity to be replaced by its Indian name—Waconia.

The entryway and steeple were added to the meeting house in 1910. (See page 148 for an earlier view of the building.)

CHAPTER 5

F.O. Nilsson and the Scandia Baptist Church

After building cabins and planting crops, the immigrants' religious commitment was their most important consideration. On August 1, 1855, nine settlers organized into a church, Scandia Baptist, in Andrew Peterson's cabin. This was the mother church of the Minnesota Swedish Baptist Conference. Besides the Reverend Nilsson and his wife Soffia Ulrika, the group was composed of Andrew Peterson, John and Maria Christina Anderson, Alexander and Sara Johnson, and Jonas Peter and Greta Johnson.[1]

On August 16, Peterson said, "Nilsson went today to Chisago Lake, and Root River [Chisago and Houston Counties, Minnesota]." Nilsson's journey also extended into Iowa, because Peterson mentioned his homecoming from there more than eight weeks later.

Perhaps Nilsson's compatriot, Per Daniel Anderson, shared in promoting a mutual missionary objective. Seven days after Nilsson returned, Peterson mentioned that Per Daniel had also returned from Iowa. Although Per Daniel, whose brother John was Andrew Peterson's brother-in-law, lived in St. Paul at the time, a claim was being held for him in Scandia *(map 35)*.

Nilsson's exile from Sweden, asylum in North America, settlement in Carver County, founding of the Baptist congregation in Waconia, missionary visits to the Swedish settlements in the St. Croix Valley—particularly Taylors Falls and Chisago Lake—were facts repeated in fiction by Vilhelm Moberg. One can only imagine Moberg's reaction when he unexpectedly found Peterson's ink-penned notes in the ledger revealing the name of one of the chief leaders of Sweden's religious awakening. Moberg's brief biographical sketch of Frederick Nilsson that exists in some editions of the *Last Letter Home* described the challenges Nilsson faced during missionary visits to Chisago Lake.

Contemporary reports say Nilsson found favor with many of the immigrants of that day. So did Moberg's Baptist preacher, F. O. Nilsson. Nilsson had gained the sympathy of the immigrants because of his persecution in the homeland. Now the settlers deliberately went against the warnings that had been issued from their church pulpits and helped Nilsson find places to preach and attended his meetings.[2]

1. Jonas Peter Johnson was one of several who, in the earliest days of settlement, studied for the ministry, was ordained, and later left Scandia to preach the gospel. He sold his improved land located in Section 9 *(map 45)* in several pieces, including one part to John Lundsten. Lundsten reconsidered his purchase and sold out the same day he bought it. The farm passed on to Swan Halling and eventually to the families of Hans Hanson, Thomas P. Johnson, Henry Rietz, and Henry Peterman. (See Sources.)

2. In Dr. Norris Magnuson's article, "Our Unsung Heroines," in *The Standard*, May 15, 1977, he said of Nilsson's persecution in Sweden: "Unfortunate as the sentence was for the Nilssons [whippings, imprisonment, and banishment], it became a great victory for the cause of the Baptists and the larger free church movement. Newspapers carried the story of the Nilsson trial to all of Sweden and abroad, and large crowds turned out to hear the now-famous preacher. Nilsson's dignified and clearcut presentation was well received by audiences that included a number of sympathetic Lutheran believers who were soon to become Swedish Baptist leaders."

Under Nilsson's strong leadership, the Scandia Baptist Church membership numbered thirty-two by the end of 1856. Following the organization of the church in Andrew Peterson's cabin, this small group continued to meet in members' homes. The first baptismal service took place during this time, when Magnus and Christine Peterson were baptized in an opening in the ice in Clearwater Lake on February 17, 1856.

Andrew Bergquist, the founder of this lakeshore settlement, played an important role in the life of the church. During April, 1856, Andrew and Ellen Bergquist were baptized, and on Sunday, June 8, Peterson wrote, "We all had communion at Bergquist."

The church members met to learn English and for choir practice. Andrew mentions on April 4, 1857, "We had a language meeting at Johannes [Peterson's brother-in-law]. We had a real good time. Nilsson and I beat Johannes at words."

In the spring of 1857, work began on a meeting house for the congregation. The timber was already at the site (though when they hauled it there is not clear) when Peterson wrote on April 13, 1857, "Forenoon- Had a meeting at Bjorkquist's [Bergquist's] house. P.M. had a raising bee at the church building." ("Raising bee" probably refers to the workers' installation of the uprights or the framework.) This structure was a log cabin 20 by 26 feet in size.

Six months later, finishing touches were made. Peterson wrote in the combined entry for October 9 and 10, "I worked at the church. We put in the windows." The following Monday he wrote, "I worked at the church for Johannes. We put in the doors." Then, "In the forenoon I was alone at the church. Finished hanging the door and put up the facing."

The scarcity of ministers on the frontier prompted Philip Otto Johnson and Josephine Helen Brown from the nearby Swedish settlement called Götaholm at Swede Lake to seek Nilsson's services in the newly built church. They walked eight miles with their bridal party to Scandia. Nilsson performed the sacrament of marriage for the young Lutheran couple on December 24, 1857.

After their hike back to Götatholm (near Watertown), they arrived at their cabin only to be scolded by the bride's mother. She had prepared a rabbit dinner and was concerned that their lateness might have spoiled the meal.

Philip and Josephine were grateful for their wedding gifts—an overall dress, a pair of wooden shoes, and a hoe. Among the furnishings, which Philip had made himself, was a poster bed, supported by stakes of wood which were driven into the packed-earth floor of the cabin.

Church officers handled matters requiring disciplinary action in the community. On one occasion, Peterson recorded that a member was called up before the church officers for jumping a claim, although he does not say how the case was decided. In another incident, injuries were apparently inflicted upon Peter Fisher's farm animals by a dog, but no specifics were given in this entry. Peterson did explain, however, how financial restitution was made in this case involving a neighbor who was not a member of the same church. On April 4, 1857, he wrote: "Nilsson and I went over to Fisher to be reconciled to him. This is the way we decided. Nilsson paid him $10.00 but if the sheep should die he was to pay $6.00 more, and, if the cow should calve within the next 9 days and the calf should die, then he was to pay for that besides $2.00 Nilsson gave Fisher so that he should call off the case against me. I am to pay Nilsson these $2.00." And on April 16, he wrote: "First I was with Mr. Nilsson to Fishers when he paid him $7.00 for the calf which was dead. Mr. Fisher promised he would ask no more damages for injuries that the dog had done."

According to studies carried on by Professor Roger McKnight, Nilsson's journals indicate the minister, who was a missionary worker and circuit rider, traveled little outside of Carver County during his first two winters in Minnesota. On January 28, 1857, he related the harrowing experience of a traveler who had taken the wrong path home. He had finally been forced to turn back by a wolf pack which had supposedly been a threat to him, and Nilsson and his wife took him in for the night.

Nilsson was to have a similar experience. While traveling in July, 1857, on a poorly marked trail from Washington County to Scandia, he was consoled by the thought that he should eventually establish his bearings when he encountered the scheduled pony express rider. He missed the mail carrier, however, and later wrote:

> I had 33 miles left to Shakopee. I even had to ask about the road, which I then found difficult to find, since in these new counties they have surveyed the roads but have not managed to build them. No mail carrier came, and I actually lost my way once, but after extreme exertion in the forest succeeded in reaching a house, where I rested a while and found

out about the road, which was rather badly cleared. My new road was a rather fresh wagon track, and I had to literally crawl on my hands and feet at one point in order to detect the above-mentioned wagon track in the long grass. From the above-mentioned house I was shown the course I had to take through thickets, without any path, for two miles to an open road. Towards the afternoon I came to a place called Spring Lake. I had now hiked by foot nearly 60 miles in two days, in a heat of over 90° celsius *[sic]*, and had today had no chance to eat since breakfast, but had sweated and drunk unreasonably.[3] I was now so sick that although I had merely eight miles left to Shakopee I had to stay at Spring Lake.

In March of 1859, Nilsson described another life-threatening situation as he sought shelter from a raging winter storm. He said:

> The blowing and snowing gained terrific strength and was accompanied with severe cold. When I had crossed a creek about a mile from Stillwater so much snow had fallen that it became impossible for me to see where the road was. The horse took off to the left from the proper route—a thing I discovered a while after it happened. But since the horse seemed especially eager to pursue her new course I let her carry on, hoping in the meantime that by instinct she was headed for some out-of-the-way farm place. That hope was happily realized. For when I had ridden for awhile I came upon a rail-fence, which I followed around its curves until I at last was right up by a fine farm house which on account of the blinding snowstorm I failed to see until I was close to it.

Nilsson spent the night with a widow and her two sons and reported he made slow headway—only fifteen miles during the forenoon—because of the drifted snow.

The first conference of the Swedish Baptists in Minnesota was held in the log church. Four congregations, with a total of 160 members, participated—Scandia, Houston, Chisago Lake, and Wastedo (in Goodhue County). Peterson recorded this event in his diary on Saturday, September 18, 1858, "In the Afternoon we went to a prayer meeting in preparation for the Conference." Sunday services were held as usual and on Monday he wrote that "the Conference started," and ended the following day.

According to church records, the Sunday school was organized in 1858 with John Erickson as superintendent. Later (in connection with English language lessons), "the first public school in the vicinity held its first class in the church, the teacher being Frank Bergquist."

Peterson's diaries frequently mentioned sharing rides with neighbors to the Swedish communities at Götaholm as well as to "King Oscar's Settlement," where Elsa, Peterson's bride-to-be, lived. This settlement was located three miles southwest of Carver. (Eventually the name of King Oscar's settlement, given in honor of the King of Sweden and Norway and growing numbers of his Norwegian subjects who had also settled therein, was changed to the Union Settlement.)

In either the fall of 1853 or the following spring of 1854, the Reverend P. A. Cederstrom, the Lutheran pastor from Chisago Lake, and others sponsored by the Lutheran Synod of Northern Illinois, were the first to provide the Scandinavian families in Union Settlement with formal spiritual enrichment. This was the religious preference of the Protestants establishing their log buildings in the river town of Carver and beyond to Oscar's Settlement.

Some of the early families in Oscar's Settlement proposed that the forty-acre tract (which had not as yet been claimed) was to be sold with a contingency that provided for a future building site for church purposes. Thus, even before the congregation was organized, the sanctuary of the East Union Scandinavian Lutheran Church (about 30 feet wide and 36 feet long) was built on a three-acre tract. Until the church was established in 1858, some of the settlers apparently experienced emotional or spiritual unrest caused by the missionary efforts of the Baptists, Methodists, and various fly-by-night preachers, including a Lutheran minister who allegedly had problems with alcohol.

One of the first responsibilities assumed by the newly installed church deacons at the Union Settlement church was to plan their school, which became the forerunner of Gustavus Adolphus College in St. Peter. They also wrote some regulations designed to guard themselves and their congregation against preachers or laymen who were not followers of the true evangelical Lutheran doctrine. Speakers found it necessary to show church authorities their licenses or letters of recommendation before delivering messages from the pulpit at Oscar's Settlement church.

From the time members in the congregation organized at the Union Settlement, the community had been pushing farther west. Some families who were now located four or more miles beyond the church discovered the reality of Minnesota's un-

3. Nilsson probably meant to write the word Farenheit instead of Celsius, since 90° Celsius converts to a Farenheit reading of 194°.

predictable and often harsh winter weather. Traveling even a few additional miles became a critical factor during an era when most pioneers depended upon a few fortunate sled-owning families to pick them up along the way to Sunday services; otherwise they walked. These factors prompted these distant members to seek support for their effort to build another place of worship.

In 1858, the East Union settlement church board approved a request made by some of its members to build a second church, creating two congregations of the same Lutheran denomination. Thus, the East and West Union churches came into being in 1858. In 1876, other members asked the board to consider a second request to build a place of worship closer to home. It was granted and the Salem Lutheran Church was built in Carver.

Some of those who made a permanent break away from the East and West Union congregations had been ministered to by Pastor A. G. Linden. Following his withdrawal from the West Union church with some of its members, these families held services in the post office at Gotha.[4] They were affiliated with Ansgarius Synod but eventually merged with the Mission Covenant Church.

Still others who were being ministered to by the Reverends F. O. Nilsson and Gustaf Palmquist met in private homes. In 1879, they built the Swedish Methodist Episcopal Church, said to have cost $1,000, near the homestead of Marvin White, located on Section 10 in San Francisco Township. However, neither of these splinter groups survived in their isolated surroundings.

Peterson remarked on May 2, 1858, that "The German took communion with us today" in reference to a Baptist neighbor. Several German families in Scandia, as well as in the nearby settlement of Minnetrista, became Baptists. Encouraged by their Swedish friends, this small assembly organized a church, "The German Congregation of Baptized Christians in Minnetrista, Minnesota," on November 20, 1858.

4. The post office was located one mile west of West Union on Section 1 in Hancock Township. It faced the general store—a brick building (now abandoned) which still stands and marks the place called Gotha. Although it is generally agreed that those who broke away from the existing church met at the Gotha post office, other statements differ as to what denomination the faction parties adopted. According to the *Compendium of History and Biography of Carver and Hennepin Counties, Minnesota* (page 244), the dissenters worshiped at the Gotha post office until a frame building was completed at a cost of $800 on Section 1. The *Compendium* claimed the religious character of the church changed in 1874 "from Lutherianism *[sic]* to Methodism."

The Reverend Nilsson officiated during ordination of the church's first pastor, John Wendt. Wendt became the pastor of the church—the first German-speaking Baptist church congregation in Minnesota.

On Easter Sunday, April 24, 1859, Peterson wrote, "We had a German meeting when two Germans were baptized." Peterson also told of spending the night at Wendt's home, a cabin that served as a place of worship for nine years until the first log church was built in 1868.

Fifteen years later, in 1873, the Germans constructed an impressive brick-faced building. Members of the Peterson family attended the dedication. The Baptists in the area still use the same sanctuary, which is now called the Minnetrista Baptist Church.[5]

In 1859, George (sometimes called Erik) and Ellen Mattson donated one-quarter acre of their farm *(map 49)* for use by the Scandia Baptist Church congregation. Since the meeting house had been built nearly two years earlier, the 1859 date suggests a legal delay in issuing and recording the deed. Andrew and Ellen Bergquist donated land *(map 51)* for cemetery use in 1859.

The families in Scandia worshiped with help from other lay preachers or ministers while supporting Nilsson and his wife Soffia. Nilsson traveled 445 miles on foot and on horseback during the second quarter of 1859.

Nilsson recorded at least five trips down the Mississippi to Iowa and Illinois to attend church meetings and to promote his evangelistic crusade.[6] In 1859, his diary described some of the dangers he experienced: once he floundered waist deep in a swamp; another time he was pinned under his buggy. He was repeatedly confronted with the perils of washed-out bridges.

In 1860, when Nilsson returned to Minnesota

5. The book *Minnetrista Baptist Church, St. Bonifacius, Minnesota* (published to celebrate the centennial in 1958) lists 451 baptisms. It also reported that others in the congregation had been received into the fellowship by letter.

A pictorial book entitled *Directory of the Minnetrista Baptist Church in Commemoration of the 125th Anniversary, 1858-1983* (Columbia, S.C. 1983) provides members with a memento of this congregation's birthday tribute. On July 16, 1983, members and friends celebrated during a homecoming picnic and also attended special services throughout the week of October 9-16.

6. McKnight's discussion of Nilsson's memoirs mentioned contact made with Gustaf Unonius (the gentleman farmer from Pine Lake, Wisconsin) who was then an Episcopalian minister in Chicago. Nilsson also described his visits to the Bishop Hill commune in Illinois.

from the settlements in Galesburg and Bishop Hill, Illinois, he found a letter waiting from the Twenty-fifth Street Baptist Church in New York City. Members had voted on May 11, 1860, to support a missionary program in Scandinavia, and asked Nilsson to accept the call to return to their homeland. The furor of religious intolerance had died down in Sweden following the repeal of the Conventicle Decree in 1858.

Even before Nilsson accepted the proposed assignment, the pulpit vacancy in Scandia had been filled by Alfred Johnson, a newly licensed minister and a Scandia resident *(map 35, 36)*. Peterson's October 2, 1859, report was: "Sunday. Mr. Gail from Minneapolis and a preacher from Shakopee were here and we have today chosen Alfred [Johnson] and Erickson as teachers to preach God's word."

During this transition period in the Scandia Baptist Church, the missionary preacher of the Augustana Synod Lutheran Church, the Reverend Eric Norelius, described his journey through Waconia on December 5, 1860. He mentioned the evening devotional service, which was held at the home of a Lutheran family by the name of Borrow Swanberg at a cabin located on the west side of the lake *(map 3)*. Although the pioneers listened reverently, Norelius remarked there were too few people to organize a Lutheran church.

After staying overnight with the Swanbergs, Norelius traveled across the ice on Clearwater Lake to Scandia, where he reported the settlement was composed of twenty-five to thirty families. He accepted an invitation to preach in the Scandia Baptist Church. His message to twenty or more persons was taken from the bibical text, Zechariah 12:9-13. Later, he discovered there was some dissension about a theological issue relating to the doctrine on elections (the belief that it is not our own initiative but the work of the Holy Spirit which brings humankind to Christ).

Norelius spent the evening with George Mattson, who was from Ockelbo, Gastrikland, in Sweden.[7] Norelius was impressed with Mattson, who was described as a lovable man who was unusually well-educated for a farmer. He knew enough Greek to read the New Testament in Greek quite well. Norelius judged that Mattson had been shaken in his faith and hoped he would eventually return to the church he had departed.

When Norelius left the settlement on December 7, 1860, he continued his journey through the forest to Götaholm where, he said, the Swedes had settled around the small body of water called Swede Lake, about two miles from the village of Watertown.

Alfred Johnson's ministry at Scandia was of short duration – 1859 to 1860 – since Johnson and several unnamed others rejoined the Lutheran church through the preaching of the Reverend Peter Carlson from the East Union Lutheran Church. A baptismal service was subsequently held at Johnson's cabin. Johnson placed a basin of water on a three-legged stool, then reached for the baby in his wife Mary's arms, and dropped to his knees as he instructed his youngsters – Robert, who was five; Frank, three; and Lila, two – to form a circle around him. Carlson baptized them, as well as several other older children from other families who had also withdrawn from the Baptist church.

Without mentioning Alfred Johnson's departure, Peterson's May 27, 1860, entry was, "Sunday. [Reverend John A.] Peterson was today chosen as our pastor in the church. [Andrew] Norelius and Nilsson's brother are here today, also Granlund, Svedlund and Mortenson."[8] That meeting continued throughout the following day. Peterson's remark about a "love feast" which was held during these sessions meant the participants had broken down the barriers that separated them because of wealth, culture, or other outward manifestations of status. By sharing a meal or eating and drinking together before partaking in the sacrament of Holy Communion, they had expressed the very nature of the church – their equality in the eyes of God.

7. Mattson, according to the 1860 Census, was a thirty-four-year-old farmer. He and his wife Ellen and their children, George Henry and John William, then two and three respectively, left the settlement in 1863, but maintained close ties with the Petersons and returned to visit them in Scandia after settling in California.

8. The Reverend Ernest G. Nelson's article, the "Historical Sketch of the South Isanti Baptist Church" (formerly the Swedish Baptist Church of Isanti) in the *Centennial Program of the One Hundredth Year Jubilee (1860-1960)* noted the Isanti church was organized with help from the Reverend Andrew Norelius of Vasa on May 27, 1860. He acted as chairman while the Reverend Anders Wiberg (former Lutheran pastor and educator) served as reader confirming the Baptist Principles of Faith. Among the charter members of this congregation (who met at Olaf Eastlund's home) were the parents of Andrew Norelius, the Baptist preacher, and son Eric, a Lutheran preacher.

Allen Kastrup's book, *The Swedish Heritage in America,* 202 (St. Paul, 1975), said Andrew Norelius also served as a chaplain in the Union Army during the Civil War and finally settled in Iowa.

On June 5, Peterson recorded, "Forenoon we went and said goodby to Mr. Nilsson. Today he started on his return trip to Sweden."

The special respect which the members had for their spiritual leader is shown through Peterson's statements. He addressed the minister and his wife by their last name although he used first names while making references to people in general.

Elna and Nicholas Swenson settled themselves in the home formerly occupied by the Reverend and Mrs. Nilsson. They had been baptized in Sweden and joined the local church on July 26, 1861. Even so, Peterson seemed to have little reason to mention their presence during their beginning days in Scandia.

Since the Reverend Johnson had been preaching while Nilsson was away on his missionary circuit, the sequence of events suggests the Reverend John A. Peterson *(map 11)* had been devoting his time and energy to help organize the public schools at the same time that the church was in transition. Peterson had his farm, his ministry, an acting (then official) superintendency of the Laketown Township schools, and his teaching responsibilities—clearly more than a man described as frail and physically weak should have been expected to handle. He was minister for two years, until 1862. Peterson's spiritual and intellectual strength were his most notable characteristics. The Reverend Peterson has been remembered primarily for his writings, as well as for the book of songs called the *Trumpet of Zion* or *Sions Basun*—the first Swedish Baptist hymnal published in the United States.

The name of John A. Peterson is not mentioned in Peterson's diary for several years until November 19, 1871, when he noted that "Sunday. John A. Peterson from Blue Earth is here." Court records suggest that the minister's empty dwelling may have been abandoned, because seventeen years passed before Axel Jorgenson's name appeared on the property title.

The church grew rapidly during its first seven years. In 1862, it had sixty-two members, but this was its high point. Membership dropped, then made a comeback, but never again in those early years did it have that large a membership. (Unlike many churches in which infants are baptized and counted as members, the children of Baptist parents are not included on membership rolls until they make a public confession of faith and are baptized.)

Peterson brought attention to circumstances requiring consideration by the church board on January 10, 1859, when he wrote, "In the afternoon we had a special meeting in regards to the legitimate complaints Nilsson had against some of the church members."

Nilsson's journals reveal he was not timid about defending and maintaining the discipline of the church. After a discussion about an unmarried couple (the woman was pregnant) who were members of the church, Nilsson said, "when offenses of that nature occurred exclusion was the rule."

The subject of integrity became a central issue after Sven Abrahamson voiced a personal protest of duplicity against Nilsson. He charged that the minister gave two different groups varying explanations of predestination. The congregation favored the minister in this debate.

On April 18, 1862, two years after Nilsson's departure, Peterson wrote, "Had a meeting when Abrahamson left the church."

In January, 1875, Scandia Baptist was at its low point, with only fifteen members. While families moving away accounted for some of the decline, internal dissension and social and religious reaction following the Civil War also contributed to the loss in membership. Over the next fifteen years, approximately twenty-four members were dropped from the rolls.

Peterson remarked on March 9, 1875, "Went to the election and in the afternoon to the meeting in Scandia. Peter Carlson from Carver [East Union] preached and organized a Lutheran Church." Some of those new members had formerly been associated with the Scandia Baptist Church.

The Waconia Swedish Lutheran church declined in numbers and the German Lutherans who moved into the area established Trinity Lutheran Church (Missouri Synod) in Waconia.

In mid-1875, Scandia Baptist Church began to experience a revival. Of twenty-six people baptized during a special service in June, twenty new members were of the second generation—sons and daughters of the pioneers. The Reverend John Erickson was pastor at the time, and Peterson's brother-in-law John Anderson, who was then at Vasa, came to assist him. The building too was renovated that year, with siding put on to cover the logs.

Andrew Peterson wrote on July 4, 1876, that "The Lutherans and we celebrated together in Scandia. John Anderson from Vasa made the opening speech." He did not mean the Augustana Synod

Lutherans from East and West Union or Götaholm but rather those who had split from the Augustana Synod Lutherans over religious differences.

Although it is not known when the crude benches were exchanged for pews in the church, Peterson provided information about the first pulpit on March 9, 1860. He wrote, "Was at the meeting house and helped Hammarberg *[sic]* make the pulpit."[9] This podium served speakers and ministers until October 31, 1876. Then Peterson revealed, "Elsa [Andrew's wife] and I went to Waconia, then I hauled the pulpit and book case to the meeting house, and then I dug up grape vines."

In these gradually changing surroundings, preachers from various denominations were welcome at the Scandia church as well as the Peterson home. Political candidates also used the church as a meeting house, regardless of party affiliation. Thirty-one student pastors profited by their experiences from this church pulpit.

In writing of the many who used his home and the church to speak, Peterson wrote on September 16, 1871, "In the afternoon we had a Covenant meeting in our house. J. A. Peterson and O. Hakanson are here." In 1876, he wrote, "I attended the Lutheran services in Scandia." A year later, he said, "A Methodist minister from Carver preached." Then in 1879, "In the evening we had a meeting in the chapel at Scandia. The Methodist pastor from Carver and a Covenant preacher, by the name of Franzen, preached." In October of that same year he noted, "Last night Gondt and the Lutheran minister, Hogelstrom, from Cokato came here so tonight we have a meeting in Scandia."

In February, 1880, he said, "Sunday. The Lutheran ministers, Fogelstrom, preached in the morning, and Person, in the evening." That following day he said, "In the morning I did nothing. The Lutheran minister, Person, was at our house for dinner, and then we went to the meeting in Scandia."

By 1881, the Baptist congregation at Scandia had contracted with the Lutheran minister from Watertown for ministerial services. After the last service, preached on September 25, 1881, Peterson explained, "Sunday. Fogelstrom preached. He has now finished the year that he had promised us."

Even while serving other congregations, the Reverend John Anderson (Peterson's brother-in-law) frequently returned to Scandia to deliver sermons. "Today [March 1, 1882] we had a meeting in the church when John Anderson preached. We also had a communion service. We also came to an agreement with John Anderson that he should hold services once a month for us." These monthly visits continued for several years.

In addition to the 1859 contribution of land made by Ellen and Andrew Bergquist for cemetery use, the neighboring family, Peter and Sophia Johnson, enlarged the burial ground in 1882. It was their donation of just a fraction less than half an acre which was adjacent to the cemetery *(map 51)* that caused Peterson to make his December 4, 1882, entry. "In the morning I went to Waconia and had a deed written for the grave yard." He said on December 30, "I rode with Freed *[map 41]* down to Chaska and turned in the deed for the grave yard that it should be recorded. I rode home with Birrel Nilson *[map 43, 44]*."

Most holidays in Scandia were observed with church meetings. Although Christmas was a special day at the church, Peterson did not mention Christmas gifts. In 1887, he wrote that the church had a decorated Christmas tree, and after that one each year. Although evergreens were scarce in this part of Minnesota, the settlers apparently took turns furnishing the tree, cutting one from their own woods. December 25 was a day of rest or visiting, and sometimes involved a church meeting. Thanksgiving was a church day, but it was not observed every year in the early days of the settlement. After 1861, the Fourth of July was another day designated for worship services. In later years, the meeting included a picnic on the church lawn. Sometimes this was a gathering of former members who had moved from Scandia and returned for yearly reunions.

By 1890, the membership of the church was up to fifty-six after fifteen persons had been baptized on June 8, 1890. In February of that same year, the missionaries Andrew Sisell and L. Eklund were in Scandia. Sisell preached every evening that entire week. Eklund was back for several days that following April and preached on Easter Sunday.[10]

From 1855 to 1930, a total of forty-six ministers—mostly students—served the Scandia congregation. From time to time, these preachers were tem-

9. Sources differ as to the correct spelling of John and Hedwig Maria Hammerberg's name. Also spelled Hammaberg as well as Hammerburg.

10. Andrew Sisell was also a diarist. His records have been translated from the Swedish language by the Reverend Ernest G. Nelson. The notes were compiled into a small book entitled, *A Missionary's Notes and Experiences on the Red River Valley Field* (Countryside Lithographic, Isanti, MN., 1982).

The Reverend and Mrs. F. O. Nilsson

The Reverend and Mrs. John Erickson

porarily replaced by visiting missionaries and college graduates. One such preacher was Professor Eric Sandell.

Thirty-seven years after the Lutheran minister Eric Norelius first visited Scandia while on his way to Götaholm in 1860, he revisited it and described the changes he saw in 1897: there were well-graded roads in every direction, and a railroad on each side of the lake. The edge of Clearwater Lake, long since divested of the woods along its shoreline, seemed to be a disappointment to him, although the beauty of the lake itself had not changed.

Although Norelius did not mention the church in Scandia, Peterson's June 21—24, 1876 entries state its appearance had also changed. Peterson purchased 200 feet of lumber and said, "Worked on the meeting house. We have torn it down and are building it over." After sheathing the walls he delivered additional lumber as well as lime, brick, and paint to the site.

In detailing the relationship of the congregation with its student preacher, Nels E. Valerius, Peterson mentioned Valerius's presence at John Johnson's house and subsequently at his own home. He related information about the manual labor performed by Valerius while he helped neighbors work on Frank Lundsten's barn.

Evidently Valerius lived with Peterson until July 7, 1897, when he moved to Nicholas Swenson's house. Later in that same month of July, more than 240 visitors from the Elim Baptist Church in Minneapolis arrived in Scandia. "Sandell- Walerius *[sic]*, one Bjorkquist and the American McKinney preached."

On September 28, 1897, he wrote: "In the evening practically everyone from the church went to Brobergs and had a surprise party on our preacher, Walerius. He leaves to go back to school in Chicago tomorrow." On February 3, 1898, he wrote: "In the morning we had a business meeting in Scandia in order to decide who we should call as our pastor during the summer. We decided to call Erik Walerius and also to allow him to attend the University in Minneapolis while serving as our pastor."

The meeting house, a simple frame structure, took on additional characteristics of a church in 1910, when an entryway and steeple were added to the building.

The Reverend Jonas Peter and Greta Johnson

Nicholas and Elna Swenson

The Reverend Nels E. Valerius, 1897-1901 seated in the home of Per Daniel and Caroline Anderson.

This photograph of Andrew and Elsa Peterson was probably used as their wedding announcement. (See footnote 1, opposite page.)

CHAPTER 6

On the Claim

In 1856, one year after settling in Scandia, Peterson wrote, "Started for Carver to look for work." He returned to his cabin for a brief period during his thirty-day stay in this busy river town. There he earned one dollar each day working for the different employers he referred to as "Noys" and "the Count." With cash in his pocket, he journeyed to St. Paul and purchased a stove and other necessary provisions.

Within a short time, Peterson was back in Carver. He bought raffia and a grafting box and started his orchard with 1,000 apple scions purchased from Neally, his former employer. Scions, or "cions," the variant spelling used by Peterson and his associates, are new, living shoots or cuttings which are grafted onto rooted plants or seedlings for propagation.

Picking up shipments of nursery stock or making direct purchases from orchardists in Carver and at the settlement called King Oscar's sometimes seemed his major reason for going there. Once he told of returning from Oscar's Settlement with sixteen plum trees. On April 27, 1858, his entry showed his annoyance at the high charges he had to pay: "Had Nilsson's mare and went to Carver after the grafts...I had to pay a dollar for freight on the box from St. Paul to Carver [via steamboat]. They said there was no bill of lading. Holm also charged $.40 for receiving and keeping the box. The hungry dogs!"

One of the reasons for Andrew's visits to Oscar's Settlement was that Elsa, the woman he was to marry, lived there with her widowed mother and family. She may have been visiting in Scandia when Peterson wrote on August 25 and 26, 1858, "Went with Elsa down to the swedish settlement at Carver." And on September 4, 1858, he wrote, "Elsa and I, together with 'Maja Stina' (sister Maria) went to Chaska in Mattson's wagon."

The existing daguerreotype indicates the purpose of one of these trips may have been to have the couple's photograph taken – an announcement of his and Elsa's forthcoming wedding to send to family and friends.[1]

When the wedding day, September 15, 1858, arrived, it appeared to be little more than an interruption in their busy pioneers' lives. Andrew described it as one filled with the usual chores: "In the morning I was over at Johannes and chopped cornstalks. At noon John went home with me and started plowing for the wheat. In the evening at 5 o'clock Elsa and my expectations became a reality, a marriage." Andrew was then nearly forty, Elsa was twenty-three years old.

According to the wedding certificate the

1. This and other photographs were found among the possessions of Andrew Peterson's brother Johannes Rydell. Along with other memorabilia, Rydell's grandson, Ivar Widéen, had them in safekeeping until the 1960s. Of the collection of pictures, it was clear to Widéen that several were of Peterson's farm buildings and his family, but at least six of the earliest prints remained a mystery. They were eventually sent to Helen (Booth) Wettstein and her sister Gladys Booth, the grandchildren of the Reverend John and Maria Christina Anderson, and subsequently sent to the Reverend Carl Tideman's widow Esther (Lundsten) for identification. Esther recognized the couple in one of these photographs as Andrew and Elsa Peterson.

Reverend Nilsson performed the ceremony in John and Maria Christina Anderson's cabin.[2] Peter Nilsson *(map 22)* and the Reverend Andrew Norelius, brother of the Lutheran minister Eric Norelius, were also there as witnesses. This document suggests Elsa's mother, or possibly Elsa herself, had been married more than once. Elsa's name is listed on this certificate as "Anderson," while family records refer to her as Elsa Engeman, a name given in Peterson's diary entry of June 26, 1891: "Today Elsa's brother's daughter, Olivia Ingman *[sic]*, came here for a visit."

Elsa Peterson's name appears on Scandia Baptist Church membership records with that of her sister Bengta ("Bertha") Cornelius as being baptized Friday, September 24, 1858. But Peterson overlooked mentioning this fact when he wrote: "Were at a meeting all day. We had a baptismal service when [Taylor] August Johnson and his wife, Magnus Johnson's wife and Cornelius' wife ['Bertha'] were baptized."

Throughout her marriage, Elsa was to live a godly life, one of total submission to her husband and family. Her peaceful and quiet disposition was a reflection of quiet assurance. She was content to live and work in the shadow of her husband, a man whose no-nonsense characteristics were sometimes described as being blunt.

Elsa was well-cared for by her mate, a determined person whose nature it was to create and care for essentials even while preoccupied with nursery stock and other demands. Within the beginning months of their marriage, Andrew recorded these typical chores: making a sled for Peter Nilsson's son, mending kitchen and wash kettles and coffee pots for his sister Maria Christina and Mattson, making wooden shoes, and scooping and shaping shovels and watering troughs for the livestock out of trees. He hooped barrels and washtubs and made a lantern, milk shelves for the cellar, benches, a dog chain, a molasses kettle, and a case for a clock he had received as payment of a debt. Andrew told of fixing shoes, patching clothes, and making soap. He also added a trundle bed to the furnishings in the cabin.

Elsa helped in the field, cooked, cleaned, washed, and did other household chores, as well as bore and took care of their children. Together they harvested ginseng roots, honey, and farm products and exchanged them with the merchants in Carver, Chaska, and Waconia for pantry staples and other essential items. Peterson swapped tools, farm equipment, and labor. From time to time he also sought short-term loans from relatives and friends. He wrote on October 11, 1858, "I went down to the Oscar settlement to borrow money. I got $10.00 from my mother-in-law. I have also borrowed $20.00 of Andrew Swanson today."

During a week-long stay in 1858, Peterson recorded that Elsa's sisters, "Anna and Elizabeth have taken the wooden shoes to Carver and then have been after Anna's cloth." Elizabeth returned to Scandia with her husband, Olaf Engelbrectson, on December 18, 1858, and visited through Christmas, no doubt spending time with sister Bertha Cornelius, their widowed mother, and friends. Socializing also included fellowship at the Nilsson cabin. Peterson wrote on January 3, 1859, "Cornelius' family and we were invited over to Mr. Nilssons for a dinner when we talked about spiritual matters."

Following mention of the sale of Cornelius' home and claim on July 22, 1859 (its location was not explained), the Corneliuses settled in the Litchfield area of Minnesota. They continued to keep closely in touch with Andrew and Elsa.

Before the birth of their first child on August 4, 1859, Peterson succinctly reported that "Elsa got sick" in the evening. He told of traveling to Erickson's *(map 33)* "and then to Hammaberg" and being back at 11:00 p.m., but did not explain that a midwife was with him. (The 1860 census lists Hedwig Maria Hammerberg [Mrs. John] as the midwife in Scandia.) On the day of his daughter's arrival he wrote, "Stayed in all day. 12:30 a girl, Ida Gustava was born and all is well."

For each of the Petersons' other babies, who were to occupy the same cradle Peterson had made, there was only a single entry noting the person who may have assisted Elsa. Others were never mentioned.

In contrast to the abbreviated information recorded about family matters, it is interesting to note the importance Peterson attached to his investment on the farm. He kept records of his expenditures in his bookkeeping ledgers and made a point of recording incidental charges in diary entries as he did on October 15, 1860, when he told of paying $1 for his naturalization papers at Chaska. He detailed the names of animals as well as breeding dates and in most instances revealed the places his stock had been taken to be bred.

Peterson made a trip to Chaska to pay his

2. Andrew and Elsa Peterson's marriage certificate is with papers inherited by Sarah Peterson. The name difference appears on charts prepared by Clyde C. Waters. (See Sources.)

mother-in-law's taxes in 1860, suggesting Elsa's mother rented or leased her property and lived with other members of her family. She briefly took care of her grandchildren – Ida, George, and John, who were then four, two, and one years of age. Caring for the toddlers and helping with household chores helped free Elsa for livestock, garden, and field work. The women also found time to visit during several afternoons with Per Daniel's wife, Caroline Anderson, while socializing and quilting.

Elsa's mother remained in Scandia from May 19 until October 1, 1863. Then Peterson wrote, "Today Mother left us to go with Magnus Person to St. Paul."

In November, without explanation, Peterson contacted an attorney who practiced law in the same area in which he had lived and worked for Neally in Iowa. On November 4, 1863, he said, "Today Bergquist sent the draft to a lawyer in Village Creek."

Local concerns were so overriding that the larger issues of the country did not merit even a single paragraph. Oddly, Peterson did not mention personal encounters with the Indians, political issues (although he worked for third-party movements), or even the assassination of President Abraham Lincoln. The Civil War is only briefly mentioned, when Peterson was helping Caroline Anderson, the wife of Per Daniel, who was serving in the Union Army. He also mentions observing a day of fasting and prayer as set aside by government proclamation. Otherwise he made no comment on social or political issues.

Neighbor helped neighbor in a myriad of ways in that era. Peterson tells of hauling a butternut log to Waconia and then heading for Olaf Anderson's farm *(map 12)* where he picked up yellow dye for a fabric he called jean cloth. Olaf cut Peterson's window opening in his corn crib, and Anderson's daughters, Christine and Johanna (then about eleven and twelve years old), helped harvest his potatoes. Peterson hauled rocks from Olaf's land for the foundation of his buildings and used Anderson's oxen to team them with his own.

Another friend Peterson frequently mentioned was a man he called only "Ahlstrom." Even after he was assigned to represent him as power of attorney, this concise September 19, 1863, reference is typical: "Went to Chaska. P. Nilson, Hakanson, Nils Person, Halling, Lundsten, Nicholas and his wife went along. I also went to Carver and sold Ahlstrom's wagon for $7.00." Ten days later he wrote, "Philip Otto Johnson has been here today and paid me $145.75 for Ahlstrom's land." An entry dated April 27, 1864, revealed Peterson sent a money draft to Ahlstrom, who was at Pike's Peak in Colorado. He also retrieved Ahlstrom's possessions at Swen Monson's home in Carver, but did not explain how he disposed of them.

Perhaps Peterson was too short of cash to buy Ahlstrom's wagon for himself, because soon after this one of his priorities was to secure the necessary materials to make a wagon. Until February 20, 1864, he had borrowed a wagon when he needed one. Then he wrote, "Nicholas and I went to Andrew Swenson *[map 23]* and to Anderson to saw off some wagon wheels, but they had no log that would do." On June 27, he cut slabs from the rounds of trees for wheels. He made axles and finished this crude carrier, which was called a roll wagon, in seven days. He managed with this mode of transportation for four years, after which time he told of purchasing a new one for $85.

In addition to comments about the sale of farm products – grape vines to Mrs. Bengston *(map 38)* and wool to Miss Salter *(map 55)* – Peterson also demonstrated acts of kindness on behalf of neighborhood women whose husbands were no longer living or were absent from the settlement. For example, he delivered wood to them. He also mentioned on June 11, 1864, that the wives of Jonas Peter Johnson *(map 45)* and Alfred Johnson *(map 36)* accompanied him to Chaska. This trip was made four years after Alfred's departure from the Scandia Baptist Church. During that intervening period, Alfred and his neighbor, Taylor August Johnson (also known as August Taylor), served as volunteers with the Ninth Minnesota Infantry. Before Taylor's enlistment, he worked on Peterson's claim. He helped build a cowshed, cleared ground for an orchard, and cut hay during the weeks of growing unrest between the Indians, government, and the settlers.

Peterson told of washing himself as well as his team in Clearwater Lake, and during cold weather he bathed himself in a heated bathhouse at the Andersons'. He failed to identify the particular Anderson family and did not mention if others from his family joined him.

In 1867, work on the new Peterson house was begun. This time, much of the labor on it was done by paid workers. Two of them, referred to in the diary only as Mattias and Olaf, cut the logs for it. Three years later, on November 14, 1870, the house was at a point where the family could move in. At that time there were six Peterson children: Ida Gustava, eleven; George Andrew ("Sture"), ten; John ("Axel"), nearly eight; Charles ("Carl"), five; Frank, three; and the baby, Emma, five months. The youngest three, Anna, Josephine, and Oscar, would be born in the Petersons' new home.

Even after the family was living in the house, work continued on it. John Nelson, a close friend and member of the Scandia Baptist Church, worked at the house, doing the more skilled carpentry work such as making window frames. Contrary to the normal application of wainscoting, which is usually used as a facing for the lower part of an inner wall, Nelson nailed this paneling on the interior *ceilings* of the house. The wainscoting apparently solved a problem involving the continuing work on the house after the family had moved in. The walls of the rooms were not all lathed or plastered at first. The wood ceilings probably enabled the family to live in the house with a minimum of disruption, even as the workers plastered the walls. These surfaces exist to this day; although they have been painted over, there is no mistaking the grooved panels.

There were four bedrooms on the second floor, and after the new kitchen addition was completed in 1881, there were two first-floor sleeping rooms. One of the smallest of three rooms, 9 by 12 feet, located on the main floor of the house, served as the original kitchen. It is difficult to imagine how Elsa managed to preserve and prepare huge quantities of food in quarters occupied by a cooking stove, woodbox, dry sink, and an oblong table large enough to serve her family and guests. This kitchen was finally replaced by a larger working area (15 by 24 feet) on the north side of the house eleven years after the family first moved in. The new chimney followed through the first floor and was enclosed in one of two pantries located within the kitchen and along the entire north wall of the room. A doorway chopped through the original rock foundation provided access into the basement area below the main part of the house.

There was always room in this modest home for the large Peterson family, along with occasional boarding teachers who taught during the school term, and an endless succession of visitors. Everyone who came through—relatives, horticultural experts, salesmen, and even passing tramps—stayed overnight. Of one of the latter, Peterson noted on May 13, 1897: "Last night a tramp by [the] name of Anderson stayed here. He was full of lice."

Much of the farm work followed a seasonal cycle. A spring task was the shearing of sheep. This seems to have been the special province of Elsa and, later, her daughters. When the boys worked at it in 1887, they "helped the women folks to shear the sheep." Soon after the clippings, Andrew and Elsa made an overnight trip to Minneapolis to sell the wool, hides, and usually some butter.

Housecleaning, another spring chore, included taking down the woodburning heating stoves for the summer and ridding the chimneys of their winter's accumulation of soot.

By the 1870s, the making of molasses from sugar cane was an extensive fall project. "In the evening Nicholas, Lundsten, Freed and Per Daniel came over and we made up our account in regards to the cane mill." The total amount came to 128 gallons for several families.

The settlers made other sweetening too. Because white sugar was costly or not available, they forced hollowed-out pieces of sumac, or wood spigots, into holes bored into the trunk of sugar maple trees in late winter when the sap was rising. The liquid was collected, drop by drop, in wooden buckets, then poured into a large flat pan or vat. This vat was positioned over a fire and rested on twin cement supports which formed the sides of an outdoor fireplace.

Approximately forty gallons of sap boiled down into one gallon of syrup. Reducing the sap to syrup and maple sugar required an enormous amount of firewood. As the years passed, maple sugaring became a larger operation. Andrew mentions tapping 311 trees one year.

In a detailed entry for May 16, 1873, Peterson said: "In the morning I did various things. Malmborg *[map 39]* split rails. In the afternoon I hauled stumps and roots. Plowed the new part of the orchard. Burnt the last grub, and brush on the grubbed field. Elsa and the children finished raking the brush today. Malmborg started grubbing in the meadow. Today Hank from Chaska and an reaper agent from St. Paul were here. I bought a Wood's reaper with the latest improvements from them for $235.00 with the freight which is $25.00. The freight I am to pay at once, then $100.00 in June, 1874, and the rest $110.00 in June, 1875, also I am to pay 10% interest."

Throughout the years, Peterson's diary entries mentioned a wide range of personal, civic, and political activities. He was with his German neighbors when they looked for a shortcut to Chaska, and on April 7, 1858, finally said, "We made a road towards Chaska for the school children." He told about hauling rock from the island in Clearwater Lake, selling barley to the brewer, and coming home from jury duty in Chaska at 10 o'clock at night. He sought signatures from neighborhood residents to change the road to Chaska he had mentioned earlier, and he got signatures to endorse a canal project in 1874–a proposal called the Fox-Wisconsin water route from the Mississippi River to Lake Michigan. With growing farmers' unrest over high railroad rates, another shipping alternative was in the settlers' best interest. Since Peterson was familiar with canals after having traveled them in Sweden and at least partway on the Erie Canal (extending 350 miles from Buffalo to Albany, New York), the canal project seemed to offer a practical solution.

Even though Peterson did not say so, it was the third-party movement that was providing much of the momentum for reform among the agricultural population of the United States, which was organizing into clubs and granges in opposition to the dominant Republican Party. They were endorsing canal proposals–favoring in particular the Fox-Wisconsin water route. The idea proved to be impractical. However, existing boat and barge traffic benefited because this effort was followed by substantial river improvements.

Although a housewife and mother of nine children, Elsa spent a great deal of time working outdoors. She remained remarkably strong physically. Seventeen years her husband's junior, she received help from her eldest daughter, Ida, but little assistance from anyone else except on the infrequent occasions when she was not well.

Once even during the early stages of an illness in 1866, Andrew and Elsa doggedly continued their efforts in the field. Peterson said of this, "We have picked potatoes for a few minutes at a time." Elsa's recovery from the illness was very slow. She required an extensive recuperation period and it was "Nils' wife" as well as "Anna Erickson" who baked bread and cared for the children.

Elsa was badly hurt after tumbling down a flight of stairs while almost at term during her seventh pregnancy in 1872. Nevertheless, she cooked syrup the following day and for several days thereafter. Although Ida, who was thirteen at the time, cared for the children and managed other household chores, there were still other excessive demands on Elsa–washing clothes, shearing sheep, gardening, skimming milk for calves, making cheese, collecting and preserving cream for butter, churning butter, preserving fruits and vegetables, and cooking three meals a day for family, boarders, and visitors. These responsibilities were all part of her daily routine.

Awkward as Elsa was during the last part of her pregnancy, the seasonal work came first. Eight days before the birth of Anna Isabelle, while still bruised from her fall, Elsa, as reported in Peterson's diary, still kept busy. "Lundsten's wife [Maja Lisa] and Elsa sheared the sheep. I did various things and helped them with the sheep."

None remained idle. At eight years of age, Charles was working in the fields planting, hoeing, husking and cutting corn and sorghum with his older brothers Sture and Axel.

If the boys were not outdoors planting or harvesting, they were kept busy cutting wood or grubbing stumps to clear more land. Their duties included searching for and driving the cattle into the stalls in the barn, milking and feeding the livestock, hauling manure to the fields, taking horses to the blacksmith when they needed to be shod, and digging quackgrass. There was enough work to keep them all very busy.

The baby Anna was hardly five months old in 1872 when, "Elsa, Per Daniel's wife [Caroline] and I went to Chaska." Then Peterson explained, "We went to Dr. Lars and I made a bargain with him. If he could remove the growth that Anna has, I will pay him $25.00, but if he was not successful, he is to have nothing, not one cent." (Peterson's previous experience with Dr. Wickfield in Shakopee, where he took his son Axel for a similar problem a few years earlier and was forced to return a second time, was evidently still fresh in his mind.)

Neither Andrew nor Elsa could tailor. Although Andrew recorded that he mended various pieces of apparel, the clothing needs for the entire family were met much the way they had been among peasants in Sweden–through bartering or, when cash was scarce, an exchange of labor. Peterson recorded, "Johanas Peter has made over a coat for me. I am to work for him one day to pay for that."

Fifteen years later, the Petersons seemed to be prospering. After describing an April storm that brought six inches of snow in 1871, Peterson said, "Lars Nilson started to work for me today. He is sewing clothes for the boys."

In the following weeks, Lars cultivated corn with the oxen, hoed all day, cut down logs for the wood shed, cut hay, plowed, worked on the road, cleaned out the sheep barn, and hauled brush and rotten straw from the barn roofs. Eight months later, Peterson commented that Lars was making and repairing old clothes for Caroline, Per Daniel's wife. His hired man was probably living in the vacant cabin—the first of Peterson's two dwellings. Every year, until it was demolished in 1886, Andrew or Elsa whitewashed the interior.

Evidence of continuing prosperity came from Peterson's record of cash payments made to a succession of tailors who worked at their home. On November 30, 1872, he said, "Andrew Lundsten has sewed five days this week and four days last week. I paid him $.60 a day and that is good wages."

Andrew Peterson
October 20, 1818—March 31, 1898

Elsa Peterson
October 8, 1835—March 8, 1922

Ida	**George**	**John**	**Charles**	**Frank**
	("Sture")	("Axel")	("Carl")	
8- 5-1859	2-19-1861	12-16-1862	4- 8-1865	10-29-1867
2-11-1900	12-21-1928	3- 6-1930	10-30-1941	6- 22-1921
	m			
	Ida Tapan			

Emma	**Anna**	**Josephine**	**Oscar**
4-11-1870	5-14-1872	8-13-1875	12- 3-1878
5-17-1943	9-19-1889	10-18-1908	7-24-1941
		m	
		Nels Carlson	

Refer to the chapter, "Family Legacies," for the complete family chart.

On September 24, 1855, Peterson wrote: "Made a carpenter's bench, a last, etc." The bench, winnowing basket, two-man bucket carrier, woodbox, barrels, tools, and tinware were sold during the farm auction held at Peterson's homestead in 1969.

CARVER COUNTY
HOLLYWOOD
WATERTOWN
Watertown
Gotäholm
Lake Minnetonka
St.Bonifacius
Mayer
CAMDEN
Waconia Lake
Waconia
WACONIA
Scandia
Victoria
LAKETOWN
Augusta Station
CHANHASSEN
Eden Prairie
Norwood
YOUNG AMERICA
Cologne
BENTON
DAHLGREN
Chaska
CHASKA
Shakopee (Scott County)
Carver
East Union
West Union
HANCOCK
SAN FRANCISCO
San Francisco
Minnesota River
N
POPE
STEARNS
SWIFT
CHISAGO
Sunrise
Lindstrom
Chisago Lake
Taylors Falls
Mississippi River
Forest City
Grove City
Litchfield
Acton
KANDIYOHI
MEEKER
WRIGHT
ANOKA
Scandia
St. Croix River
CHIPPEWA
Montevideo
Camp Release
Maynard (Leenthrop)
Granite Falls
Upper Sioux Agency
YELLOW MEDICINE
Wood Lake
RENVILLE
McLEOD
Hutchinson
Glencoe
HENNEPIN
Minneapolis
Fort Snelling
RAMSEY
St. Paul
WASHINGTON
Stillwater
CARVER
Shakopee
SIBLEY
SCOTT
DAKOTA
Birch Coulee
Gibbon
Henderson
Redwood Falls
Lower Sioux Agency
Redwood Ferry
Fort Ridgely
LeSueur
LE SUEUR
NICOLLET
St. Peter
Waterville
Vasa
Red Wing
Cannon Falls
LYON
REDWOOD
New Ulm
BROWN
RICE
GOODHUE
Mankato
MURRAY
COTTONWOOD
WATONWAN
BLUE EARTH
WASECA
STEELE
DODGE

CHAPTER 7

The Sioux Uprising

In mid-1862, there arose in Minnesota a conflict between the Dakota or Sioux Indians and the white settlers which has come to be called the Sioux Uprising or Dakota War of 1862. The war took place for a variety of reasons and resulted in the deaths of many white settlers and Indians. Most of the battles in the war took place east and south of Carver County, but throughout the conflict settlers in the area heard alarming reports of the imminent arrival of Indian warriors.

Philip O. Johnson, who lived in the Swedish colony at Götaholm, recalled the settlers' reactions to the Indian disturbances. His description of the local situation was written in Swedish and included in a weekly series of newspaper articles reporting the early beginnings of this settlement located on the shore of Swede Lake near Watertown. Although it is not known when Johnson wrote the report, these articles appeared between March 1 to April 5, 1877, in *Minnesota Stats Tidning,* a Swedish-language newspaper. The translation follows:

> It was especially from Meeker and Kandiyohi Counties and from Fort Ridgely and New Ulm that the terrible reports came. Also the little town of Hutchinson (which was only 30 miles from Watertown) was the scene of action for the redskins; and from there to our settlement the Indians, of course, could come in several hours. Also rumors reached us daily of how the Indians burned the houses, murdered men and children and violated the women, how the inhabitants of Hutchinson were put in a state of seige, and so on.
>
> This caused the people in Watertown to think of defense and they also began the building of a sort of fortification of logs and earth, which was put up on the highest point in town.
>
> It was one day in the middle of August 1862 that one of my neighbors and I were busy with haymaking about two miles from home, when suddenly one of our nearest neighbors approached us rapidly and shouted, out of breath: 'Run, run for your life and death! The Indians are coming here to murder and burn!'
>
> To our question as to where they were, the man answered: 'They are not far from here, and the people at home have taken out their household things and hid them in the tall grass in the woods or in the cornfield. Everyone who has horses and carts must load as much as possible on them, and everyone must flee.'
>
> We hurried home immediately, and on the way we met a number of people both on horses and on foot. Everyone hurried away as fast as they were able to. One kind neighbor had informed my wife about the impending danger and helped her to hide away a part of our belongings. The good man had taken our one child by the hand and my wife by the other (a two-week-old boy in her arms) when I met them a mile from home. We made our way to Watertown like the others. There people gathered from all directions and they began to ask each other if the rumor that the Indians were so near was really true. A horseman was sent out in all directions and although no Indians were to be seen, there was still a chance, being only several hours away from our settlement.
>
> Most of us returned home the following night. Others looked for a place of refuge on an island in a nearby lake [Waconia Lake]. Some people went to Carver or Chaska, others to Minneapolis, Yes, some continued on as far as Illinois or other States. Most of them came back again however.

Johnson's neighbor, Milton Jadwin, at Oak Lake, sent his wife to St. Anthony. Jadwin remained at his farm and used his horses to transport messages and mail between the settlements. He helped build the fort at Watertown. He also delivered the mail to Hutchinson, a distance of about twenty-five miles from his home, after he learned the community had been without mail delivery for several weeks.

The communities along the Minnesota River, even if not threatened directly by the war, saw many of the preparations carried out to fight it. River steamers transported soldiers and their supplies on the Minnesota River, beyond Carver to the region of the outbreak, which extended to a few miles below St. Peter. The Carver settlement was an important shipping point in those days – all the goods and supplies for Glencoe, Hutchinson, Forest City, and other points to the northwest were warehoused there before being hauled to their final destination.

When the steamer *Favorite* carried former governor and now General Henry H. Sibley leading the first soldier forces from Fort Snelling to Shakopee and the wharf at Little Rapids on August 18, 1862, the steamship captain, Edwin Bell, recalled:

> When we rounded the point below Carver, a sight I shall never forget was seen. Men, women and children were on the bank of the river, many in their night clothes, just as they left their beds to flee from the Indians, who were reported to be nearing the town. There was much rejoicing when they saw that the soldiers on the boat had come to their relief. We went about three miles above Carver (or to the rapids), there left the remaining soldiers, and then returned to Shakopee.

Although Frank Lundsten was only five or six years old when the alarm spread to Scandia, he repeated the story about his experience throughout his life. His parents, John and Maja Lisa *(map 42)*, were in the midst of family prayer when a neighbor pushed open the cabin door and shouted, "This is no time for praying, Lundsten, the Indians are coming!" There was a sense of urgency and even panic as settlers poured into the region from miles around.

Those who fled to the island in Waconia Lake peeled bark from dead elms and made lean-to coverings in an attempt to protect themselves from a steady drizzle. Some of the families who thought to bring hams and other provisions shared their food supplies with those who had none.

Members of the Andrew Anderson family recalled that their grandparents, Per Daniel and Caroline *(map 35)*, were said to have dug a hole in the ground near their cabin and buried valuables such as their clock and sewing machine before fleeing to the island. On August 20, 1862, Andrew Peterson wrote in his succinct fashion of the event, "We had an Indian scare so we fled out on the island in Clearwater Lake. We stayed until the evening of the 21st then went home."

On August 24, at the time of the important battle at New Ulm, Andrew Peterson reported: "Sunday. Just as we started the meeting Andrew Swenson came and told us we must leave at once to fight the Indians. The meeting broke up and we all hurried home to get ready but then we decided to wait for more definite orders." On Monday he wrote, "Went to Nobles for a meeting and to be examined by the doctor to find out if I was fit for war duty." (On January 19 and 27, 1865, Peterson said the sergeant signed an affidavit saying he was too old for war.)

Although Andrew Peterson did not describe the situation in Waconia, residents there had already built a fortress on the summit of the hill overlooking the lake and the island. The remains of buried stumps from the uprights of the fort were found while men were working on the basement excavation for the veterinary hospital at 116 West First Street in Waconia. This building is still being used for veterinary purposes.

After learning about the other battles at Birch Coulee, Acton, and Fort Abercrombie (on the Red River in Dakota Territory), the alarm spread on September 2 and 3 that the warring tribes were then in Forest City and at Hutchinson.

The soldiers from Company B of the Ninth Minnesota Infantry had been recruited at Fort Snelling between August 15 and 23, and were soon engaged in combat with Little Crow and his followers at Kelly's Bluff in McLeod County (bordering Carver County on the west), but were forced to seek refuge at Hutchinson. The new recruits took their stand after three infantrymen were killed. Eighteen soldiers were also badly wounded.

In response to the urgency of this situation, Company H of the Ninth Minnesota Infantry (also known as the Carver County Company) marched eighteen miles straight west of Waconia into McLeod County and Glencoe on September 3. From there Captain William R. Baxter, a Chaska man, and Company H accompanied the soldiers who finally drove Indian leader Little Crow and his warriors out of Hutchinson. Company H included, from Scandia, Sergeant Andrew Mattson, Private Godfrey Hammerberg (son of Hedwig Maria and her husband John), Taylor August Johnson, and Alfred Johnson.[1]

Peterson's September 5 and 6 entries revealed: "Did nothing as we had another Indian scare. We carried our stuff out in the brush and intended to flee to St. Paul."

Even though Peterson's Sunday, September 7, entry was, "We are more peaceful about the Indians today," the existing situation was far from being stable. In fact there were several more battles, but on September 23 the uprising ended with the Battle of Wood Lake (located five miles north of present-day Echo).

1. According to information received from Jeanette Servin, a Darwin resident and granddaughter of August Julius Johnson, her great-grandfather, Taylor August Johnson, was a native of Linköping, Östergötland. At the time Taylor Johnson enlisted in the army (August, 1862), he and his wife Christina Louisa were parents of Hulda, six; Frank Victor, three; Albertina (Abbie), two; and Clara, born in August. (Membership records from the Scandia church reveal Taylor and his wife left the church several months earlier, in June, 1862.) After Taylor returned from the war he and Christina Louisa moved their family to Mooers Prairie (an extinct settlement formerly located within the townships of Stockholm and Cokato) in Meeker County, where seven more children were born. They were Godfrey (who died at the age of four months), August, Elva Josephine, Ida, Alice, Hulda (named after her eldest sister, who had passed away), and Nathaniel.

Taylor Johnson, a professional tailor and farmer, died on June 12, 1920, at the age of eighty-eight. Christina Louisa died at about the age of seventy-two, probably on January 19, 1907, although sources differ slightly. Both Taylor and Christina Louisa were buried in the cemetery at Dassel–a community where they lived out their lives after leaving Mooers Prairie.

Andrew and his sister Charlotte Anderson pose with their niece Lillie Larson and their parents Per Daniel and Caroline.

CHAPTER 8

Per Daniel and Caroline Anderson

Per Daniel Anderson, born in Sweden on May 5, 1828, left the parish of Västra Ryd in the province of Östergötland, and traveled to America with his brother John (who married Andrew Peterson's sister Maria Christina) and sister Louise. Then, even before his brother and others of that group left Iowa, Per Daniel moved to St. Paul where he hauled lumber at a sawmill and served on St. Paul's first fire department.

It was during Peterson's forced stay in St. Paul in 1855 (others on the same riverboat trip proceeded to Scandia before him) that he first mentioned Anderson in his entry of May 17: "This day, Thursday, Mr. Nilsson and Per. Daniel went up river to St. Peter but my health is still such that I must remain here."

During those initial weeks of clearing and building cabins, Per Daniel explored the wilderness surrounding Clearwater and Parley lakes, but after choosing his eighty-acre homestead (map 35), he returned to his work in St. Paul. By that time Peterson was already established on his own claim and wrote on April 11, 1856, "Built on P. Daniel's shanty."

Each time Per Daniel returned to Scandia, he delivered supplies to the settlers and spent brief periods of time in his cabin while clearing his land. He also traded services with others and paid Alfred Johnson $60 for holding his claim.

On July 15, 1858, two years after his shanty was built, Per Daniel married Caroline Johnson, the housekeeper in charge of domestic help at the residence of Alexander Ramsey, territorial governor of Minnesota from 1849-53. According to church membership lists, Per Daniel and Caroline were baptized on July 3, 1859, while they were still living in St. Paul.

The year Per Daniel and Caroline were married, Republican candidate Ramsey and his running mate Ignatius Donnelly were barnstorming communities in Minnesota. Ramsey sought election to the governor's position in 1858 while Donnelly campaigned for election into office as lieutenant governor of the newly formed state.

On March 31, 1859, Andrew Peterson told of being in Chaska "after Per Daniel's things." Among the possessions Caroline cherished the most was a chest of silverware she received from Mr. and Mrs. Ramsey.

Per Daniel fit in with the cooperative spirit of Scandia. He helped Peterson deliver rye to Broberg's house for his (Per Daniel's) brother, the Reverend John Anderson. Per Daniel and Peterson plowed together; they hauled rye and fall wheat, and stacked wheat and hay.

Peterson wrote on September 3, 1859, "In the afternoon I cut rails for Per Daniels. In the evening we went fishing on the lake." They also dug a well and made shingles. After melting snow for the ash barrel, he wrote on November 19, 1859, "Per Daniel and I made a shelter for the oxen [and] also cooked soap."

They hewed logs, went to the mill, made a small yard for the oxen, grubbed, and planted corn and potatoes. On June 15 and 16, 1860, he said, "I went to Per Daniel and joined the foundation to his house." After they laid the last row on the side walls, Peterson worked on the rafters. He installed the ceiling planks and mouldings around the windows, made a door, hung doors in the house, and installed panels. Then he built Per Daniel's cow barn.

Although most of Peterson's walks in the vicinity of Per Daniel's homestead were for the single purpose of going to help others, neighbors also observed him veering off in the direction of Parley Lake, where he soaked basswood logs to make into rope. A typical entry is that of July 14, 1862, when he wrote, "In the afternoon I stripped raffia from the basswood at Per Daniel's place." He apparently had found the logs at the proper stage; now he could pull and twist the basswood fibers into rope.

In addition to everyday concerns, Peterson and other area residents were considering an appeal being made by military authorities for men to defend the Union during the Civil War. In order to avoid a draft, government officials in Carver County offered a bounty of $250 for each enlisted man and agreed to remit property taxes for those who volunteered. Even so, the able-bodied men were reluctant to serve. They were poor. Their families depended on them.

Peterson wrote about matters pertaining to the recruitment effort as well as local campaigns calling for financial support. On February 26, 1864, he said, "Today Nicholas went to Chaska and let his boy, Hans, enlist." On July 4, 1864, he explained, "We had a meeting and took up [a] subscription for the three that had been drafted for the war. I promised $40.00."

It is not clear whether this subscription was meant to pay for exemptions or aid to support the families of men already in uniform. After a day of fasting and prayer, Peterson revealed a neighborhood decision. On August 22 he reported, "Then I went to a business meeting when we collected money for Nicholas who had been drafted." Without exemption status for Nicholas, his wife Elna (who was pregnant at the time) would have been alone with Nels, nine; Nelie (reports show this spelling to be consistent), eight; Bertha, six; Roegenus, four; and Godfried, one.

On August 24 and 27, Peterson wrote, "went to a meeting in Witsik's school house for the gathering of money for soldiers," and then, "This evening the Swedes went down to enlist."

Per Daniel Anderson was one of the men Peterson mentioned as having enlisted. He was mustered into the army on August 30, 1864, with Otto Broberg, Swen Bengston *(map 38)*, and Andrew Swanberg. These recruits served with Company A of the Fourth Minnesota Regiment.

Peterson's concern for Caroline Anderson and her children – Louise, six; Charlotte (Lottie), four; and Alice, two – was evident. He helped her throughout the entire period of time, nearly a year, that Per Daniel was gone. In one instance, Peterson revealed Caroline was not completely alone. He mentioned that her "hired maid" helped his family dig potatoes. On October 6, 1864, he wrote, "Until 10 in the morning we threshed at Hakanson, then I went and butchered a pig for Carolina and in the afternoon I hauled manure on the field for rye," On the tenth of that month he also "threshed for the old woman, Hanson from Dalicarlia *[sic]* in place of Caroline."[1]

He fixed the stalls in Per Daniel's cow barn and made a pigsty. Olaf Hakanson helped him haul hay. The following month, Peterson said he "butchered a sow for Carolina and fixed her door[;] also put mouldings on the floor by the walls." In December he "went to Waconia with grist for Caroline and carried home mine."

The pioneers continued to struggle in Scandia. They longed for peace, praying for the safe return of their loved ones who were with General William T. Sherman, moving from the smoldering ruins of Atlanta.

Peterson reported he was hauling cornstalks on December 27 and 28, 1864, but he also wrote, "Per Daniels, Carolina, and children are here." During those several days that week, the conversation in the household undoubtedly included the news President Abraham Lincoln had received from General Sherman – that the Union forces had captured Savannah on December 22.

Early in the new year (January 18-20, 1865), Peterson disclosed, "Hakanson and I hauled hay for Carolina and in the morning I went with the surveyor and laid out the road between Bengston's and Per Daniel's land [map 38, 35]."

One reason for Peterson's concern for Caroline

1. Although "the old woman" Christine Hanson lived in Scandia until March 20, 1866 *(map 45)*, others Peterson mentioned who were from the province of Dalarna appeared to be transients. Erick Sund, Andrew Sigfridson, and Louisa Taylor were among the Dalecarlians who "rippled and brake the flax," led the bullocks, hoed around the apple trees, cut wood, cut and cocked hay, and cradled rye for Andrew Peterson.

is that she had a baby while Per Daniel was serving with the Union Army. On April 1, 1865, Per Daniel wrote to Caroline, "I see further in the letter that we have gotten ourselves another daughter and it pleases me very much that you have gotten along as well as you have."

On April 8, he said, "I forgot to do what you asked me when I wrote the last letter namely to give the little daughter a name. Minna Carolina, but if you want to change that, I have no objection."

Caroline named the child Carolina Wilhelmina.

That same year, the Union Army entered Richmond, Virginia, and on April 9, 1865, General Robert E. Lee signed the papers of surrender at Appomattox Courthouse, Virginia. Not long after, April 28, 1865, Per Daniel wrote to Caroline from Raleigh, North Carolina:

> My beloved wife, God's grace and peace be with you for Christ's sake. I want to use this time to write a few lines to you again, because at this time things are changing rapidly, you hear one thing one hour and something else another. But now we have authentic news that the rebellion has been crushed on the whole eastern part of Mississippi Reserve. Therefore we will be going north toward our homes within 40 hours, this is what General Logan told us last night. I must tell you I am in good health. I have however caught a little cold, as the nights are chilly but the days are warm. I must say I have great cause to thank God for His abundant grace granted me both body and soul and this grace is everlasting. I forgot to mention in my last letter that we had a visit from General Grant on the 25th of April. I haven't any other news to report this time except that the soldiers are very happy and full of fun for the great expectation of soon returning towards their dear homes. May God be praised and not man.
>
> I will close for this time with a dear greeting from your dear husband. Papa also sends very dear greetings to his dear children – that you should be very good children because then when you get hungry your mama can give you food. The children down here in the South are often very hungry where we have gone through, so when they ask their mother for food she often has very little to give them because the northern soldiers have taken the food. I can greet you from carpenter Erickson from St. Paul. He was with me yesterday.
>
> P.D. Anderson
>
> Greet friends in Scandia from me.
>
> We have not received any money as yet.

After this, Per Daniel participated in the memorable grand review of the national armies which was staged in Washington, D.C., on May 24, 1865. Then on June 22, 1865, Peterson wrote, "Today our soldiers from four regiments came home again."

Throughout the entire forward thrust of the Union Army, some soldiers were detailed to move on ahead before daylight to forage for food. When the troops caught up with them, the foragers, or *bummers,* as they were sometimes called, often had the wagons filled with corn, sweet potatoes, meal, molasses, bacon, hams, and poultry. Cows, oxen, and mules were also brought back tied to those wagons.

Per Daniel was one of the soldiers detailed to forage, and in later life he told children and grandchildren of kneeling behind wagons loaded with food supplies as he prayed for forgiveness. The message he had written to his children reiterates his compassion for the families suffering from the ravages of war. He was following orders when he confiscated the supplies found in those wagons.

Per Daniel was a devoted family man and adhered to strict conservative and Christian principles. He served as a deacon in the Scandia Baptist Church, participated in the Sunday School program, supported the Republican Party all his life, took keen interest in temperance reform, and, together with Caroline, raised ten children – Anna Louise, Charlotte Augusta, Alice Florence, Carolina Wilhelmina, Isabelle, Abbie May Susan, Andrew Oscar, Charles Benjamin, Fritchof James, and Almer John.

Andrew Peterson told of attending wedding festivities when Per Daniel's daughter Louise was married at Anderson's home on May 11, 1887. He said, "After dinner we went to a wedding at Per Daniel's house when [Oscar Erick] Larson and Louise were married." He reported their arrival from Minneapolis and visit at the Peterson home one year later, May 12, 1888, and wrote of the Larsons again when their daughter Lillie, born October 7, 1890, was seven years old. On January 6, 1897, he noted, "Peter Anderson's and Larson's families visited us."

Louise and Oscar Larson's children, Edith, Lillie, and Myrtle, spent summer vacations with their grandparents in Scandia. They learned the words and music to a number of army songs ("Tenting Tonight" seemed to be a favorite) as they accompanied grandfather Per Daniel in the family buggy. They traveled together while on various errands to nearby places as well as to St. Bonifacius, where Per Daniel collected his veteran's pension.

Lillie also spent vacations, usually of several

Per Daniel and Caroline Anderson

Per Daniel Anderson	**Caroline Anderson**
May 5, 1828—January 10, 1906	**September 22, 1835—February 10, 1913**

Anna Louise	**Charlotte Augusta**	**Alice Florence**	**Carolina Wilhelmina**	**Isabelle**
m		*m*	*m*	*m*
Oscar Erick Larson		Charles Norman	G. Arvid Hagstrom	John Swanson
Edith Lillie Myrtle		Maude Wave Florence Le Roy Floyd Clifford	Marion*	

Abbie May Susan	**Andrew Oscar**	**Charles Benjamin**	**Fritchof James**	**Almer J.**
m	*m*	*m*	*m*	*m*
Charles Peterson	Beda Peterson	Hilda C. Schock	Amy Johnson	Florence ?
Grace Marion*	Donald Benjamin Virginia Lucille Leonard twins	Earl Katherine Gilbert Gladys Grace	Janice Charlotte Gerald	Carl Robert

*After Abbie May Susan (Mrs.Charles Peterson) and her daughter Grace passed away Carolina and G. Arvid Hagstrom adopted Marion.

weeks' duration, in Scandia with Andrew and Elsa Peterson's family. They were indirectly related; grandfather Per Daniel's brother John was married to Andrew Peterson's sister Maria Christina. Lillie was fond of being treated as if she were one of the Petersons' grandchildren, and the Petersons undoubtedly also enjoyed the fantasy since they had no grandchildren of their own.

Lillie Larson loved farm meals—especially the treats, such as maple sugar candy filled with butternuts, and hot apple pie. She later mused nostalgically about the pleasant sight of wooden shoes lined in a row beside the back door of Peterson's home. Although they looked cumbersome, the shoes made by Peterson of basswood were light and easy to slip into to wear for barnyard chores.

Picking apples in the orchard became a tedious job, but Lillie always did her fair share of work as family and friends harvested fruit from more than 600 trees. Her memories of vacations in Scandia included hiking across the meadows with Josephine Peterson and enjoying the beauty of the settlement and the farms surrounded by acres and acres of split rail fencing, rolling hills, beautiful trees, and lakes.

Per Daniel and Caroline Anderson with daughters Charlotte, Carolina, and granddaughters Edith, Lillie and Marion. Back (from left): Per Daniel, Caroline, Edith Larson, Charlotte Anderson, and Lillie Larson. Front: Carolina Hagstrom and daughter Marion, Hildegard Carlson, and another visitor from Chicago.

John and Catherine Broberg

CHAPTER 9

John and Catherine Broberg

John Johnson and his wife Catherine arrived in America from the Gällaryd Parish of Jönköpings *län,* Sweden, in 1854. They were accompanied by John's sister, Maja Lisa, and her husband, John Danielson. During the brief period of time that they lived in Andover, Illinois, Danielson was an apprentice tailor. Encouraged by reports from the missionary pastor Fredrick O. Nilsson about the new country being opened up in the northwest, they resolved to work their way to Minnesota Territory.

After cutting wood in Red Wing and St. Paul, they completed their journey to Scandia on June 10, 1856. All of their worldly possessions were piled in a wagon pulled by a yoke of oxen. Johnson claimed lakeshore property adjacent to settlement founder Andrew Bergquist's *(map 61),* while his sister's family located themselves to the east *(map 42, 43, 44)* beyond the claims of Nilsson and Andrew Peterson.

Frustrated by the number of new arrivals with similar names, John Johnson decided to change his. Combining the Swedish words *bro,* meaning bridge, with *berg,* or mountain, he formed the word *broberg,* and thereby became John Broberg. John Danielson, his brother-in-law, chose the words *lund,* meaning grove of trees or forest, and *sten,* or stone, and became John Lundsten.

Andrew Peterson's references to John and Catherine Broberg were first noted when he borrowed their oxen during the fall of 1857. Then he told of making a new tongue for their wagon and a hayrake. (The latter was to be available for Peterson's use as well.) In the meantime Broberg worked to repay Peterson's skilled labor by helping him deliver two loads of hay for the roof of Andrew's cowshed.

Peterson later wrote that he had spent two and one-half days crafting a new tie for Broberg's wagon; later Jonas Peter Johnson *(map 45)* and Broberg returned from their trip to a mill, and Peterson received his portion of the flour. This is a typical entry, which was made September 18, 1857: "Broberg was again here and plowed the small field. We also made up our accounts. He was owing me one and a half dollar[s] for corn meal. I had raked three days on what I owed him."

While Peterson helped to join the foundation to Broberg's cabin, he noted that John Erickson *(map 33)* and his children were at his claim during his absence. They were husking his corn for him.

Broberg and Peterson also accepted a great deal of responsibility for public projects. Broberg was general foreman of road crews at a time when local roads were being developed. Peterson was road supervisor. Both appointments were made by the county commissioners. Broberg was appointed and certified as school trustee in 1860, serving with Alexander Johnson *(map 34)* and Andrew Peterson.

In 1857, Peterson agreed to make a sled for Broberg and selected, chopped down, and split the tree to make the runners for it. Peterson was preoccupied with this effort until December 22, 1857, when he wrote: "Worked on Broberg's sled and finished it. I have worked on it 9 days except for a few odd minutes. He only wants to pay at the rate of $.75 a day but I am determined to have $7.00 for the work as was first agreed." January 4,

1858, "Began to make a door for Broberg." He worked for two consecutive days and finally wrote: "Went to Broberg and hung his door and for that he is to give me a day's work. I am to have $3.55 for the door and $.05 for a hoe handle."

John Broberg's brother Otto arrived in Scandia, making his presence known through Peterson's diary entry of October 26, 1858: "Thrashing – That which was thrashed by the thrashing machine for me was 25 bushels rye and 7½ bushels wheat. We that worked with the machine were Jonas Peter, Lundsten, Torsten, Otto Broberg, three of Hammerberg's sons, John and I. I had to pay $5.00 to the owner of the machine and I owe Broberg one day as he provided the oats for the horses."

Otto's brother-in-law, John Lundsten, made a $200 payment (probably with financial help received from his neighbors) to maintain exemption status from draft in the Civil War. After receiving his second notice, Otto served as John's substitute. Otto was not married, and he was concerned for his sister, Maja Lisa; he felt John should remain at home to care for his family, which consisted of Maja Lisa and their five children: Sara, eleven; Frank, seven; John, five; Emily, three; and Joseph, then one year old.

Otto was mustered into the Union Army on August 30, 1864. After his discharge from Company A, the Fourth Minnesota Infantry, on January 12, 1865, Otto returned to Scandia for a short while.

He still might have been in the settlement when his brother, Peter Broberg, Peter's wife Christine, and her sister, Stina Cajsa, and husband John (Magnusson) Monson, first appeared in Scandia. These relatives seemed to have arrived on the scene following Peterson's mention of a wagon train on May 3-4, 1867. Peterson said, "There were 9 families with 12 horses here from Moline. They are going to take out homesteads."

From the beginning, Peter Broberg cut wood, hauled hay, and plowed for Peterson. Christine was first mentioned on April 21, 1868: "Per [Peter] John Broberg cleaned the hazelbrush roots off the new broken land. Broberg's Christine was carrying sap to the kettle yesterday and today she is husking corn." Throughout the following weeks, Christine separated rye kernels and picked weeds from wheat, hoed beans and corn, hoed the turnip field for half a day, cut corn, helped pick rutabagas, and spread manure on the south field. She cleaned sheep manure from the shelter and helped wash sheep. With all this, she also found time to help Andrew and Elsa plant corn, beans, and squash on the rye field near the cabin; then she helped Elsa and the children hoe beans for several days. Day after day, Peter burned brush and cultivated corn. He helped Per Daniel and Peterson butcher hogs. While Peterson was working at Per Daniel's place installing ceiling boards in his cabin, Christine and Elsa were digging carrots.

On September 10, 1869, Peterson wrote, "Threshed over at Jonas Peter's place *[map 45]*. In the afternoon Christine Broberg and I shocked the flax. We also butchered a ram. Christine worked here all day."

Peterson labored just short of a week harvesting rape, a forage crop which is related to the cabbage family. Although it is used to feed sheep and hogs, the seeds yield rape oil, also called Colza oil. Peterson listed Frieberg, Christine Broberg, Malmberg, and Lundberg as his helpers. After screening some of the harvest for seed, he hauled two loads to Waconia. This crop weighed 2,621 pounds.

Peter's and Christine's days in Scandia were filled with endless hours of backbreaking labor. When they purchased the forty acres situated next to and west of his brother John's claim *(map 66)* from Joseph Hartman, their own responsibilities allowed less time to help Peterson. When they did help, they traded services. These arrangements between relatives and neighbors did not always turn out to be of mutual benefit, however. Estimates of the fair value of goods in relationship to the hourly worth of labor in these exchanges often caused disturbances, even between brothers.

Without revealing the nature of past problems, Peterson's May 6, 1876, entry was "I went with Peter Broberg to help him get reconciled to his relatives."

Although the Monson family had arrived with Peter and Christine Broberg at Scandia, they settled close to Willmar in Kandiyohi County. They visited Peter and Christine in the settlement in 1877 and several times thereafter.

On one occasion, Peter Broberg and Andrew Peterson started for Chaska with a load of wood on a sled but had to turn back because the snow had melted off the road. Peter continued to haul wood to Chaska, and also helped break ground on the place called an "island"–the high ground surrounded by the dried-up swamp on the south end of Peterson's property (map 46).

Without reference as to circumstances, Peterson wrote on September 16, 1880, "We buried Per Johan Broberg." Peter was fatally injured after sliding down from the top of a wheat stack onto a pitch fork. Although Peterson's diary did not even suggest, much less describe, the tragedy that claimed Peter's life, the facts relating to the incident were published in the Carver County *Weekly Valley Herald*. Other accidents similar in nature were reported throughout the county. Articles in the September 9 and 16, 1880, issues of the newspaper warned farmers about the dangerous habit of standing pitch forks against their stacks.

During the endless days of Peter Broberg's suffering, he asked Per Daniel Anderson to complete the necessary arrangements for his will. Per Daniel then submitted an order for admission of Peter's will to probate. The document stated:

> Peter Broberg said to me P. D. Anderson, that Stina may have all the property that is left after the debts are paid up to her death to use it as she wishes, but after her death what is left shall go to Peter Broberg's daughter Tilda Justina Nelson.

Five days after Peter's burial, Peterson wrote, "I went to Broberg's place for the inventory." On October 21, he traveled to Chaska with John Lundsten and "went bond for him as administrator for Christine Broberg."

Peterson attended Peter Broberg's livestock auction on November 26. During a December morning he reported that Lundsten and I went "over to Christine Broberg to see if we could settle the real estate question between her and Andrew Broberg." This matter probably referred to the purchase by Andrew Broberg, John's son, of the farm *(map 66)* on December 18, 1880, for $997. No doubt Lundsten and Peterson participated as witnesses when Christine sold the estate with the understanding that Andrew would own and work the land while she would rent or simply occupy her dwelling until ready to leave. Then, on April 28, 1882, Peterson wrote "after dinner Elsa and I went to Stina Broberg's auction." Christine was never mentioned again, and it is thought she returned to Sweden.

Although Peterson reported the burial of Kate and Andrew Broberg's son on Sunday, May 17, 1885, he did not give the boy's name, cause of death, or age. Before long, Peterson's diary entries shed light about Kate's (she was Andrew Bergquist's daughter) and Andrew Broberg's intent to build another home, which was to be situated on the farm they purchased from Christine. He also said his own son, Carl, had been at the depot to pick up lumber needed to construct Kate and Andrew's new home. Then Peterson recorded that a double wedding took place at Kate and Andrew's dwelling on November 20, 1885, without mentioning who was married or which of his children attended the event.

Before the year 1885 had drawn to a close, Andrew Broberg's father John also passed away. After that particular New Year's Eve, Peterson wrote, "Last night Jonas Broberg died." He recorded blizzard conditions for several days, and then wrote on January 5: "Today we went to J. Broberg's funeral. We undertook no work. The weather is clear and beautiful." John died leaving his wife Catherine with four children at home—Amanda, eleven; John William, thirteen; James, seventeen; and Theodore, eighteen.

After John's death, his son Theodore's work at the church did not pass without notice. He had been cleaning the sanctuary and caring for the fire before Sunday school and worship service. When he received an offering from a special collection, it was probably to help his widowed mother. On September 4, 1886, Peterson, Lundsten, and G. B. Nilson attended a meeting at Catherine Broberg's house to help her settle matters of real estate.

One year after John's death, Catherine's property was flanked on both sides by that of her sons, Andrew and Enoch. Andrew and Kate were already raising their family on the farm Peter and Christine once owned. Then Enoch, who lived in Minneapolis, purchased Bergquist's former homestead *(map 50, 52)*. Although he did not live in Scandia, he was discussing his intent to build on the tract east of his mother's home. Since Enoch was employed at Smith Lumber Company in Minneapolis, it seems Peterson agreed to supervise the general contracting. Peterson mentioned Frank Lundsten on February 21, 1887, and told of writing up an order for building materials.

Meanwhile other daily activities included a wedding (the bride and groom were not identified) at Catherine Broberg's place, Andrew's work with his threshing machine at the Peterson farm, and a missionary meeting at the Broberg home. Peterson's son Frank hauled ice for Broberg, and his daughter Ida stayed with Kate when the latter was not well.

Peterson's son Sture and John Lundsten's son Frank continued to work until they finished the detail work on Enoch Broberg's new home. Enoch's open pavilion or picnic shelter is thought to have been completed in 1889.

On December 19, 1889, Peterson wrote, "Mama [Elsa] went over to Broberg's house as Mrs. Broberg was suddenly taken ill. In the evening at 6 she died." She was 57 years old. On December 21, he wrote, "Carl [Peterson's son] helped A. Broberg to dig old Mrs. Broberg's grave in the Scandia grave yard." And on December 23, "Today old lady Broberg was buried. Practically the whole congregation attended."

Eight Broberg children survived their parents: Andrew, Joseph, Enoch R., Annie Mathilda, Theodore Otto, James Gustaf, John William, and Amanda Christina. The eldest son Theodore inherited the family farm and continued to live on it. By this time, Enoch was the manager of operations at the City Lumber Company (now known as the Justus Lumber Company) in Minneapolis. Since he was also selling real estate, there is reason to believe his investment in the lakeshore property was speculative, because the new home seems to have been rented from the time it was completed. After leaving his family home in Scandia, he did not live in the settlement even briefly. He married Mayme Holmquist in April of 1893, and the couple lived in Minneapolis.

Enoch Broberg

Several months after Enoch's wedding on June 15, 1893, Peterson wrote: "Today Prof. Sandell and his family moved into Enok [sic] Broberg's house in Scandia to live there three months. Axel drove them over." Sandell preached at the Scandia Baptist church that summer. There was mention of a surprise party at Broberg's house on August 23, 1893, and another on September 18, 1893, when Peterson wrote, "In the evening all from the church were gathered to a surprise meeting at Prof. Sandell in Scandia."

On December 10, 1896, the name of John's and Catherine Broberg's son Theodore appeared on the title for lot 4 *(map 66)* in place of Andrew and Kate

Broberg. Before the property changed hands, Peterson mentioned that his daughters (they were not named) were at Andrew Broberg's house making clothes for Kate and Andrew's children.

Perhaps the limited acreage no longer supported their family needs, or perhaps Kate longed to be closer to her parents, who had moved to Minneapolis. In any case, the couple moved to Minneapolis in 1896, where Andrew found employment as a night watchman.

It is possible that Enoch's brother John William and his wife (existing records do not reveal her name) lived in Enoch's new home before they purchased the property Peter and Christine Broberg once owned. Enoch's father-in-law, James W. Holmquist, could have used the place as a summer home even before he bought the property on August 27, 1898, since it was located on the shore of Waconia Lake. This sale removed the Broberg name from the land east of the original homestead.

Apparently other family members were not interested in buying the property. Joseph Broberg married and moved to Eagle Bend, Minnesota. James lived in National, Washington, where he operated a sawmill. Annie moved to Brooklyn Center, Minnesota, and Amanda to Westwood, California.

Theodore sold the farm Andrew and Kate formerly owned to John William on October 1, 1898. Before the year was out, John sold it and moved to Seattle.

Of John and Catherine Broberg's children, Theodore, who had inherited the homestead, was the only one who remained in Scandia.

John (Johnson) Broberg **March 11, 1831—December 31, 1885**	**Catherine Broberg** **June 26, 1832—December 19, 1889**

Andrew **March 18, 1856** *m* Katherine M. Bergquist – –	**Joseph** **January 27, 1858** *m* Katie Kelsey from Delano on February 3, 1897	**Enoch R.** **January 17, 1860** *m* Mayme Holmquist – April 13 or 18, 1893	**Annie Mathilda** **April 9, 1865** *m* Nathaniel Bergquist – October 1, 1887
Theodore Otto **September 4, 1867** *m* Johanna Gustafson – February 28, 1899	**James Gustaf** **December 6, 1869**	**John William** **November 24, 1872** *m* – – –	**Amanda Christina** **August 24, 1874** *m* Oscar Hawkins –

Maja Lisa and John Lundsten

CHAPTER 10

The Lundsten Family of Sunny Hill Farm

John Lundsten, his wife Maja Lisa, and infant daughter Sara Carlotta left the Swedish parish of Gällaryd for America on May 7, 1854. They were accompanied during their ocean voyage by Maja Lisa Lundsten's brother, John Broberg, and his wife. They arrived in Boston on July 5, 1854, but moved to Andover, Illinois, before traveling on to Minnesota Territory.

During a brief stay in Red Wing, the men cut wood to fuel the river steamers. With the money earned, John Lundsten purchased a team of oxen needed to pull Broberg's wagon, and spent his last dollar to buy an ax. The families continued their journey, stopping in St. Paul and finally arriving at the Scandia settlement on June 10, 1856. The Lundstens chose a site east of Andrew Peterson *(map 42, 43, 44)* and the Brobergs on the shore of Clearwater Lake.

The events during August, 1856, held both joy and sorrow. John and Maja Lisa were baptized and became members of the Scandia Baptist Church on a pleasant summer day, August 3. Two days later, on August 5, Maja Lisa gave birth to baby Clara, but the baby died three days later.

As was the custom, the families in the neighborhood exchanged labor, use of farm animals, and sometimes goods. "Lundsten gave me half a pound of butter for my old songbook," wrote Peterson on October 18, 1856.

Peterson helped build the first of Lundsten's two cabins. Later he mentioned starting out on a trip with him to a mill in Eden Prairie, which was eight miles east of Scandia. Because of a sudden downpour, the two men turned back after traveling only a few miles. Even though the kind of load was not stated, the weight of the wagon as well as its contents would have surely turned the road to mire, making it impossible to reach their destination.

On April 30, 1857, Peterson measured out potatoes for distribution for use as seed potatoes or supplemental food reserves: "Three bushels for Jonas Peter [Johnson], five pails for Lundsten, two bushel for [John] Erickson and four bushels for Mr. Nilsson," wrote Andrew.

Peterson helped Lundsten hew ceiling planks November 6, 1858. During the next several years, the two men stacked wheat on the south forty, delivered corn, and threshed. Andrew also finished breaking a new field using Lundsten's oxen and Nicholas Swenson's bullocks.

Sara Carlotta Lundsten became an older sister when Frank was born in 1857. John George arrived in 1859, and in 1861, Emily Caroline became the second daughter to survive.

The *Compendium of History and Biography of Carver and Hennepin Counties* reported John Lundsten's interest in community and church development. Although the years he served as treasurer on the town board were not made part of the biography, the report stated that John was instrumental in starting the Scandia Baptist Church Sunday School in 1858 and served as its superintendent, a position he held for twenty-five years. His son Frank took over in 1883.

Lundsten's ongoing cooperative effort included helping Peterson rethatch the roof on his cowbarn, husking corn, and sharing a trip to the flour mill on January 26, 1863. Peterson wrote, "Jonas Peter, Lundsten, [Christian] Shilling *[map 9]* and I went to Waterville's mill," which was about forty miles south of Scandia. On January 28, he made note of their return at 4:00 p.m., and his yield: "Out of the 12 bushels Club wheat I got 437 lbs. of flour, that makes 38 lbs. flour to the bushel. From the rye I had 197 lbs. of flour, that makes 28 lbs. to the bushel."

Through the years, the Lundsten family continued to grow with the births of Joseph Oscar in 1863, and the twins Otto Wilhelm and Alice Wilhelmina on February 28, 1866. The next year, Peterson told of attending the funeral of John and Maja Lisa's first-born, fourteen-year-old Sara Carlotta, and then two years later, August 23, 1869, he wrote that he had "Made caskets for the Lundsten children." Although existing records do not mention multiple births when baby Lotta arrived on August 16, 1869, Peterson's statement suggests she was one of twin babies who died soon after they were born.[1]

By the time John Lundsten's brother Andrew appeared in Scandia, in 1872 or 1873, John and Maja Lisa were already settled in the second log cabin – a building eventually incorporated into the well-built dwelling that stood for many years on Sunny Hill Farm. During Andrew Lundsten's residency, he lived with his wife and children in John and Maja Lisa's vacated cabin. He made clothing for Elsa and Andrew Peterson and helped with neighborhood field work before moving on to Wright County a few years later.

Despite infant deaths, John and Maja Lisa's family continued to expand through births and marriages. Emily, at nineteen, became Mrs. Jacob Franklin Schreiner in 1880, and four years later brother Frank, then twenty-seven, and Mary C. Hawkins were wed. After Frank's marriage, he and his bride moved into his parent's home at Sunny Hill Farm and shared the work responsibilities with John and Maja Lisa.

John Lundsten, Jr., was married in about 1881 or 1882, and the couple settled in Minneapolis. But tragedy befell this family, too. John and Julia lost their daughter Verna, and soon after, Julia lost her husband as well. On August 26, 1888, Andrew wrote, "Sunday. Today we buried John Lundsten, Jr. from Minneapolis here in [the] Scandia grave yard."

1. The information included in this chapter (except where otherwise stated) has been recorded in Rhoda Lundsten's unpublished papers called, "The Saga of Sunny Hill Farm."

Joseph Lundsten married Anna Steinhorst in 1886.

Alice's twin brother Otto, at eighteen, found clerical employment in Waconia. His interest in business subsequently led to an apprenticeship with prominent businessman George DuToit. He roomed and boarded with the DuToit family in Chaska, during which time he assisted DuToit at the Carver County State Bank at Chaska and helped to establish banking facilities in Waconia, Norwood, Chanhassen, Augusta, Lester Prairie, Belle Plaine, and Excelsior.

During the latter part of the nineteenth century, he became cashier and bank director at the State Bank in Lester Prairie. In addition, Otto purchased his own business in Lester Prairie. His brother Joseph then managed the Lundsten Livery Stable for him.

Otto Lundsten was twenty-seven when he married Alice Bardwell from Excelsior, Minnesota, on May 24, 1893. She had good reason to admire Otto's enthusiasm and aggressive good nature. By 1907, he had purchased controlling interest of the bank at Hutchinson; while he was president of that bank, Joseph joined him in another business venture, becoming manager of the Lundsten Lumber Company. Otto and Joseph operated lumber yards in Mayer, Maple Plain, and Delano. By 1919, Otto Wilhelm Lundsten purchased the Minnetonka State Bank in Excelsior from his mentor, George DuToit.

Sunny Hill Farm became the hub – the focal point – of a great deal of family activity. Frank and Mary's children, Clarence, Frances, Amy, and Mabel, were privileged to grow up with considerable attention from visiting relatives as well as grandparents John and Maja Lisa.

Grandfather (John Lundsten) was described as a tall, well-built man who seemed stern, and, with his full beard, rather forbidding. Yet he had a sense of humor and, although he was always hurried and busy, he sometimes took time to play with his grandchildren.

These young people became an interested audience whenever Frank, their father, spoke to them about the primitive conditions in Scandia when he and their aunt Sara Carlotta were growing up. He used to say, as he got older, "I would much rather ride in an auto than in the vehicle I rode in as a boy–four slabs, six inches wide, sawed off a large tree and made into a wagon drawn by a yoke of oxen." Frank was referring to a roll wagon. Riding in it was, he said, "like shooting the bumps in an amusement park." This cumbersome carrier squawked and squeaked because the wheels were made from the rounds of trees. The rides were noisy, too, since there never seemed to be enough lard to adequately grease the wheels.

About one month after the birth of Frank and Mary's daughter Rhoda, Peterson wrote on March 21, 1894: "We were plunged into bitter grief today. At 11 o'clock we received word that John Lundsten had suddenly died. Frank [Peterson] went over there at once by the short cut, and then he went to Waconia after Frank Lundsten. Mama and Emma went over to Lundstens. I am not well enough to go over there. Axel also went over. I had to stay in bed." On March 24 he noted: "Today John Lundsten was buried. Mama and I stayed at Lundsten's house as I was not able to go to Scandia."

After his father's death, Frank carried on his own work in construction while he managed the family farm. His wife Mary and his mother Maja Lisa continued to share the responsibilities with help from the children and hired farm hands.

It was customary for Frank and Mary to help grandmother Maja Lisa cater all of the family celebrations. Andrew Peterson referred to one on June 20, 1895: "In the afternoon at 5 we went to a wedding at Lundsten's house. Rev. Linder and Alice Lundsten [Otto Lundsten's twin sister] were married by C.F. Lindberg. We got home at 12 o'clock midnight. Lindberg and a Rev. Lindholm with his wife stayed with us over night."

With all of Maja Lisa's children married and their families coming and going, she thrived in these warm and busy surroundings. She could usually be found in the rocking chair soothing one of her grandchildren, or cradling infants Donald and Rhoda. Donald (Otto and Alice's son) and Rhoda (Frank and Mary's daughter) were born February 26 and 27, 1894, respectively, only one day apart.

In the evening at Sunny Hill Farm, the children often played in their night clothes on the brown moon-patterned quilt grandmother Lundsten spread out on the floor. The tune Maja Lisa hummed as she rocked them in her arms seemed to instill peacefulness, even among those children who had been restless while romping on the floor. Gradually even the most active among them were overcome, and nodded weary heads in sleep. One song, "Tryggare Kan Ingen Vara" (translated "More Secure Can No One Be") – known in English as

John (Danielson) Lundsten
March 9, 1828-March 21, 1894

Maja Lisa Lundsten
September 7, 1828—March 27, 1913

Sara Carlotta 1853-1867	**Clara Christina 1856-1856**	**Frank Gustaf 1857-1939**	**John George 1859-1888**	**Emily Caroline 1861-1949**
		m Mary C. Hawkins	*m* Julia M. Mahala	*m* Jacob Schreiner
		Clarence, Frances, Amy, Mabel, Rhoda, Esther, John, Hazel, Frank	Verna	Alice, Olive, Edna, Verna, Florence, Raymond

Joseph Oscar 1863-1931	**Otto Wilhelm* 1866-1956**	**Alice* 1866-1954**	**Lotta w/twin? 1869-1869**
m Anna Steinhorst	*m* Alice Bardwell	*m* Lawrence Linder	
Ruth	Donald, Clifford, Malcom, Dorothy	Miriam, Lorimer, Wilma, Helen	

* Twins

Lundsten family members in 1891. From left: Clarence, Maja Lisa, Mary (Hawkins), Frank, Frances, Amy, and John Lundsten.

Emily Lundsten married Henry Rietz's nephew, Jacob Schreiner.

The Reverend Lawrence Linder and Alice Lundsten Linder, 1895.

"Children of the Heavenly Father"–was one of many sacred melodies from the homeland the children heard Maja Lisa quietly sing and hum.

The family circle at Sunny Hill Farm soon widened to include Esther, born to Frank and Mary in 1896, John Everett, born in 1898, Hazel Vivian, 1900, and, the youngest, Frank Rueben, born in 1905. Three years later, in 1908, the family mourned the death of Frances, then a student at Hamline University in St. Paul.

Daughter Esther, born May 26, 1896, brought the second minister into the family when she was twenty-three. She married the Reverend Carl Tideman of the Scandia Baptist Church (he was the recipient later of the first diary Andrew Peterson had kept, telling about his experiences during his ocean crossing).

While pain and sorrow frequently entered their lives, there were other moments filled with the joy of weddings, baptisms, and get-togethers. Such gatherings included the Brobergs and other neighboring families. Of those days, John Everett Lundsten has written:

One of the most fortunate things that ever happened to Dad was when he married the girl who became our mother. . . . Dad was a hard worker all of his life and yet those of us who knew him best are aware of the fact that he was also interested in many better things of life. There were always plenty of books and periodicals available in our home and as I ended formal schooling with the grade-school I have always been grateful for the regular copies of the Christian Herald, Literary Digest and National Geographic which were full of good, educational reading. His interest in church and Sunday School was, I think, the prime motive of his life, but he was always interested in any humanitarian project...During the years when the Prohibition Party was a political force, he was active in it locally. One of my first memories of him was when he took me with him to see a Prohibition parade in Minneapolis. I was only eight or nine and we walked to Victoria on a warm June morning to catch the ten o'clock train. I can still see Clara Salter *[map 55]* hoeing in her garden and as we walked by she looked up and said 'Well, Frank, I see you are still true-blue.' It was hot and dusty but it seemed as I remember those words that I held myself a little straighter as I walked beside him.

Frank Lundsten

Elsa Peterson, Maja Lisa Lundsten, and Caroline Anderson in 1904.

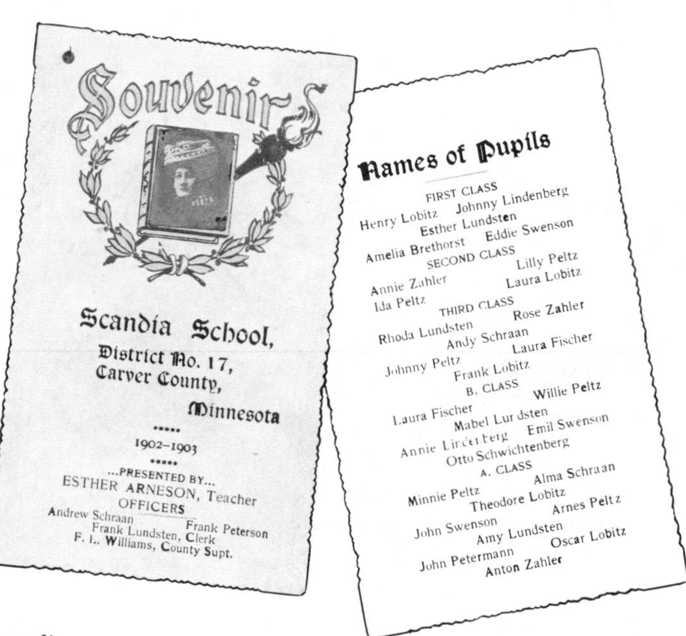

Souvenir

Scandia School,
District No. 17,
Carver County,
Minnesota

1902–1903

...PRESENTED BY...
ESTHER ARNESON, Teacher

OFFICERS
Andrew Schraan Frank Peterson
Frank Lundsten, Clerk
F. L. Williams, County Supt.

Names of Pupils

FIRST CLASS
Henry Lobitz Johnny Lindenberg
Esther Lundsten
Amelia Brethorst Eddie Swenson

SECOND CLASS
Annie Zahler Lilly Peltz
Ida Peltz Laura Lobitz

THIRD CLASS
Rhoda Lundsten Rose Zahler
Andy Schraan
Johnny Peltz Laura Fischer
Frank Lobitz

B. CLASS
Laura Fischer Willie Peltz
Mabel Lundsten
Annie Lindenberg Emil Swenson
Otto Schwichtenberg

A. CLASS
Minnie Peltz Alma Schraan
Theodore Lobitz
John Swenson Arnes Peltz
Amy Lundsten
John Petermann Oscar Lobitz
Anton Zahler

The class of 1874 at the second school in Scandia.

CHAPTER 11

District 17 The Scandia School

Although ministers and missionaries started some of the educational programs for children before Minnesota became a state, Susan Hazeltine is recognized today as the first public school teacher in Carver County. She taught classes during the fall of 1855 in a cabin located in Chanhassen Township, even before school districts were organized in the county. During the winter of 1855-56, the people in the village of Carver in San Francisco Township established their first school and school board, according to law. They became School District 1 in Minnesota because theirs was the first school outside of Minneapolis. District 1 was recognized as such until 1958, when the statewide numbering system changed. Ten days after Statehood Day, on May 21, 1858, Peterson wrote "we had a meeting at Fisher's house to organize a public school and decide where to build the school house."

Some time after this meeting, Andrew Bergquist's son Frank established a public school program at the Scandia Baptist Church. Bergquist's salary was probably paid by members of the congregation.

The location of public schools had been a matter of considerable debate. Territorial and state legislative committees had favored a plan in which each township would be a school district, but the plan met with opposition; most families preferred the old neighborhood schools. In older states, schools were established in the center of populated areas; the township plan called for schools to be built in the center of the township. In Carver County, as in other places in Minnesota, enactment of this plan would have caused schools to be built in swamps or at great distances from those who lived at the far corners of the township.

Andrew Peterson did not explain how the local farm families came to choose the site for their first school, although township records reveal he referred to a spot located on the Reverend F. O. Nilsson's property *(map 47A)*. On July 12, 1858, he wrote, "I went with Forssten and Hamberg [Hammerberg, a member of the Scandia Baptist Church] and helped them stake out claims on the school section."

Early records from the school districts in Carver County (some of which had to be translated from the German and Swedish languages) reveal that the families in the districts were assigned quotas of logs with which to build the schoolhouse.[1] They were to hew them to precise dimensions and deliver them to the site of the school.

Andrew Peterson mentioned chopping and

1. Rudolph Siewert (translator of school records) received his education in the parochial and public schools in Carver County and his advanced professional education at Mankato State Teacher's College and the University of Minnesota. He established his teaching career in the local area in 1927. He was elected to nine consecutive four-year terms (1934-1971) as superintendent of schools in Carver County and, while on leave of absence, served with the United States Army from 1943-1945. He was also appointed by the Carver County Commissioners for a one-year term as administrator of schools (1970-1971) to complete the consolidation of public schools, which had started in Carver County in 1946 and continued until 1970. Scandia was consolidated with Waconia School District 44 and is now District 110.

hauling logs for the school on February 11, 1859. After several days of carpentry work and the installation of a fireplace in his own cabin in March, 1859, Peterson said he worked the entire day of April 27, 1859, on the school.[2] Once again that fall he told of working at the school. He did not record the names of those who lifted timbers into place or who otherwise helped to build it.

Payment of $1 was made on May 29, 1860, to the Reverend and Mrs. F. O. Nilsson by John Matezold *(map 57)*, Andrew Mattson *(map 23)*, and John Erickson *(map 33)* for the schoolhouse site. The parcel of land was approximately 103 by 206 feet. The agreement read, in part, as follows:

> We, Frederick O. Nilsson and Soffia U. Nilsson hereby agree to let the above named school district have ½ (half) an acre of land of my premises being in the N.W. corner of the N.E. quarter of Section 17, town 116, range 24, for the use of building a school house on it, for said school district, and to have use of said premises as long as the district shall use it for school and public meetings; and furthermore I agree that all property owned by the district on the said part of land or school house site, they shall be empowered by this agreement to remove when they please.

Peterson's remark of July 4, 1860, in which he said, "We had a meeting and celebration with the school children," may have been an open house or special observance with Frank Bergquist's students, to introduce them to the location of the new school.

On September 20, 1860, Peterson wrote, "Broberg, Alexander and I went to Gustafson and were certified as school trustees." The following month, on October 2, he wrote, "J. A. Peterson [the Scandia Baptist Church minister] was here yesterday and made a tax list for the school district." The next day, "We have contracted with Peterson that he is to be our school teacher this winter and have $15.00 a month." The school year was short. Rudolph Siewert, former superintendent of Carver County Schools, said classes started November 1 and continued through the end of March, with a brief summer session to conclude the term.

John Broberg, Henry Schraan *(map 63)*, Alexander Johnson, and John A. Peterson held a district school meeting at Andrew Peterson's cabin on December 26, 1860. All but J. A. Peterson were school trustees and were officially elected to serve as school board directors April 27, 1861, during a meeting at the first school. Peterson said he was certified the following month.

On May 7, 1861, Peterson wrote that "Mitchel *[sic]* was here with $16.00 for the school master," suggesting that John Peterson's salary included $1 for janitorial services, since the contract for that winter term had been quoted as $15 per month.

The school district was divided into subdistricts, of which Scandia was Subdistrict Number 2. Taxes were levied in the amount of $.40 on every $100 of valuation of the taxable property. The receipts for the Laketown School District, received by the treasurer for the fiscal year April 1, 1861, to March 1862, amounted to $288.72. Payments to subdistrict teachers were as follows:

Ernst Miller	1859	$26.35
Miss Lena Meyer	1860	24.00
O. G. Johnson	1860	28.78
H. Gerdsen	1861	43.90
F. Salter	1861	42.90
G. Hammerberg	1861	33.00
E. C. Rogers	1861	25.50

The treasurer's fee was $2.26, other disbursements totaled $226.69, and the balance in the treasury was $26.03. A note had been entered on the same page by Henry Gerdsen *(map 30)*, town clerk *pro tem*. He wrote, "The teacher of sub district number 2, having left without furnishing the proper register, the board is unable at present to ascertain the exact amount due to said sub district." And Andrew Peterson's entry for January 27, 1862, had been, "Among other [things] we saw to it that we got rid of the school master." Peterson did not elaborate on that statement although the cause given by Henry Gerdsen (that the teacher did not have the proper credentials) was probably not an isolated one in this era. In those days, the superintendent was responsible for checking the teachers' credentials. Officials could have chosen a braggart, especially if no one else had applied for the job. On the other hand, the conservative element of society, mired in ancient prejudices, would have rejected applications from women, no matter how appealing their credentials might have been. Such men would not be willing to abandon tradition, based on their interpretation of Sacred Scripture, which had the effect of excluding women from public activities. The particular treasurer's report for the teachers within the subdistricts, from 1859-1861, illustrates that even when women were hired, they were paid considerably less than men.

2. A photograph shows the fireplace chimney was no longer part of the cabin on May 4, 1885. See page 80.

At a township meeting held in the home of H. Witzig on March 27, 1862, the schoolteacher John A. Peterson was named school superintendent. Peterson submitted a bill, which was paid for services rendered as the superintendent of schools as well as for clerical duties during the election on October, 1861.

Peterson wrote this April 7, 1866, diary entry with no additional information. "In the afternoon we had a meeting in the school house regarding the starting of a private school."

Andrew Peterson was elected treasurer of the school board in 1869. One of his first acts was to draw $100 to purchase books. He also stated: "I fixed the schoolhouse door."

It soon became evident there were problems to be resolved with the building itself after the structure started settling into the ground. William Peltz recalled that his mother Ida and his aunt attended classes in this log cabin – a place where the runoff from melting snow and rain covered the classroom floor. According to Rudolph Siewert, it was not unusual for schools in Carver County to close in late January or February or whenever the spring thaw started, because most of the buildings were without floors.

At a meeting held November 4, 1871, twenty-one votes were cast in favor of rebuilding the Scandia School at a new location; seventeen voters wanted things left as they were.

Nothing further was done that year. Then in 1873, the board purchased a one-acre tract of land in Section 8 from Louis Fisher *(map 39)* for $20. Hubert Lohmer *(map 59)* was appointed chairman of the building committee; other members were Jacob Jenni *(map 37)*, Andrew Peterson, Louis Fisher, Henry Reitz *(map 56)*, and Peter D. Anderson.

School records from 1871 list forty-one boys (five of them between the ages of eighteen and twenty) and thirty-eight girls (all between the ages of five and seventeen years) residing in the district. Actually enrolled in class were twenty-six boys and twenty-five girls. In that year, of the Peterson children, only George, ten, and John, eight, were in school.

Ida was fourteen when she started to attend sessions with the class of 1873. Charles also began school in this year, but Frank, then six, remained at home. By 1874, the only children in the Peterson family under school age were Emma and Anna. (Josephine and Oscar were born in 1875 and 1878, respectively.)

In 1873, Peterson's diary described hauling boards from Chaska to the school. On January 15, 1876, he chopped and hauled wood to heat the school, delivering his family's quota of firewood.

During those early years and even after the turn of the century, the school term was seven months. Although the state appropriated $50 for each student if classes were held for the required period of time, this goal was not easily reached. Teachers were scarce. The weather was often adverse and so were the roads. Moreover, it was useless to start school before November, because harvesting had to be completed first. Even then, not all of the pupils enrolled at the start. They came when they could. From time to time, Peterson recorded, "The boys are in school," as if it were the exception. Although the superintendent and board members were responsible for enforcing attendance, it was difficult to take action against neighbors if officers were not willing or able to set the proper examples themselves. For some children, even the minimum forty-day attendance requirement during the school term was not always possible. They could, however, make up those days during the summer session.

A new schoolhouse was built some time during these years, but records do not give the year it was completed. Several photographs, although faded, show what the interior looked like. Large blackboards as well as shiny new desks with chairs replaced small slate boards and benches used by students at the first school. Kerosene lamps and metal light reflectors were held in place with wrought iron brackets attached to the classroom walls. A wood-burning stove heated the room and kept the occupants comfortable most of the time.

The teachers evaluated the pupils as to attendance, interest, and ability. They were classified as very slack, slow to learn, too irregular, careless and indifferent, industrious, bright but careless, quite bright, very bright, careless and indifferent.

Pupils of all ages were in one large room. Often the older students helped the younger ones with their studies because the teacher had so many children to help in various grade levels.

Although pioneers built schools within walking distance of every child (according to the neighborhood plan), the children always looked for shortcuts. Some of them crawled between the rail fences that marked property lines. Pupils were often taken to school or fetched with the team. Then as now, families shared rides much as they do in modern-day car pools. In winter, the bobsleds slipped smoothly across the countryside, but after the snow melted, mud and ruts caught at the wagon wheels.

Water kept in pails satisfied the children's thirst, and they shared a common dipper. Normally the water had to be carried from the nearest farm because schools seldom had their own wells. In later years, the students used folding cups which were packed in molasses pails containing their lunches.

Students remembered what it was like to be in class with odors blending from lunches waiting to be eaten; wood smoke; wet, woolen mittens; and shoes their young owners had worn as they hurried through the barnyard chores. At home or at school, it was the same—when the temperature dropped, it was never very comfortable to sit on the cold boards in the outside privy.

Although strict discipline was supposedly required in these early schools, then as now things did not always run smoothly. Peterson wrote about a teacher named Mr. Krassey who simply closed the doors and left five weeks before the end of the term because of his pupils' behavior. There was no mention of a replacement. School was over for that year.

"Tipping the bell" was a favorite prank among the schoolboys. A few good pulls and the long rope carried the bell up and over itself. The rope wound around and around the bell's axis.

More than once, the mischievous students ignored an order to stay after school and pick up the ladder at the Lindenberg farm to retrieve the bell rope. Instead, they jumped out the windows and ran out of the schoolhouse door. A student and former school board member, Albert Schwichtenberg, vividly recalled his classroom experience after one of the board members entered the school before class was dismissed the following day. This man, who was of considerable size, bellowed, "If youse boice chump out of the fenster [window] again, I will bring myself a loonch [lunch] and a big stick and keep youse after school till youse all gets a blue belly!"

In another related episode, Schwichtenberg told about the young female teacher who lived with Charles Klatt and his family during her stay in Scandia. She found it was not easy to come and go without the entire household knowing about it. On one occasion, one of the gentlemen in the settlement came to take her to Waconia in a buggy. As they traveled, a musk-like odor became increasingly strong. When they stopped to investigate, they found a civet cat had been placed under the buggy blanket. The young teacher had few doubts as to the perpetrator.[3]

A succession of teachers roomed at the Peterson house after the family moved from the log cabin. Stephen Booth was one of them. Eventually he married Grace Anderson, daughter of Peterson's brother-in-law and sister, the Reverend John and Maria Christina Anderson.

During the school term, oral examinations judged by members of the school board were held. On February 25, 1870, and a number of instances thereafter, Peterson mentioned being "at the examination of the school children all day." These sessions were always considered a big day in the life of the students.

The State Department of Education was compelled to make special provisions for families who depended on help from their children. Boys and girls who completed their education through the eighth grade could be excused from further schooling providing they passed their state exams. This opportunity also applied to the parochial students who were required by law to take these tests, administered by the public school teachers.

The year closed with class picnics and presentations and awards from the teachers to the students. Each child received a souvenir booklet featuring verses of poetry with a high moral tone. These keepsakes were usually treated with care and were often kept among their cherished possessions.

The country school served an important function in the lives of the people in the community because the building itself served as a community center. It was a central gathering place for social events, not all of which were school-related.

Some of the graduates of the Scandia school were inspired to become teachers themselves, and these included Kate Bergquist, Amanda and Kate Broberg, Emma and Anna Freed, Mabel and Rhoda Lundsten, Edna Nelson, and Arnes Peltz. Other graduates became farmers, public servants, bankers, builders, business- and tradespeople, professors, homemakers, and nurses.

3. A civet cat is a spotted skunk, a small, tree-climbing animal native to North America. Skunks and civet cats (a colloquial expression) are unprotected wild animals found in Minnesota. See *Minnesota Game and Fish Laws*, 119 (Minneapolis, 1980).

Class of 1911. Back row (from left), Henry Lobitz, Hazel Lundsten, Albert Schwichtenberg, Minnie Groth (teacher), Clara Schwichtenberg, Harry Lobitz, and Everett Lundsten. Front row (from left): Roy Pofahl, Mabel Peltz, Myrtle Pofahl, Myra Peterson, George Lindenberg, and Irwin Schwichtenberg.

Minnie Groth's class picnic, 1911, including some visitors who dropped by. From left: William Peltz, the Reverend Carl G. Tideman, Frank Peterson, John Klatt (seated), and to the far right—Mrs. Selby Peterson holding baby Ruth.

Ethel Pettijohn's class picnic in 1912.

School picnics were often held on the Simon Peltz pasture by Parley Lake.

Evelyn and Harold Lobitz, children of Carl and Clara Lobitz (Ernestine's grandchildren), are shown with their teacher Edna (Nelson) Cutkosky (left, rear). Sarah Peterson, Leonard, and Lucille Anderson are also pictured with this class.

Classmates in the horse-drawn sled in front of the Charles Klatt home in Waconia.

Former Scandia students (from left): Esther Lundsten, Malinda Pofahl, and Lillian Peltz at the high school in Waconia.

From left: Ida Peltz with Edith Burgstahler, brother Bill, and sisters Mabel and Lillian.

Andrew and Elsa Peterson

Carver County Historical Society

CHAPTER 12

Peterson's Family Life (1876-1898)

Peterson often recorded the harsher aspects of human events in his diary along with the more agreeable ones. On January 22, 1876, he wrote, for example, "The boys are attending school without missing a day," then he told of purchasing wooden shoes for his young children in Waconia, and plastering the granary. It was tight – the rats would no longer be able to work themselves in. Then he worked on a privy.

Elsa's mother was the first to be taken from the family in death. Peterson said on October 6, 1876, "Drove Elsa over to Watertown as she is going to Litchfield to see her mother who is dying." He did not elaborate except to say when they returned twelve days later that Josephine (who was then a toddler, barely one year old) had accompanied Elsa.

Outdoor activities on the claim included digging a well in the barnyard as late as December. Peterson hewed timber for the well curb, while John Nelson *(map 10)* and Peterson's sons dug down a distance of seventeen feet in two days. By the time this project was completed, the well was twenty-six feet deep and had been lined with brick.

In addition to the never-ending chores on the farm, Andrew Peterson was responsible for all the church clerical work for a thirteen-year period. He also served as a church deacon, on the district school board, and on the Laketown Township board. He was a road supervisor, served on jury duty, was a witness during a court trial, and performed a host of other civic duties.

Through 1876, Peterson's writings included personal reminders about supplies being lent, borrowed, or traded. These entries were eventually crossed out after each of the specific transactions had been satisfied. In one instance he wrote, "Nicholas Swenson has borrowed a 24 lb. can with sugar, 23 lbs. sifted rye flour in a sack and 44 lbs. middling flour in a sack." He also said, "August Taylor borrowed 29 lbs. of salt from me." In another entry he noted, "I borrowed the small tin pitcher full, or slightly heaped, with lard from Jonas Peter. I also borrowed 7 lbs. of pork from him. It was a middle piece without bone."

Peterson's cash records include income from the sale of nursery and farm products. His expenditures show salaries paid for field and carpenter help and reveal the cost of clothing, fabrics, hardware, lumber, photographs, and furnishings as well as food and pantry items. His expense column often included favors of "mixed candy" for the family. On one occasion he paid $4 to "Lindahl" in Watertown for photographs of Elsa, Ida, and Sture, which was the cost of eighteen pictures – six of each. There were other entries such as Axel's "boots for plowing," $2.50; wooden shoes for Axel, $.35; six suspender buckles, $.10; a shooting jacket for Sture, $.80; nine and one-half yards of mattress goods, $1.40; and a doll for Josephine, $.30. Josephine later received a doll house and a hat with ribbons. Andrew Peterson also said he purchased a winter cap and a coat made of buffalo hide for $24.50.

Peterson may have been a chronic complainer, but he worked hard and he was getting old. He repeatedly mentions his lack of physical well-being, including, among other things, lameness, back problems, colds, lumbago, neuralgia, influenza, rheumatic pain, and spells of heart palpitation. In his search for relief, on January 31, 1876, he traveled with his brother-in-law, John Anderson, to Red Wing where he consulted a Norwegian woman doctor who may have been a heart specialist. He did not mention the results of his examination or how he cared for himself other than admitting he remained idle when he was "not well."

The newspapers and magazines of that day were riddled with gaudy ads promoting patent medicines with featured endorsements by those who had supposedly been cured. Peterson was not immune to these appeals. He wrote of picking up a shipment of medicines at the depot, and although he referred to his use of an oil substance, he did not say if he spread the lubricant on his skin. He also used a cupping device to draw blood to the surface of his flesh – a popular "remedy" of the day – and confined himself to bed after these treatments.

While great numbers of people moved to Minnesota in the belief that the climate was a great restorer of health, Peterson's records reveal most families faced serious health problems. Doctors were scarce, and conditions were primitive and far from sanitary. If medical services were available, doctors and patients alike had to travel great distances during the heat of summer and cold of winter with a horse and carriage. Peterson said that a Dr. Davis, a Minneapolis physician, visited his home on February 18, 1880. After staying overnight, the doctor was to keep an appointment at one of the Broberg family farms.

Although the family tried to escape illness, they were not always successful. On one occasion, Axel and Frank went to Victoria to be vaccinated by a Dr. Lewis, but they waited in vain – the doctor never arrived. Peterson also said, "Part of the family are sick. Perhaps it is the grippe or influenza." It was not unusual to read that the family was sick with colds or simply, "We are not well." He also wrote of being dosed by local practitioners skilled in the practice of homeopathic medicine.

Peterson often wrote about the weather and other natural events. Sometimes it was so cold that the family could do no work except for essential chores like feeding the livestock and milking.

Twice their livelihood was threatened by natural disasters. Grasshoppers wreaked havoc on Minnesota agriculture for three years. When the pestilence started in 1875, farmers plowed and hoed the grasshopper eggs under the ground in the fields to kill them. When they descended on Scandia, Peterson said the swarms were so thick that it looked as though it were snowing when he looked into the sun. His boys caught hordes of them in wire nets and dipped their snares into barrels of kerosene to kill them. Then they were burned.

Statewide, the situation prompted the governor to proclaim April 26, 1877, a day of prayer, and the settlers joined the petitions being made for deliverance. Disaster was averted on the Peterson farm. Although the apple trees suffered minor damage, the crops were saved.

Peterson's family was not as fortunate the following year when a vicious summer storm swept through the settlement on July 30. "I have never seen anything like it," Peterson remarked. "Hail stones as large as goose eggs. Thirty-five window panes were shattered in our house by the hail stones. The wheat was pounded down and so about 250 bu. of wheat destroyed and 6 acres of corn. The sorghum also was destroyed, but worst of all was that the bark was scaled off the apple trees. In other words, everything in the path of the storm was destroyed."

In the spring of 1878, the activities of the youngest children were hinted at in Peterson's diary. Emma, Anna, and Josephine couldn't help but enjoy entertaining themselves with the wagon he made especially for them. After Andrew arrived at home with the new churn, which he had purchased for $7, they probably watched in wonder while Elsa and sister Ida poured fresh cream into it and slowly turned the cream into butter.

Later that year, they were joined by another brother. Peterson never mentioned his son's retardation, so it is not known when his condition became apparent. His birth on December 3, 1878, seems to have been normal, according to Andrew's laconic entry – "Today we did nothing. Oscar Benjamin was born today." Throughout this young man's life (he lived to be in his 60s) he was well thought of. He was friendly and loved music. He often entertained himself as well as others by playing the violin. He could recall names, dates of events, and birthdates – sometimes to the chagrin of the women at church whom he greeted with comments that revealed their ages.

When the man who was taking the 1880 Census stayed as an overnight guest, Peterson reported it, and on November 3, 1880, reflected on his growing dependence on his children to care for the farm. He said: "Today Elsa and I started for Litchfield. Sture took us to the railroad station in Delano. We visited in Litchfield and Grove City until the 12th."

Members of the family all participated in daily devotions, and Peterson's diaries indicate they worked closely together in the home and at the church. The young people had their fun during spelling and cornhusking contests, visiting in one another's homes, having socials and parties, and taking occasional trips to Minneapolis or other places to attend young people's church conferences. On May 29, 1882, Peterson said, "This morning John Anderson and his daughter, Ruth, together with Ida left for the conference in Grove City."

Although declining in health and advancing in years, Peterson's March 14, 1883, entry reveals a resourceful and youthful spirit. He said: "Sture and I went over to Jons Nilson's house *(map 10)* and came to a decision about the trip to Dakota." One week later they were on their way to Aberdeen, South Dakota, "for the purpose of taking out homesteads."

Peterson accompanied Sture and August Nelson, John Nelson's son, in their search for farmland. Their mission proved to be a disappointment, however, since the territory had not been surveyed and the three men were not willing to establish squatter's rights to hold their claims. Peterson wrote of returning by train and walking along the railroad track, a distance of eleven miles, to reach Scandia. Soon afterwards, Sture traveled to Milbank with three friends—John, Meyer, and Andrew Jhalm. They searched for acreage, but apparently the results were not good there, either.

Peterson and his family also took part in the prohibition movement. Following a meeting in Scandia on November 1, 1883, the speaker, a Colonel Hamilton, and a merchant from Carver who also bore the name of Andrew Peterson, visited Andrew and Elsa at their home.

On December 5, 1883, Peterson remarked, "I had all my teeth, nine in all, pulled" by Dr. Brae in Young America. That same day Peterson checked Thomas's Russian apple trees and spent the evening hours with a cattle buyer, negotiating the sale of a cow he called "Lady."

It wasn't until May 14, 1884, that preliminary work first started on his dentures. He wrote: "After dinner Dr. Brae from Young America came and took an impression for the upper and lower plates he is to make for me. He also pulled a tooth for Carl and one for Anna. He will stay overnight." There were several similar visits by the dentist while Peterson's dentures were being fitted.

Peterson's finances had improved to such a degree in the 1880s that he was able to purchase a breaking plow, a bed, four chairs, and two mirrors during a single trip to Carver. (Until then, most of the family furnishings seemed to have been handmade or purchased at local auctions.)

On Christmas Eve, 1883, Peterson purchased an organ at the "Halriger" store in Chaska with the help and advice of a schoolteacher, Hilma Brunius. Young Emma began taking weekly lessons in Waconia, and, after she developed some skill, she played for church meetings and eventually became the regular organist.

The tour of the famous Swedish singer Kristina Nilsson, during which she appeared in Minneapolis and Stillwater, was referred to by Peterson on June 10, 1884. "Sture went to Minneapolis to hear Christina Nilson *[sic]* sing." In later years, friends of the Peterson family recalled their collection of classical records and sheet music. They enjoyed playing their musical instruments and listening to recordings as well.

After a day of "sultry, storm-brewing weather," Peterson said on July 24, 1885, "I went to the Waconia mill with grist. Mrs. F. O. Nilson *[sic]* from Houston and her sister-in-law, Mrs. C. Nilson *[sic]* from Spring Garden rode with me home. They are here to visit and greet old friends and renew their memories of dear old Scandia. It is now 25 years since F. O. Nilson moved away from here." Four days later he said, "The very hot, sultry, storm brewing weather continues. We have heavy soaking rains also but no change in the weather. Mrs. F. O. Nilson and Mrs. S. C. Nilson and Frank Peterson are here." Then the following day, "Today Mrs. F. O. Nilson and Mrs. Christian Nilson went to Broberg's place. Mama drove them over there. Tonight they are leaving for Minneapolis."

Comments suggest the journey itself must have been an exhausting experience for Soffia Nilsson and her sister-in-law.[1] Peterson said it was so hot,

1. The Reverend F. O. Nilsson resumed his ministry when he returned to Sweden, eventually taking up residency in Gothenburg. He moved back to Houston, Minnesota, in 1868, where he lived until his death in 1881. (See McKnight, "Nilsson Journal," 17.) After Andrew Peterson wrote on May 27, 1871, "I met F. O. Nilson *[sic]* in Carver and took him along home," Andrew never mentioned him again.

May 4, 1885: "This afternoon Charles Norman and Widmark, a photographer, came to take pictures of my buildings so we were hindered in our work the rest of the day."

Andrew wrote on May 8, 1885: "In the morning Widmark took a picture of the house from the southeast and then a picture of the whole family." On that day their ages were Andrew, 66; Elsa 50; Oscar, 6; Anna Isabelle, almost 13; Josephine, 9; Ida, 26; Emma, 15; "Sture," 24; "Axel," 22; "Carl," 20; and Frank, 17.

Ida Peterson

George ("Sture") Peterson

John ("Axel") Peterson

Charles ("Carl") Peterson

Frank Peterson

Emma Peterson

Oscar Peterson

with so much electricity in the air, that it was almost impossible to work.

Having failed in their search for homesteads outside of Minnesota, Peterson said on November 10, 1885, that he paid $1,500 for a farm with 240 acres of suitable land in Chippewa County near Maynard.

The Waconia banker George Mix sent the money to a Mr. Barker in Howard County, Iowa. Barker apparently owned the land, because he sent the deeds to Andrew Peterson. Peterson then forwarded them to his brother-in-law, John Anderson, who was minister of the Leenthrop Baptist Church on the outskirts of Maynard, to be recorded at the courthouse in Montevideo. A renter apparently lived there for seven years, until Sture assumed possession.

Per Daniel Anderson notified Peterson's family he had received a dispatch telling him that John Anderson (Per Daniel's brother and Andrew Peterson's brother-in-law), had died on the morning of November 14, 1887, in Granite Falls. Peterson told of traveling there with Elsa, Per Daniel, and Caroline for the burial. "The Leenthrop Church was packed with people who mourned with us in our deep sorrow and like us miss our departed loved one."

On December 12, 1887, he wrote, "At two o'clock a dispatch arrived from Granite Falls that my sister 'Maja Stina' died last night. It is just four weeks between John Anderson's death and the day his wife, 'Maja Stina' died, so they were almost allowed to go together to meet their Lord and Saviour."

In addition to their own six children, the Andersons had raised a boy from a troubled home. Perhaps this lad helped replace the loss of their son Ludwik, who died while the Andersons were living in Scandia. Grace, the youngest, was eighteen years when her parents both died. She later married Stephen Booth, and in due time gave birth to Helen and Gladys. Stephen Booth was one of the succession of school teachers who lived with the Peterson family during the school term in Scandia.[2]

Peterson wrote that, "Oscar Norman [sister Anna's orphaned son] went with us home from Leenthrop" after John Anderson's funeral. Norman apparently had been staying with relatives near Granite Falls, because he returned there on July 16, 1888. While he lived with his aunt and uncle in Scandia, he worked and attended social events with his cousins and helped Frank Lundsten and the Peltzes. After a brief period of employment with "Latham" in Excelsior, Norman quit his job and returned to Granite Falls.

After writing, "This morning I went to Scandia and set up a bulletin board on which I nailed a notice of the county fair," Peterson purchased boards and studding in Carver to build "our privy by the Scandia meeting house." He also worked on the church stables. Son Frank planted ornamental trees on the church grounds as well as those of the school. Then Andrew indicated that his children helped maintain and care for the church building and grounds. Frank and Carl "put up the stove at the church" in the fall. In the spring Carl "cleaned off and raked the yard by the church," and "Ida and Josephine scrubbed the church floor." During those early years, cuspidors were located at the ends of the benches on the men's side of the room in the church. Some of the farmers were remembered for well-placed, long-distance spits of tobacco. It is not known when these receptacles disappeared or when the congregation changed their seating arrangement. The women sat on the left side of the aisle, the men on the right near the spitoons.

His entries also told of social gatherings. On May 16, 1889, he wrote, "In the afternoon the folks from Litchfield came here. They were Andrew Johnson and his wife and his sister Josephine, and his brother, Edward, and Anna Ingemanson." (They were apparently related to the Peterson family through Olaf Johnson. In an earlier reference, Peterson had said, "My brother-in-law Olaf Johnson, from Litchfield came here from the Farmer's Alliance meeting in St. Paul.")

The day following the arrival of their guests, Peterson reported, "Frank is entertaining the Litchfield visitors." On Saturday he said, "Andrew and Edward Johnson went down to Minneapolis today. After dinner the rest of the Litchfield visitors and part of our folks went visiting to Andrew Brobergs [map 66]. In the evening Andrew and Edward Johnson returned from Minneapolis." On

2. Grace and Stephen Booth were both teachers. After their marriage (See Waters, "Genealogy," 15), Grace worked in the post office at Montevideo, while Stephen served as the postmaster at Clara City. Their eldest daughter Helen was born at Clara City in 1900, and Gladys arrived during her father's assignment at the Census Bureau in Washington, D.C., in 1904. The family returned to Minnesota in 1915, and Stephen resumed his career as postmaster in the United States Postal Service where he was employed until his retirement. Clyde C. Waters did not state the period of years Booth worked for the Census Bureau or the year he retired.

May 20, 1889, he wrote, "The Litchfield folks and our children are visiting Jons Nilsons *[map 10]*." The next day he said, "This morning at eight our Litchfield folks started for home." And the following day he wrote of another group from Litchfield. "In the afternoon my brother-in-law, Cornelius' children from Litchfield came here." Although he only identified Emanuel and Charles, there could have been other guests. These visitors also spent part of their time in Minneapolis and left Scandia the following week.

Elsa's relatives bore the name of Johnson, but that surname appears on Andrew's side, too, since his sister Gustava married a Johnson. Peterson remarked, "In the morning [Saturday] I went to Waconia and met Fred Johnson and his wife Ruth.[3] Axel and Fred Johnson spent time fishing before the guests left for Minneapolis on Monday morning.

Peterson mentioned the death of Anna Johnson, a former resident of Scandia and the daughter of Peter and Johanna Nilsson. Anna was buried May 8, 1890, beside her mother and brother in the Scandia graveyard.

In the late 1800s, a national organization called the Farmers' Alliance (of which Peterson mentioned a meeting attended by his brother-in-law, Olaf Johnson) became popular in Minnesota and Carver County. Its proposals to combat unfair railroad practices were similar to those supported by the Grange. Peterson joined the Alliance and described a meeting he attended on May 26, 1890: "The Farmer's Alliance had a meeting out on the island by Waconia. Dr. Fish (This Fish of the Great West Paper) from St. Paul made two political speeches. Sture, Carl, Ida, Josephine, and I were there."

Carlton Qualey noted Peterson's change of political allegiance when he wrote the following in an article for *Minnesota History:*

> Although he [Peterson] voted the Republican ticket in 1868 and 1872, as recorded in his diary, he wrote on February 3, 1874: 'This evening our Grange was organized.' More conclusively, he reported on January 31, 1885, that 'I attended the Farmer's Alliance meeting in our school house in the afternoon.' On November 4, 1890, he wrote: "This morning Axel, Frank and I went to the election when we voted the Alliance's ticket.' On May 9, 1891, he recorded that he attended another Alliance meeting, and on August 30, 1892, wrote: 'In the afternoon we were at Waconia and listened to a political speech by Ignatius Donnelly.' Again on July 7, 1893 [should be 1894], he 'went to Waconia to the People's Party convention.' He made no mention, however, of issues or of why he supported the Populists.

An important event occurred in the lives of several of Peterson's children, as well as for young people from several neighboring families, on Sunday, June 8, 1890. Andrew wrote: "Today we had a baptismal service in Scandia. The following from among our young people were baptized. From our family Frank and Josephine, P.D. Anderson's family, Charlie and Andrew, Broberg's family, James, William and Amanda, Jons Nilson's family, Henry and Inez, Freed's family, Emma and Anna, then B. Nilson's hired man, Frank Dahl, and Lundsten's hired man, Anton Dahl, Nicholas Swenson's family, Martin and Joel—altogether 15 persons."[4]

Peterson mentioned other family experiences in the 1890s: Sture and Carl working with harvesters in Granite Falls and Frank attending school in Minneapolis (without giving the name of the school or any specific classes).

During the month of September, Andrew and Elsa had a near-fatal accident while returning from the Carver County Fair with Frank, Ida, and Josephine. Their team of horses almost collided with that of a brewer from Shakopee. Although their wagon overturned, the family miraculously escaped with only minor injuries.

As the year drew to a close on December 20, Peterson also revealed that Sture and Emma were visitors at John Nelson's farm, and said the other boys "went skating on Peter Anderson's Lake." His December 29 entry said, "In the evening all the church young people came here and surprised Emma, giving her a gold ring, because she plays the organ at the meetings."

Elsa and Andrew finally purchased their first household convenience in 1891—an icebox. It took the combined manpower of Axel, Carl, and Andrew himself to haul the oversized cabinet home from Waconia. It stands to this day in one of the sheds.

On May 29, 1891, Peterson also disclosed that he "went to Waconia and agreed with Glashan to drill a well for me at $.95 a foot." After Peterson's son Carl hauled the drilling equipment from

3. Andrew Peterson's grandniece Ruth Anderson and grandnephew Fred Johnson were first cousins.

4. Emma Peterson's baptism had been recorded on July 5, 1885. Other family names appear only on the church membership lists.

Waconia to the farm, the first attempt to locate water seemed hopeless. Upon reaching a depth of 300 feet, the men abandoned the site because they failed to locate the water table. During the second try, the well diggers were finally successful. They reached good water at a depth of 180 feet. The men had drilled during that entire summer and then completed the project by hooking the well to a windmill. On October 19 of that year, Peterson reported that son Frank "painted on the wind mill."

By now, Andrew and Elsa's prosperity through initiative and inheritances was also such that they could afford to be generous with other members of their families. His February 9, 1892, entry revealed their thoughtfulness. "Today I sent the letter to Wingren in Chicago subscribing for 'Nya Vecko-Posten' for my brother Rydell and my sister-in-law, Elizabeth Pearson in Portland, Oregon." Whether his order was for a newspaper or magazine is not known.

Elsa sometimes attended or gave quilting bees and set the warp in place on the frame of the loom, making it ready for weaving. Elsa also assisted in the fields when needed. On August 24, 1892, Andrew wrote, "Stacked the wheat from the large piece of the south field. Mama is 'the nodding crow' (driver) most of the time because I am not well. Josephine [the youngest daughter] loaded the bundles on the wagon." Two days later, they stacked the wheat from the other side of the track and he wrote, "Today I was well so I was the 'nodding crow'."

Andrew reported without any explanation on November 25, 1892, that "Josephine teaches her last day in school today." The statement is interesting because Josephine was seventeen years old.

Andrew and Elsa's eldest son Sture was thirty-one when he left Scandia and, with Carl's help, started farming in Maynard. In the same year, 1891, he met the woman he would marry. Andrew first mentions her on July 16, 1892, as a "school teacher from Hastings." Her name was Ada Tapper, and she was a friend of Sture's cousins, the children of John and Maria Christina Anderson. She spent her first trip to Scandia, which coincided with one of Sture's visits home, on Waconia Lake fishing and boating. "The folks from Maynard" also visited friends and relatives in Scandia. When Ada was next mentioned in the diaries, on August 30, 1893, she was Sture's bride. Andrew wrote: "Frank went to Waconia with a load of wheat and then he met Sture and his wife when they came from Hastings. They are newly weds."

When the railroads came west, one line was built across the edge of the Peterson farm. The Minneapolis and St. Louis Railroad Company tracks were laid in 1881; later, Andrew noted that the boys "hauled cordwood out to the railroad."

Having the railroad cross one's land had its disadvantages. During a period of drought in 1894, coals from a passing train set off a large, persistent grass fire. On July 10, Peterson said, "Today the railroad train dropped some coals in our meadows, so the boys had to fight fire all day, and the women folks had to help them." The next day the fire broke out again, and the boys were still fighting fire past midnight. On the third day, Andrew pruned grapevines while the boys tried to extinguish the smoldering embers.

The early morning rapping sound at Peterson's door on November 17, 1895, came as no surprise to the Petersons. It had been expected, because the family had been aware of the vigil Elna Swenson's family had been keeping. Only the day before, Saturday, November 16, 1895, Peterson wrote: "In the afternoon Lindberg and I went over to Nicholas Swenson's house to see Mrs. Swenson. She is so very weak now so she can not live over the night." His next entry read, "Sunday. This morning at 5 o'clock Mr. Swenson came to us and told us that Elna, his wife, died last night at two o'clock."

After Elna's death, Ida and Josephine worked at Swenson's house cooking for the threshing crew. Ordinarily Peterson's daughters received little mention in his diaries. Ida seems to have spent her entire life in Scandia with the exception of brief intervals at the farm that Carl and and Frank owned in Maynard, for by 1897 they owned a home and farm near Sture's and Ada's farm. In January, Frank and Carl made a down payment of $200, and on October 26, Peterson recorded, "Frank and I went to Waconia and borrowed money at the bank to pay for the land that Carl and Frank [both bachelor brothers] bought in Maynard, and then we bought checks for $1,350.00 and sent it to Carl in Maynard."

None of the three Peterson sons settled permanently on their Maynard farms. Sture and his wife moved into the town of Maynard, where he worked as a carpenter with Lawrence Sanner. His farm is still being cultivated and his home in Maynard, located close to the business district, still stands and continues to reflect the quiet dignity of its former owner.

Frank returned to Scandia where Axel (also a bachelor) had remained all of his life. Carl (also known as Charles) stayed in Maynard while his sister Emma, sometimes relieved by Josephine, kept house for him. Finally, after Frank died, Carl also moved back home to live with Emma, Axel, and Oscar.

Upon Frank's return to Scandia, he continued to live at home following purchase (for rental purposes) of the farm formerly belonging to his father's longtime friend and correspondent, George Mattson *[map 48]*.

During the time Peterson's children lived on their farms near Maynard, they attended the Leenthrop Baptist Church located next to the cemetery in which their aunt and uncle, Maria Christina and the Reverend John Anderson, were both buried. Eventually the Leenthrop congregation merged with the Baptists in Maynard, and the former church in Leenthrop, where Anderson once preached, was sold to the Christian Missionary Alliance congregation and then moved to another location. Members salvaged some of the foundation stones and built a pulpit-shaped marker. It defines the place where the church once stood and serves as a tribute. It honors the memory of sod home beginnings and people blessed with the spirit of God.

Before the parsonage and barn were moved away, part of the house was removed. The extension or addition was hauled to the farm owned by Carl and Frank Peterson (Peterson's family called it Fairview) and joined to the side toward the back of the home. The room became a new kitchen.

Peterson frequently sent his children containers of grapes, maple syrup, and molasses. He also sent the school sleds (presumably because they were no longer of use to the children at the Scandia school) and the family sulky, a two-wheeled buggy.

Leenthrop Baptist Church and parsonage, built in 1884, where the Reverend John Anderson was minister. He and Maria Christina are buried in the church cemetery.

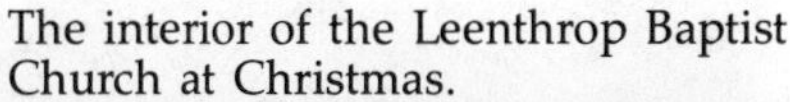

The interior of the Leenthrop Baptist Church at Christmas.

The Reverend John Anderson family. From left: Julia, John, Grace, Maria Christina, and Ruth. Back: Henry, John, and Frances.

The buildings once owned by the Petersons in the Leenthrop-Maynard area are currently surrounded by productive farms, vast open spaces, and the homes of several generations of families who are still cultivators of the soil located on the prairie—the heartland of Minnesota.

The greatest sorrow Andrew and Elsa experienced in their lifetime was the death of their daughter, Anna, at the age of seventeen. Other than saying "Anna is sick with rheumatism" on July 9, 1888, and mentioning taking her from place to place for treatments (the method was not explained), the situation seemed hopeless. In one instance, he said, "Anna did not take the treatment as they [Elsa and Anna] doubted the doctor's ability."

Peterson's suffering was revealed in a longer-than-usual paragraph on September 19, 1889. One sentence from the diary reads: "She was always so kind, quiet and tolerant that our loss and sorrow is heart rending to all of us, but in all our deep sorrow, we have this comfort that she went away happy in her faith on her dear Saviour, Jesus Christ." He told of sending a telegram to the boys in Maynard, ordering a casket, and making a frame for Anna's grave.

Andrew and Elsa's material fortunes were rising in the years between 1876 and 1890. Roger McKnight wrote that "His farming prospered, he branched out in earnest to apple orchardry. . . . While the memories of pioneer farming faded, this middle period was, at the same time marked by a persistently increasing list of family tragedies."

The years between 1890 and 1898, McKnight wrote, serve as a "time of calm in the author's life. Before this time the journals provide the picture of a man engaged in heavy farm labor. But now he becomes a sedentary figure, patiently observing people as they come and go while he quietly remains at home, grafting apple trees or hoeing in the garden."

The grown children of the
Reverend John and Maria Christina Anderson.
Back (from left): Grace and Frances.
Front: Henry, Julia, Ruth, and John.

Nicholas Swenson with sons Willie and Joel at home in Scandia.

CHAPTER 13

Neighbors

Iron Mike

In the 1850s, Michael ("Iron Mike") Reichenberger transported his worldly possessions on his back, tramping approximately fifteen miles through the wilderness, from the steamboat landing in Carver to his claim in Laketown Township. His choice for the site of his log dwelling was a spot close to the Hennepin County line *(map 14)*. As owners of this homestead, Mike and his wife Margaret eventually provided public right-of-way for a road and railroad access through their land.

A native of Bavaria, Mike seemed to have had little in common with his Scandinavian neighbors, especially in the beginning years when farmers traded labor and shared rides. It was then that he lugged sacks of grain or corn on his back as he traveled a distance of at least thirty-five miles to the mill in St. Anthony (later Minneapolis). His trips were finally shortened in 1867 after a gristmill began operations in Waconia.

The Reichenbergers befriended the Dakota Indians who passed their way and eventually these "friendlies" taught Margaret to use a certain root which had an analgesic substance to give to her teething children. Although Margaret also learned how to make beverages from herbs and basswood blossoms, she found their friends preferred the white man's brew. It was not unusual for them to drink at least several cups of coffee during a visit.

Probably Mike's most memorable encounter with the Indians occurred when his field work was interrupted by a group of agitated Dakotas asking the whereabouts of several others who were presumed to be from the same tribe. He avoided telling this search party that those they looked for could be found hiding behind the haystack located closest to the edge of the clearing.[1]

The 1860 census records that Michael Reichenberger, then thirty-two, lived with his wife Margaret, then twenty-eight, and children, Elizabeth, three, and Mary, one. Another immigrant farmer from Bavaria, Mathias Auer, then twenty-eight years old, also lived with the Reichenbergers. School records of 1872 listed as registered students in Scandia Elizabeth, sixteen; Mary, thirteen; Catherine, nine; John, seven; and Michael, five.

Although the Reichenbergers were German Catholics and did not share a common ethnic or religious background with their Swedish Baptist neighbors, Andrew Peterson does tell of going to the Reichenberger farm with his stock to use Mike's cattle for breeding services. Like others in the vicinity, the Reichenberger children also assisted their neighbors with field work.

Iron Mike remained at home after Margaret died June 27, 1894, while his son John and wife Mary (Noterman from Chaska) occupied a second dwelling centrally located on the homestead property. When John's wife Mary also died on July 28, 1915, the eldest daughter Esther was only ten years old. From that time on (until she was an adult and left

1. These people who returned each summer to their ancient home in Carver County were most likely from Chief Rattling Moccasin's band of *Wah-pay-tons* (otherwise known as the Little Rapids Band) and his successors.

home), Esther became the homemaker in charge of younger family members—John, Ed, Mike, Regina, and Loretta. The grandfather, Iron Mike, lived with them until his death on September 27, 1919. The young brothers Ed and Mike stayed in the settlement after others in the family left home. They worked with their father and as hired hands on neighboring farms until their father died in 1944. Then they assumed responsibility for the entire operation of the farm.

Although several in the family continue to own portions of this homestead, they no longer live in Carver County. But as of 1980, John, seventy, and Ed, sixty-seven, were still working the land. They had eighty acres under cultivation and were raising at least one hundred head of cattle.

Making Caskets

Most of the soldiers held prisoner during the Civil War returned home as invalids. Andrew Mattson, the thirty-two-year-old sergeant from Scandia *(map 23)*, had been held captive at Guntown, Mississippi, while serving with Company H of the Ninth Minnesota Infantry. He fought during the Sioux Uprising, witnessed the mass execution of Indians at Mankato, and later accompanied General Sibley's Indian expedition to Dakota. Upon leaving the garrison at Fort Abercrombie, his unit finally joined forces with the entire Ninth Minnesota in Mississippi in the fall of 1863. Following Mattson's capture by the Confederate Army in Mississippi, the Minnesota regiment marched through Arkansas, Missouri, Tennessee, and Alabama.

Although it was not until August 24, 1865, that soldiers of the Ninth Minnesota were finally discharged, the events that transpired in Mattson's life reveal that he had already been at home in Scandia (the date of discharge is not known) several months before others in his unit were released.[2] Soon after his homecoming he died, reportedly from a disease he had contracted while held as a prisoner in Mississippi.

2. Information from the Ninth Minnesota roster reveals that the person in charge of Andrew Mattson's division was Captain William R. Baxter. Baxter, a soldier from Chaska, lost his life during the battle at Brice's Cross Roads on June 10, 1864. Although Godfrey Hammerberg, Mattson's companion from Scandia, was shot in the head at Guntown, Mississippi, his injury was not fatal. Hammerberg was mustered out of the army on August 24, 1865, with his neighbor, Taylor August Johnson. The former Baptist minister, Alfred Johnson, received his discharge in 1865 while hospitalized with other wounded veterans.

Without mentioning Mattson's illness or other circumstances relating to his friend, Andrew Peterson explained on May 29, 1865, that he "started to make a casket for Andrew Mattson and worked on it all night." He followed that statement with, "We buried Andrew Mattson and then I went to bed and slept."

Perhaps some of the special planks made out of butternut logs and other timber that Peterson mentioned taking to the mill in Waconia were set aside solely for constructing caskets. Even though it was customary for families to keep boards on hand for this purpose, Peterson, it appears, kept a larger stock than usual in his reserves. This was illustrated four months after Mattson's burial when Peterson made this entry, "Erickson *[map 33]* is here making a casket for Andrew Mattson's boy."

Peterson, it seems, took charge of handling the remains of many of the settlers. His reports frequently mentioned making caskets, especially during the beginning years within the settlement.

Farewell to Ellen and Andrew

In spite of the affection Andrew and Ellen Bergquist held for their friends and strong personal ties they had established throughout the county, they decided to leave Scandia. Peterson said on May 2, 1866, "Today Bergquist moved to Minneapolis." Before leaving the settlement, Bergquist incorporated John Johnson's farm *(map 52)* with his original homestead.

The oldest Bergquist son, Frank, who was a farmer and a schoolteacher, continued to live on the home place while providing postal services for the patrons in Scandia. This service was merged with the Waconia post office in 1870. (Although the settlement postal address was changed to Waconia in 1870, the familiar name of Scandia continued to be identified as such until 1880. After that year, the name disappeared from local plat maps and the site no longer existed within the rural area outside of Waconia.)

As in most farms of substantial size, the property lines of the Bergquist estate were eventually altered as specific lots were sold to a succession of new owners. In this instance, court records reveal the names of Peter Swenson, Charles Lundgren, Peter Magnus Johnson, Enoch Broberg, James Holmquist, Andrew Anderson (Per Daniel Anderson's son), and August Nelson (John Nelson's son).

The Petersons and Bergquists maintained close ties through Frank's continued residency. Daughter Kate Bergquist married Andrew Broberg,

Annie (daughter of John and Catherine Broberg) and her husband Nathaniel Bergquist.

and son Nathaniel married Annie Broberg. (Another daughter, Henrietta, married William B. Fruen, the founder of the Fruen Milling Company, one of the first mills in Minneapolis.)

The Bergquists first found their church home at the First Baptist Church in Minneapolis. But after a short time, the Bergquists and twenty-two other members of a Bible study group requested separation from the existing church to start another Baptist congregation specifically for people of their own nationality. Then, following accepted procedure within the church structure, those individual members who requested permission to organize another church of the same denomination were given letters of transfer from the home church. Each member of the group who received these letters from the First Baptist Church in Minneapolis then met for a simple ceremony. They formed a circle, joined hands, and prayed. Thus the Swedish Baptist Church of Minneapolis was founded on June 24, 1871. (Today this congregation is known as the Bethlehem Baptist Church.)

Although Peterson mentioned Ellen Bergquist's visit in Scandia on September 7, 1896, he did not reveal that Andrew had died on February 21, 1896. Ellen passed away on December 2, 1906. Both were buried at Hillside Cemetery in Minneapolis.

Their daughter, Henrietta Bergquist Fruen, wrote a small book of poetry called *Recollections of a Pioneer,* commemorating the pioneer beginnings in Scandia.[3] It was published in 1904 by the Strandberg Press in Minneapolis.

3. Today family members spell their name Burquest.

Wilhelmina Brethorst

Pockets Filled with Treats

Stories handed down by the German family of Wilhelmina ("Minnie") Brethorst do not include the year she settled in Henderson with her first husband, Frederick Ott, or the date he lost his life in an accident. However, in 1870, Minnie and her children, Amelia, Edward, Robert, and Albertine, left Henderson and moved to Laketown Township. There Minnie met and married George Brethorst (also known as Jacob). Brethorst had lived in Scandia since December 3, 1867, on land purchased from Peter Nilsson in the general neighborhood of the Grimm alfalfa fields. The Brethorsts lived on this farm until March 13, 1871, when they traded their farm *(map 22)* with August Pofahl *(map 33).* The Pofahl property had belonged to John Erickson, a pioneer who helped clear the timber, studied to become a minister, and had power of attorney for the Reverend Nilsson when the latter left Scandia.

Since much of the property Brethorst received in the land exchange was a wetland area near Parley Lake, the family struggled to make a living. The size of the family more than doubled when the Ott children were joined by stepbrothers Louis, George, Diedrick, Richard, and Oscar Brethorst.

Peterson usually mentioned this family in connection with harvesting. But he wrote on April 18, 1888, that "Senn (Bradhouse's son-in-law) came after 20 bu. seed wheat today." This entry illustrates the difficulties Peterson had with spelling neighboring German family names, for by Bradhouse, he meant Brethorst, and by Senn, he meant Brethorst's son-in-law, Henry Sohns.

The day after Sohns *(map 27)* was at the Peterson farm, George Brethorst died of what was then called lung fever. Peterson wrote on Sunday, April 22, "In the afternoon we buried Bradhouse out by the Moravian Church." Sohns, a Moravian, probably made arrangements for Brethorst's burial in the Lake Auburn Moravian Brethren's Church cemetery, although his in-laws were not of his faith.

Somehow Minnie managed to support her children. She sheared sheep for neighboring farm families and worked as a midwife. Tending to the needs of expectant mothers and caring for them after the birth of their children filled an important service in Scandia. Minnie was frequently seen picking berries or carrying apples or other food in her wide apron. She took shortcuts across the fields, always managing to squeeze herself between the fence rails as she journeyed to help others or to visit her daughter Albertine, Mrs. Henry Sohns.

Albertine and Henry had fourteen children; two of them died of diptheria. In addition to farming, Henry and his sons spent most of their free time trapping animals (as did other men in the surrounding settlement) to supplement the family income. It was said he kept an extra set of clothing in the woods and changed into them before checking his traps because of the odor emitted by his quarry, the skunk. Henry was after the pure black kind since solid black pelts were worth more money than the striped ones.

The earth on the trail through the woods from the Brethorst farm to that of their neighbors Martin and Wilhelmina Maas *(map 26)* was packed like cement from constant use. Most likely Sture also used this path in helping to construct the Maas home. On May 11, 1889, Peterson wrote, "Sture continues working for Maas." He was not through there until July 25, 1889, when Andrew wrote, "Sture returned from Maas place today. They have finished the Maas' dwelling house."

Pauline and Charlie Maas, two of thirteen children, remembered looking forward to returning the loaves of bread their mother sometimes borrowed from Minnie Brethorst.[4] They already knew that when Minnie reached into the long side pockets of her dress, they would receive an assortment of mixed candy treats. Fresh loaves of bread were often delivered or carried back from the Maas farm in Minnie's apron. Because Mrs. Maas made clothes for Minnie, Minnie often delayed her return trip home, always taking time to help in any way she could.

Even though Minnie's sons worked the farm and held outside jobs, too, life seemed to be a never-ending struggle, aggravated by alcohol. On one occasion Minnie arrived at the Maas farm home and exclaimed, *"Ach! Ich bin hierher gekommen diesem Elend zu entfliehen. Da es hier nicht besser ist, so kann ich ebensogut wieder heimgehen,"* which meant, "Oh, dear! I came here to escape this misery [from alcohol]. Since it is no better here, I might as well go back home again."

In addition to raising her own youngsters, Minnie raised her granddaughter because her daughter, Amelia Ott Lietzau, had died during childbirth. The baby, also named Amelia, inherited the nickname Melee. She attended the Scandia school and was lovingly cared for by Grandma Brethorst.

Neighborhood children appreciated Melee's grandmother because she was a teller of fascinating tales. Since Minnie had attended the birth of many of these settlement children, it is little wonder that she was always ready with her candy treats.

Louis Brethorst seemed to take special interest

4. Charlie and his sister Pauline (Maas) Weinzerel from St. Bonifacius (who were both in their 80s) reminisced with relatives of the Brethorst family, including Linda (Brethorst) Dix from Young America, Gladys (Schraan) Wendland from Bloomington, Marge (Sohns) Reis from Victoria, and Esther (Sohns) Hoffman from Covington, Kentucky. The present generation of the Brethorsts are proud of their heritage and have close ties with each other. The second Sunday in September has always been set aside for a traditional celebration of the clan, during which time it is not unusual to see more than ninety people gathered for fun and fellowship. Old family photographs are conspicuously displayed for their offspring to see, while relatives share findings resulting from year-long research regarding their genealogy. Their combined effort is published in a yearly bulletin called "News and Notes."

in doing what he could for his stepsister's daughter. He never married. He was a road maintenance worker for Laketown Township and occasionally worked as a carpenter.

On one occasion, Louis drove his team across frozen Waconia Lake in winter and struck open water where the Cedar Lake Ice Company had been cutting ice. Although the horses were drowned, Louis managed to save himself.

After Minnie's children had grown, the state of Minnesota dredged a waterway from Parley Lake through the low-lying swamp area to Lake Minnetonka. The wetlands of the Brethorst farm drained into this channel. After the marsh dried, the size of the pasture area increased for the cattle.

Several years before her death, Minnie moved into the home of her daughter Albertine and son-in-law Henry Sohns. She passed away there on November 5, 1918, and was buried beside her husband at the Lake Auburn Church cemetery.

A Tale of Six Sisters

Andrew Peterson's neighbor, Henry Peterman, was born in Buffalo, New York, in 1841, the son of John and Erna ("Dorthea") Peterman, natives of Prussia. They arrived in the United States in 1836, spent several years on a farm in New York state, moved to Jackson County, Wisconsin, and finally settled in Carver County in 1867. They purchased John Maetzold's farm *(map 57),* his livestock, and his personal property for $3,300.

John and Erna's son Henry, at the age of twenty-six, was not yet married and was quite naturally attracted to the young ladies in Scandia, especially the six daughters of John and Ida Zieman, who were German immigrants. The six were Alma (who did not live in the Scandia community), Amelia, Ida, Annie, Ricka, and Otillia. In 1868, Henry married Amelia.

In their later years, John and Erna made their home with Henry and Amelia until their deaths. Peterson attended a funeral at the Peterman home on March 15, 1871, but did not say who had passed away. But on December 15, 1885, Peterson wrote, "This morning Elsa and I went to old man Peterman's funeral," and on May 28, 1888, he wrote, "This forenoon Mama, Frank and I attended the funeral in Waconia of Peterman's mother [Erna]." Five years later, a barrel factory stood on the Peterman farm, and Peterson hauled hoop poles to the factory owner.

Henry Peterman, a trustee in the Trinity Lutheran Church, built a lucrative creamery business in his lifetime. He raised a larger-than-usual dairy herd, and then invested in a small frame building, including equipment, to process creamery products. He called his company—a private business venture located in Waconia—the Peterman Creamery. It is said to be one of the first milk-condensing plants in Minnesota.

Henry and Amelia (Zieman) Peterman

Henry and Amelia raised eight children—Minnie, William, Henry, Otto, John, Emma, Annie, and Ida. There was naturally a great deal of family interaction at this and neighboring farms, since all but one of the six Zieman sisters remained in or close to Scandia and their parents John and Ida Zieman, even after each of them had been married.

Amelia Peterman's sister Ida (Mrs. Simon Peltz) remained with her parents, John and Ida Zieman, on the home farm *(map 34).* Eventually sister Annie (Mrs. Charles Klatt), who had been living in Waconia with her husband and family, moved next door to Andrew Peterson's farm, the Klatts having purchased the former Nilsson-Swenson property *(map 47, 47A).* Sister Ricka (Mrs. Frederick Maas) was situated in the vicinity of the Gerdsen school *(map 26),* and sister Otillia (Mrs. John Radde) also lived nearby.

Alma Zieman was the eldest of John and Ida Zieman's six daughters and the only sister who did not live in the neighborhood. Alma had traveled to America alone as a teenager, even before her parents had left Germany. When she arrived at St. Paul, she learned from workers at the dock on the Minnesota River that New Ulm was a German community, and decided that was the place to go. Although this journey was made prior to the Indian uprising, Alma's stagecoach was guarded by militia from Fort Snelling. She apparently found employment as a domestic worker

After Therese, the sister of Simon Peltz, married widower Philip Burgstahler, she was pictured visiting relatives in Scandia. From left: Therese (Peltz) Burgstahler, Mrs. Albert Maas (Minnie Schutz), the family dog, Ricka (Zieman), her son Albert, and husband Frederick at the Maas farm.

and eventually married John Roesoft, a blacksmith at Fort Ridgely. Alma's safety was a major concern for her family in Scandia, but she survived the Sioux War.

In 1896, Andrew Peterson recorded that he hauled milk and basswood to Peterman's Creamery in Waconia. The creamery had increased its demand for dairy products, and as a result most families in the settlement responded by enlarging the size of their dairy herds. In a few years the largest percentage of condensed milk produced by the creamery was sold in bulk to ice cream companies.

Peterman's family prospered. They had invested substantially in the creamery, and supported this effort with their continued hard work on the farm. Son William also worked with his father at the creamery and eventually married a neighbor, Elizabeth Schraan. His wedding on May 24, 1899, was followed by the marriage of his brother Otto to Elizabeth's sister, Alma Schraan, on July 25, 1903.

Otto and his bride moved into their own home, located across from the family farm *(map 45)*, which had been given to him by his parents.[5] After Henry Peterman's death in 1916, William took charge of the business and built a new home for his wife Elizabeth and daughters Dorothy and Gladys, next to the remodeled creamery. In time the Waconia Creamery Association (a co-op) purchased the entire business operation from William Peterman. After consolidating that plant into its own, the cooperative creamery moved into the Peterman building on the corner of First and Maple Streets in Waconia. This structure was demolished in 1983.

Henry's wife Amelia and daughter Annie remained alone at home in Scandia after others in the family moved away. The women employed hired men and continued to farm.[6] Amelia's son Otto and his family helped when they could.

5. The wives of William and Otto were the daughters of Andrew and Bertha (Schwichtenberg) Schraan. The Schraan property *(map 63)* bordered the fields of Nicholas Swenson, Andrew Peterson, and Henry Peterman. William's daughter Gladys took charge of his home after Elizabeth passed away in 1951, and until his death in 1967, William continued to live next to the creamery Henry had started in Waconia. The home is still occupied by Gladys and her husband, Ray Giesen. They were married September 15, 1939.

6. The August 2, 1928, edition of the *Waconia Patriot* (p. 1) reported that James Zelanka, former hired hand at the Peterman farm, was in custody at the jail in Chaska. After drinking and other problems had resulted in his dismissal from work at the farm, this vengeful worker attacked and killed the new hired man. Zelanka was found guilty of homicide and given a life sentence of hard labor at Stillwater State Prison.

Stalked by Wolves

The Peterson home was under construction for years. Andrew often made references to the work on the house. After he traveled to Chaska with a load of wheat and sold it for $1 a bushel, he wrote on January 14, 1874, "I also hauled home a load of lathsticks." Peterson hired Henry Pintz, a Carver mason, to plaster the interior of his home. The lath sticks were fastened to the upright studs or the frame supporting the walls of his home (in a horizontal position with spaces between). Then the Peterson boys made the mortar (combined with matted cattle hair) and helped Pintz apply the second coat of plaster to the lath in the upstairs rooms.

Henry Pintz immigrated from Prussia (the date is not known) and married Rosalie Peterman, Henry's sister and daughter of John and Erna Peterman, who had come to the United States from Prussia in 1836. Pintz's brother-in-law, Henry Peterman, was Peterson's neighbor. The correct spelling of Henry's surname is Pintz, although Peterson spelled it Pinz.

Pintz sent money to his nephew, Charles Klatt, in Prussia, which Klatt used to pay for his passage to America. He arrived in Carver to be an apprentice for his uncle. It was said Klatt went to church the Sunday after he arrived and placed three cents, all he had left, into the collection in gratitude for his safe arrival, a job, and a new home in Minnesota.

On May 16, 1881, Peterson wrote, "John Klatt [Peterson sometimes called him John, although his name was Charles] and the boys began to dig a cellar." Klatt helped John Hakanson and Sture haul dirt from the cellar. When the excavation was completed, he wrote, "Pinz and Klatt began to build the cellar." On August 20, 1881, "Charley Klatt began to sheath the outside of the kitchen with brick." Three days later he said, "Klatt laid bricks and Carl mixed the mortar. Pinz came at noon and helped to lay brick the rest of the day. Jons Nilson worked on the inside finishing the kitchen."

In the days that followed, Pintz and Klatt finished the exterior brick facing on the new kitchen addition to the house, built a chimney, worked on a cistern, and plastered the kitchen.

While working for Pintz (he also lived with him), Klatt often journeyed on foot to jobs located at a distance from Carver. Although he was tired at the end of the day, he was always alert for wolves, because he had once been forced to hold them at bay. This sense of uneasiness never left him.

Ernestine's New Barn

Herman Lobitz and Ernestine Ketcher were married in 1878. They lived on the farm *(map 38)* that Herman's parents, Gottfried and Amelia Lobitz, purchased from Swen Bengston on April 24, 1866. Although the Lobitz family belonged to the Trinity Lutheran Church in Waconia, they were in other ways very much a part of Scandia. The children attended the Scandia school and joined other farmhands when neighbors needed help.

Peterson once told of exchanging grape vines for cedar trees growing on the Lobitz farm and mentioned a trip he made to town specifically to pick up each of their shipments of strawberry plants.

Herman Lobitz harvested logs to build a new barn. He made frequent trips to the sawmill in Waconia across the ice on Waconia Lake, then home again with the lumber. His death resulted from an accident that occurred while he was hauling wood. It was customary to secure the load with a double chain and a pole with a twist, but neighbors believed Herman died because he had not fastened the load in the usual manner. The sled hit a ridge in the ice, the dray horses shied, and the logs began to roll. Herman passed away on March 4, 1898, several days after the accident. Peterson recorded that Axel, Frank, Emma, and Josephine attended the funeral.

Soon after Herman's death, Ernestine gave birth to a son whom she named after his father. Her other children – Frank, Henry, John, Carl, Theodore, Oscar, Laura; Lena, and Harry – were now responsible for most of the farming chores.

The Scandia neighbors, led by Simon Peltz and John Pofahl, finished Herman's project for Ernestine's family. They built the barn and attached a sign printed with the year 1898 to the peak on the front gable, under the roof. This weathered building was a beautiful sight along the lakeshore road, especially during Indian summer days.[7] It loomed up into the sky against the backdrop of brightly colored fall leaves and shocks of corn standing in the surrounding fields.

The Round-Topped Trunk

August and Augusta Pofahl purchased John Erickson's homestead near Parley Lake after they

7. This barn and other outbuildings as well as the old home were demolished in the 1970s to make room for an improvement project on the lakeshore road. Family members have since built a new but small home close to the site of the old. The area where the barn once stood has been incorporated into the road right-of-way.

Paul Pofahl's family. From left: Myrtle, Grandmother Augusta Pofahl, Mary holding Severa ("Fairy"), Roy, Paul, John, Raymond, and Arthur.

arrived in Carver County. This land in Section 9 *(map 33)* met the Peterson property. Peterson was a close neighbor and exchanged labor with August and hired him to make some clothing.

Eventually, August and Augusta exchanged places with George and Minnie Brethorst. While raising their nine children on this choice parcel of land *(map 22)*, they purchased an additional farm *(map 37)*.

After August passed away his sons Edward and Paul carried on their work at both places. Edward remained at home and Paul brought his bride Mary, daughter of Louis Schwichtenberg, to live on the second farm. Another brother, John, a building contractor, built a spacious new home for them here on the property homesteaded by the Reverend John and Maria Christina Anderson. This is where Paul and Mary raised their nine children—Anna, Arthur, Edna, Raymond, John, Myrtle, Roy, Severa ("Fairy"), and Allegra.

A cabin, perhaps the first one in Scandia, was used by John and Mary as a shed. The children thought the log building was a marvelous place to play. The floor boards in the loft were very rough. The lower level was used as a tool shed and also housed their carriage, and later the family's first car.

Mary Pofahl's nephew, Albert Schwichtenberg, still has memories of old August Pofahl and his fascinating round-topped trunk filled with fabric and tools of his tailoring trade. Albert was inquisitive, and his persistent questions caused the old man to jokingly warn him against touching the container because there were "spitzbuben" (rascals) inside. Albert's father, Herman, often said to his son, "You can ask more questions than twelve men can answer!"

Anna and Herman Schwichtenberg with baby Walter and daughter Dora.

Albert's parents, Herman and Anna Schwichtenberg (Alma Lohmar's sister), raised six children—Dora, Walter, Otto, Albert, Clara, and Irwin—on their property *(map 36)* next to Per Daniel Anderson.

Albert and his cousin Raymond Pofahl spent most of their leisure time hunting; it was a favorite recreation. They did not have to travel far to hunt, since a deer pass went through their adjoining farms and there was plenty of woodland cover.

Andrew Justus

Swan and Ingrid Swanson

Falling Timber

Andrew Justus Johanson, born in Sweden on September 3, 1866, left Värnamo Stad, Småland, with several friends when he was sixteen years of age. He traveled directly to Minnesota and spent his first evening at the Immigrant Hall in Minneapolis on May 29, 1882. He reached Scandia and the home of his aunt and uncle, John and Catherine Broberg, after a short journey by train. For the Brobergs, parents of twelve children, it was customary to provide lodging for relatives seeking help upon arrival in Minnesota. In this case, Johanson was a nephew who had lost his mother at the age of five. He and his sister Bertha had been cared for in Sweden by a stepmother, along with a stepbrother and stepsister. But when he was eleven, Andrew's father, Catherine Broberg's brother, died.

On arrival in America, Johanson decided to shorten his name. He became known as Andrew Justus. He attended church services, enrolled in the Scandia school with his cousins, and worked during vacations at the farm of Jacob and Emily (Lundsten) Schreiner in Hector, Minnesota.

Within several years of Justus's arrival in Scandia, Catherine Broberg received word from Sweden that her sister Inga or Ingrid (Swenson) Swanson and her husband Swan were preparing for the departure of several sons to America.[8] John and Frank Swanson traveled directly to Scandia, staying with the Broberg family until they found employment at the Smith Lumber Company in Minneapolis with Broberg's son, Enoch. In 1886, their brother Charles, a carpenter, also joined them in Minneapolis. One year later, John, Frank, and Charles Swanson pooled their financial resources and paid the price of passage to bring their parents to Minnesota.

While the Swansons were living at the Broberg farm, Andrew Justus moved in with Emily Schreiner's parents, John and Maja Lisa Lundsten, and later with the family of her brother Frank and his wife Mary at Sunny Hill Farm.

Andrew Peterson's July 17, 1887, diary entry revealed, "Sunday. Broms preached. William Swanson [Swenson] and Justus were baptized today."

On November 3, 1889, shortly after Justus com-

8. Peterson also spelled the name Svanson. In Sweden the children were called Svensson, sons of Sven, but this name was eventually changed to Swanson after settlement in Minnesota.

pleted his education at the school in Scandia, he transferred his church membership to the same church Andrew and Ellen Bergquist attended, the First Swedish Baptist Church in Minneapolis. Meanwhile, he was employed as a delivery driver for the Smith Lumber Company where his cousins were also working. By this time, his sister Bertha was also in Minnesota. She was hired by the Swanson brothers as their housekeeper.

Frank Swanson died a year and a half later. Andrew Peterson wrote on March 1, 1891, "Sunday. Today we buried Frank Swenson [Swanson] from Minneapolis in the Scandia grave yard. He was accidentally killed by a falling timber in the forest."

Frank's accident most likely occurred while harvesting trees for the Smith Lumber Company. Peterson also revealed on March 3, 1891, "John Swenson [brother of the deceased] from Minneapolis is here on a visit."

Andrew Justus continued to work for the Smith Lumber Company until shortly before starting a business venture in Hopkins. On April 3, 1893, he officially began the City Lumber Company, now known as the Justus Lumber Company, with his partners John Swanson and Enoch Broberg. From the beginning of this partnership, Andrew Justus and John Swanson shared an apartment located above the lumberyard office. Justus became sole owner in 1897, when he bought out his partners.

After selling their interests in the company, Enoch Broberg promoted specialty building products and real estate while John Swanson moved into the country home his parents had purchased in Scandia *(map 65)*. Then Swanson went into business for himself as proprietor of a lumber firm in St. Bonifacius. Andrew Peterson occasionally mentioned this place.

Andrew Justus and his wife, the former Hanna Nicholson, were married on January 31, 1900, in Minneapolis. They had four children, Crystal, June, Andrew, and Cavour. Andrew Justus died January 26, 1949, at the age of eighty-two. Son Andrew today owns and manages the Justus Lumber Company with the third generation of owners, his son, James A. Justus.

Trampling Hooves

The Petersons had a long and neighborly association with Andrew and Bengta Nilson, who, in 1863, purchased several tracts of land *(map 43, 44)* from John Lundsten. In 1860, the Nilsons (Andrew was then forty-nine, Bengta, forty-six) consisted of Jens, nineteen; Andrew, sixteen; Borrow,

George B. and Lena Nilson

eleven; and Nels, eight. The census records say Nels was "dumb" or unable to speak. Young Andrew was also described as "deaf and dumb."

Peterson told of attending a wedding at the Nilson cabin and the baptism of his sons, but he did not identify the bride, groom, or newly baptized children.

The Nilsons sold their property in two separate land transactions to George Birrel Nilson, presumably an older son. The entire family continued to live in the house, though. George was married and a veteran of the Civil War having served with the Second Minnesota Infantry. Although 588 men left their frontier homes from the sparsely settled villages and settlements in Carver County, George was not listed as being from Carver County. The Second Infantry Regiment was not officially organized until July 22, 1861, but many of the men had mustered in before that. George apparently enlisted from another county. This division marched as far as Pittsburgh, Pennsylvania, on its way to Washington, D.C., but turned back at Louisville, Kentucky. They participated in the battles at Mill Springs, Chickamauga, and Chattanooga. They also took part in Sherman's march to the sea, the campaign against Atlanta, and in the review of troops in Washington, D.C., on March 24, 1865.

When Peterson helped the hired man, named Rosenquist, move Lundsten's old cabin to Birrel Nilson's land, it was so that Rosenquist could live in it. Rosenquist worked for Nilson and others in the settlement, but he also spent a considerable amount of time grubbing for Peterson.

Andrew often wrote about his and Elsa's ongoing relationships with friends, neighbors, and relatives. In 1876, he said, "Birrel Nilson's relatives were here today. They brought a spinning wheel with them to us from Morse [Mooers] Prairie." Soon after Peterson reported that "Sture and Ida are helping Birrel Nilson to tie wheat bundles." On an early winter morning in December, he said, "Sture and I drove to Minneapolis. We had the two pigs, 6 sacks of wheat and one sack of beans as a load. Nicholas [Swenson] and Birrel Nilson also went to Minneapolis." Peterson's entry the following day read, "At 12:30 at night we returned from Minneapolis." Their trail may have been covered with snow as they journeyed home with only the stars to guide them. Winter can be a very dangerous time of the year in Minnesota. Dusk usually falls quickly during sudden, blinding storms, and landmarks can be impossible to see.

Peterson recorded the death and burial of Birrel Nilson's mother-in-law (Peterson's son Axel and several others helped dig her grave). Later he wrote, "Birrel Nilson drove my brother-in-law, John Anderson, and my sister, 'Maja Stina,' over to the Augusta station where they took the train to Granite Falls."

Lena and George Birrel Nilson's new home was completed four years after their new barn was raised. Then members of the Scandia Baptist Church celebrated the event with a housewarming party.

Community responsibility also was a vital part of Nilson's existence. Peterson told of signing a bond for him following his election as township treasurer.

After one of Minnesota's severe storms, Peterson and his sons Axel and Frank shoveled snow from their farm to Nilson's place—a distance of one mile. Soon thereafter Carl and Birrel hauled wheat to the Waconia elevator. Axel also helped Birrel raise his windmill.

On January 3, 1890, Peterson wrote, "Mama, Ida and I were invited to G. B. Nilson for a Christmas feast." There were other socials in these years.

Then suddenly another tragedy struck the colony. Peterson recorded an accident on October 2, 1893, writing the following: "In the afternoon Mrs. Berro Nilson was visiting with us when a message came that B. Nilson had been fatally hurt. As he was hauling wood the horses were frightened so they jumped and Nilson fell off the load and fell under the horses. In their fright the horses stepped on his head and his whole face was crushed by them. Our Frank drove for the doctor

These neighbors take a break from threshing operations at Nilson's farm during the early 1890s. *Standing* (from left): Andrew Nilson, Willie Swenson, unknown, Simon Peltz, Charles Anderson, Albert Gerdsen, John Peterson seated on rig, William Maas, John Rietz, Adolph Klatt, George Fink, Albert Pofahl, Henry Rietz, Karl Krey, Andrew Broberg, John Lundsten, and Joel Swenson. *Seated* (from left): Frank Henke, Henry Peterman, unknown, Ferdinand Buelow, unknown, Fred Zoerb, Frank Peterson, Frank Dahl, unknown, George B. Nilson, Frederick Maas, and John Yetzer.

and then stayed with Nilsons all night. Nilson died at two o'clock in the morning."

The next day, he wrote "I drove Ida over to Nilsons. In the afternoon Axel went to Nilsons and stayed all night." The following day Peterson said, "Frank and Andrew Anderson are digging the grave for G. B. Nilson. In the afternoon Frank went to Nilson's house again to keep watch during the night. Mama stayed at Nilson's today." Peterson concluded his graphic account on Thursday, October 5, when he wrote, "Today we buried George Berro Nilson. We gathered in the house of mourning at 12 noon. It was a large funeral procession. Sixty-six carriages. There were two ministers, Lindberg from Clear Lake and Landlott. Just as the funeral was over it began to rain, and the rain continued all day and the following night. Rev. Lindberg went with us home."

After George Birrel's death, the Peterson family continued to help Lena Nilson. Peterson drove Lena to the home of Henry Rietz for help concerning her estate. Peterson's sons chopped and piled stove wood and also grubbed trees for her. On March 20, 1895, Andrew wrote, "Mama and I visited with Mrs. B. Nilson and I also went over to Rietz' house and had Mrs. B. Nilson sign as a witness to the testament between Mama and me."

Lena managed the farm alone for several years. Then Peterson reported on November 2, 1896, "In the evening the young people went and surprised Lena Nilson as she and Frank Person [one of her hired hands] had married down in Minneapolis. They came home tonight."

Lena suffered another loss on January 29, 1898. Peterson wrote, "The boys went to the grave yard and dug a grave for F. Person's dead child. In the evening Mama went over to Person's house to help them." Eleven days later, February 10, Peterson wrote, "It rained all day so we could do no work. In the afternoon Emma went to Mrs. Person in order to care for her." Emma Peterson nursed Lena until February 16. Then Andrew wrote, "Josephine drove Charlotte Anderson [Per Daniel Anderson's daughter] over to Person's house and brought Emma with her back home."

The events that followed are not clear, but after a short time Lena was alone again. She lived the remainder of her life with her cousin, a schoolteacher who lived close to the Götaholm settlement near Watertown.

Lena was eighty-five years old when she died January 18, 1938. Her burial place is identified by a footmarker at the Scandia cemetery. It was placed next to the small upright gravestone inscribed: "G. B. Nilson, Company A, 2nd Minnesota Infantry."

Sunny Brook Farm

Following the baptism of Carrie and "Nils Mortenson's boys," on Sunday, November 29, 1863, Andrew Peterson also mentioned cutting rails on the north forty with Nils. But Peterson later neglected to tell about Mortenson's departure from Scandia. Julius Buelow and his family purchased Mortenson's farm. The former title-holders on their papers were John Toban, Catherina and Charles Warner, and Franz Tefler. For Julius and his wife Wilhelmina this farm in Scandia *(map 32)* marked the end of a sad voyage from Germany. They had buried one of five children at sea. Ferdinand, Robert, Frank, and Emma were the surviving children. Eventually William and Wilhelmina Buelow were born in the log cabin at Scandia.

Farming looked promising for this Lutheran family, partly because the Buelow meadow had a good supply of water for their livestock. A steady stream (the Buelows called it Sunny Brook) which had Lake Auburn as its source, flowed through the woodlands of the Buelow and Brethorst property (theirs is a low-lying area), then it spilled into Six Mile Creek and eventually into Halsted's Bay in the westernmost part of Lake Minnetonka.[9] The flowing water provided for other natural resources as well. Andrew Peterson told of using his net to gather fish there. The creek was a definite asset. Of his own situation, Peterson wrote on July 6, 1870, and many times thereafter "we dug for water for the cattle."

Little is known about the horse-related accident that claimed the life of Julius Buelow. On May 29, 1883, Peterson said: "Elsa and I went to the funeral in Waconia of the German, Bulow [Buelow]." Wilhelmina was forced to carry on with help from her eldest son Ferdinand, who was then twenty-four. In time, Ferdinand and his wife Sophia took charge of the farm while Wilhelmina continued to live with them.

Ferdinand provided special neighborhood services through the use of his saw rig as well as his threshing machine. He also sold nursery stock from his orchard, served as the township assessor,

9. The Buelows named this creek Sunny Brook, then later attached this name to their farm as well. This place is not to be confused with Sunny Hill Farm which was John and Maja Lisa Lundsten's homestead *(map 42)*. Lundsten's tract included a small pond called Pig's Eye.

The Buelow family from left: Benjamin, Sophia, George, Minnie, Grandmother Wilhelmina, (shown holding Anna), Ferdinand, Lydia, Albert, and William.

and was a member of the Victoria Creamery Board and of the Carver County Farm Bureau.

The help Peterson and his family provided while caring for George Berro Nilson's widow, Lena, may have caused him to fall behind with his schedule of work. On October 16, 1893, he wrote, "First I went over to Bylow's [Buelow's] house and asked him to make our molasses." Then his sons hauled some wood there to cook it.

The children of Ferdinand and Sophia Buelow —William, Minnie, Benjamin, Albert, George, Lydia, and Anna—attended District 16, the Gerdsen School, although the neighboring farm children, the Lundstens, attended the Scandia School.

Lydia and Anna were inspired by the beauty of the music they frequently heard at the Lundsten home. Their fondest wish was for a piano—a wish that was granted when their parents purchased one for them. From that time on, the two girls walked through the woods every week to take lessons from Mabel Lundsten. Expression through music has always remained an important part of the lives of Lydia and Anna Buelow.

The Halfway House or Village Inn

Gustaf Adolph Holmberg was born in Gettinge, Vetlanda Parish, Jönköping's *län* in Småland, Sweden, July 20, 1843. He worked as a carpenter on a boat at sea and traveled to Minneapolis about 1868, where he worked as a building contractor. He married Carrie Wedmark in Hastings on April 12, 1871. She was born October 10, 1850, in Helsingland's *län,* Sweden.

Before their move to Victoria in 1889, the Holmbergs visited Gustaf's brother, Carl Oskar, his wife, Hanna, and their five children. While they were at this prairie home, located near the present city of Renville in Renville County, Gustaf and Carrie persuaded their relatives to let them adopt their daughter, Louise Josephine, because they were childless. Louise was ten years old and the second in a family of four girls and one son.

In 1889, Gustaf and Carrie purchased a place with a small store in Victoria. All three moved into the living quarters in this building, which was located along a main thoroughfare. This road, which started from the Twin Cities, was called the Great Highway of the Northwest or the "Yellowstone Trail." This well-traveled route followed beyond Holmberg's property *(map 53)* through the center of Andrew Peterson's homestead *(map 46),* then in the direction of the Scandia School, and continued in front of the Scandia Baptist Church where it turned left along the shore of Waconia Lake. From there the road passed through Waconia and beyond to Seattle, Washington, by way of Aberdeen, South Dakota, and Yellowstone Park.

Gustaf became the postmaster in Victoria and also farmed. Then, because travelers found Victoria to be an ideal resting spot and they were located close to the railroad, Gustaf and Carrie accommodated overnight guests and became shippers of grain and cordwood as well. Thus the post office, which featured a combined supply of sundry items for sale as well as sleeping facilities, became known as the Halfway House or Village Inn.

Young Louise assisted her uncle Gustaf in keeping his accounts, and replaced him as postmaster at the age of eighteen when she was appointed postmaster for the village of Victoria. She held this position for sixteen years.

A member of the Scandia Baptist Church, Carrie Holmberg's friendship with Elsa Peterson is revealed in several of Andrew's journal entries.

Gustaf and Carrie (Wedmark) Holmberg

Post office and Village Inn ("Halfway House") at Victoria.

"Mama went visiting over to Holmberg's house at Victoria" was his August 20, 1890, comment. On January 2, 1894, he wrote, "Mama went over to care for Mrs. Holmberg. Mrs. Holmberg is somewhat better." And on August 22, 1897, he said, "Sunday. Mama went and stayed with Mrs. Holmberg over night."

The year following Gustaf's death, December 27, 1899, Louise married Theodore Nordberg. He was born in Värmland, Sweden, and arrived in the United States in 1891. Louise had met him while he was a guest at the inn. After their wedding, Louise and Theodore continued to live at the inn with Carrie. They developed a retail flour and feed business the same year they married, in 1900, and continued to sell these commodities until 1938.

Although Carrie Wedmark Holmberg was never a very healthy person, she reached the age of eighty-six before she passed away in 1936.

The Nordbergs raised three children—Mildred, Evelyn, and Rueben. Louise served a forty-five-year term as treasurer of the Women's Missionary Circle of the Scandia Baptist Church, and Theodore's elected position as a Victoria Village Council member continued for a term of twenty years. They were both active in other civic and fraternal organizations as well.

Louise and Theodore celebrated their golden anniversary in 1950, and both passed away seven years later. Theodore was eighty-nine years old, and Louise was eighty-three.

Theodore Nordberg and Louise Josephine Holmberg (seated) posed for their wedding picture March 10, 1900. Attendants Mr. and Mrs. (Tillie Holmberg) Campbell stand behind.

John and Benedicta Nelson

CHAPTER 14

John and Benedicta Nelson

John Nelson, a wheat farmer and carpenter who lived on the shores of Waconia Lake, was born in Smedstorp Parish, Kristianstads *län* on April 16, 1827. As an adult in Sweden, he was baptized as a Christian believer, on August 13, 1862. The baptismal certificate indicates Nelson then became a member of the Baptist church at Bohoult.

Nelson and his first wife (whose given name is unknown) left Sweden in 1866 with their ten-year-old son August, four-year-old daughter Albertina, and Mrs. Nelson's sister, Benedicta Andersdotter. But before they arrived in America, Mrs. Nelson became ill and died. Minnesota was apparently their destination from the outset, since, after a brief stay in Blue Earth County, the bereaved family arrived in Carver County shortly thereafter.

John and his sister-in-law Benedicta (born January 11, 1834) were married in a ceremony at the Scandia Baptist Church on October 19, 1866. The service was performed by the Reverend John Erickson and witnessed by Peter Johnson and Ola Okerson.

Soon after Nelson's arrival in Scandia, he built a cabin from which evolved a salt-box style house on the north side of Waconia Lake *(map 10)*.[1] It still stands and, although it is surrounded by modern lakeshore homes, the house looks much the same as it did 100 years ago. However, the property has been subdivided and the barns no longer remain in the farmyard.

Nelson received a large share of his income from the sale of durum wheat crops. A furniture craftsman and carpenter as well, he did a great deal of work on Andrew Peterson's house. Peterson's writings from the very beginning were usually connected with building or progress reports on the family home. Nelson made window and door frames, doors, and partitions, and laid floors.

Nelson also worked on the corner boards for Peterson's granary and made "school sleds" with Peterson's help. As with other comments, Peterson did not explain that, although the sleds were sometimes used for recreation, their main purpose was for older children to transport the younger ones back and forth from school. On other occasions, Peterson mentioned replacing the metal bands attached to the runners.

Even before the interior work in Peterson's dwelling was finished, Nelson installed rafters and sheeting on the wall of his woodshed. After the granary and shed were built, finishing work on the granary was completed, and finally a porch was added to the house.

In 1874, Nelson built a bureau for the Petersons.

1. According to the *Compendium of History and Biography of Carver and Hennepin Counties, Minnesota,* page 250, the former property owner, Joseph Frey, died a soldier's death during the Civil War. He had been one of ten men who left his frontier home in Carver County, tramped to Fort Snelling, and enlisted. Governor Alexander Ramsey had been in Washington, D.C., when the war broke out and was the first governor to offer President Abraham Lincoln his state's infantry quota to support the war effort. Frey was mustered into the army on May 30, 1861, and became part of the First Minnesota Infantry. He was wounded at Bull Run and died at Gettysburg on July 2, 1863.

In that same year, he also began work on a new barn which was completed in December. Then, in an exchange of labor, Peterson worked on the Nelson home.

During succeeding years, Nelson continued his work for Andrew and Elsa Peterson. In September, 1878, Nelson tongued and grooved boards. Peterson wrote, "John Nilson *[sic]* and I began to lay the floor on the third floor." No doubt they also installed wooden ceiling paneling, because the family was living in the roughed-in home. It took several years before the strips of wood lath on the walls were finally covered with coats of plaster.

Much more work than recreation is mentioned in the diary until 1881. After that, Andrew frequently revealed social contacts and activities. On December 28, 1881, he wrote, "Elsa and I went to Waconia and Ida, Sture and Axel went visiting to Jons Nilson's house." On January 31, 1882, he said, "Erickson and his wife went back to Delano today. Elsa and I went along as far as Jons Nilson's house when we stopped for a visit." By this time, there were six more Nelson children – Alfred, William, Henry, Edward, Solomon, and Inez.

From December, 1883, when John Nelson and Peterson's sons started to dovetail timbers for Peterson's new barn, most of Andrew's daily entries regarded preliminary work. Then on June 6, 1884, he wrote, "Today we had a barn raising. We were 17 men working, and we finished at noon. After dinner J. Nilson, and the boys put up the rafters."

Several years later, in 1886, the Nelsons suffered the loss of their nineteen-year-old son, Alfred. Although Peterson's diary does not give the cause of death, family members say it was tuberculosis, or "quick consumption" as it was called in this case. Peterson attended the funeral on January 9, a day also marked by intense cold and a sharp northwest wind.

Although personal work was of foremost importance, Peterson also wrote, "Jons Nilson and [John] Lundsten were here, and we wrote a letter to the [Swedish Baptist] conference that is to be held in Houston [Minnesota]." Again the following year, on May 17, 1886, he wrote, "This morning Jons Nilson, Lundsten, Birrel Nilson were here, and we wrote a letter to the conference." Peterson did not specify whether this or other church conferences were statewide or regional gatherings.

Peterson was subpoenaed in 1887 to serve as a witness for John Nelson regarding the damage that the north line of the St. Paul, Minneapolis and Manitoba railroad had done to the Nelson farm.[2] Per Daniel Anderson and Nicholas Swenson also testified in the case. There was no record in the diary as to the outcome of the hearing, but the three witnesses made a trip to look at the alleged damage to the land. They collected payment from the railroad company for their services.

That same summer, John Nelson built a pig barn for Peterson while Carl and Frank Peterson threshed for Nelson. In December of that year, Emma Peterson and Albertina Nelson went with "Brother Broms" (he served as the Baptist minister in Scandia for a short period of time) to help with the Christmas program at Gibbon, a community situated close to Winthrop which is in the vicinity of Fort Ridgely and New Ulm.

Petersons' orphaned nephew, Oscar Norman, and their daughters Ida and Emma spent time at the Nelson house in February, 1888, and then attended a spelling bee held in the District 42 school *(map 9)*. Although Christian Shilling had donated the site for the school, it was almost always referred to as the John Nelson School because it was next to Nelson's property line and he helped build it. Peterson mentioned that some of his own language meetings were held at the schoolhouse. This building, which was formerly located on the northwest side of Waconia Lake, stands today at a nearby location. Even the District 42 sign is still intact over the entry. Although garage doors form the rear wall, there is no mistaking its former use.

Peterson's diary notes on several occasions that Elsa was setting up yarn for weaving at one house or another. She was actually placing heavy cord or thread in place over the roller on these neighbors' looms, installing the necessary warp used in the process of weaving. Benedicta Nelson owned one of these looms, and Elsa occasionally borrowed it to make rag rugs.

John Nelson's oldest daughter Albertina learned homeopathic medicine. On September 24, 1889, Frank Peterson went to the Nelson house to fetch Albertina "so that she could dose us here at home." She stayed overnight and the following day she "dosed Mama, Ida, Josephine and myself." Then Frank drove her home. On the first of October, Albertina returned and "dosed the largest part of our family." Apparently Albertina administered a

2. The St. Paul, Minneapolis and Manitoba Railroad Company purchased 5.82 acres of Nelson's land for right-of-way purposes. The line was also known as the St. Paul Pacific, then the Sioux City Railway and, finally, the Great Northern Railway Company. (See Waconia Township, Index Book "A," Section 2, Carver County Courthouse, Chaska.)

vaccine to produce immunity to a disease. Peterson does not explain what diseases she was treating them for, however.

Peterson wrote on November 28, 1889, that "Today is Thanksgiving Day according to our president's proclamation. In the morning we had a prayer meeting in Scandia, and in the afternoon we visited with John Nilson's folks." No mention was made of a Thanksgiving dinner. On Christmas day of the same year, after attending services in the morning, the Nelson family visited the Peterson family in the afternoon, and "the two old folks are going to stay over night." Sture drove them home the following day. The four-mile drive between the Peterson farm and the Nelson home, made by horse and buggy or team and wagon in summer or sled in winter, was a picturesque one that circled part of the lake.

During the last ten years of Peterson's life, he wrote more often of their social life, although these events were often overshadowed by sickness, death, and grief. On June 8, 1890, Henry and Inez Nelson, grown children of John and Benedicta, were baptized. Soon after the baptism, it became apparent that Henry was not well. He traveled to Granite Falls with Carl Peterson to work during the harvest, but the boys returned unexpectedly on September 4 because Henry had been taken sick. Henry died at the age of twenty-three, most likely of tuberculosis. On February 24, 1893, Peterson wrote, "Frank went to Scandia and helped to dig a grave as Jons Nilson's son, Henry, has died." The next day he said, "We went to Jons Nilson's house to the funeral of his son, Henry." Several days later he wrote, "Emma went home with Jons Nilson's last Saturday, and she was not able to come home today because of the storm." On February 28, he noted that "The roads are all blocked, and the wind is blowing unabatedly." On March 1, the boys were all out shoveling and August Nelson drove Emma home.

Just two years after Henry died, a third son, William, died at the age of twenty-six. On March 26, 1895, Peterson explained, "In the evening we heard that William Nilson had died in Kansas City on his way home from California." The following day, Andrew and Elsa, together with Per Daniel and Caroline Anderson, visited the Nelson home "to comfort them in their grief." Then Axel helped dig the grave while Andrew Peterson "hauled up planks to the grave."

Peterson wrote on March 29, "In the morning Frank and I went to Waconia and received the body of Willie Nilson who had died in Kansas City, and we took it to the grave yard and put down the body in the grave, but the real funeral is to be Sunday." On Sunday, he said, "We buried Willie Nilson. We could not get a minister as Lindberg was not at home so we had to bury him without a minister."

About a year later, a fourth son, Edward, then twenty-two, alarmed the family when he became ill, but he recovered. Again the Petersons tried to help as much as they could. On January 3, 1896, Peterson said, "Edward Nilson stayed over night at our house. He was so very, sick so he and Albertine left for Minneapolis in order to get to the doctor. Our Frank drove them to St. Bonifacius." On January 8, he said, "Jons Nilson was here and paid me the ten dollars that Albertina borrowed from me."

Peterson wrote that the young people (his sons and daughters) went to John Nelson's home for a surprise party on March 10, 1896. On July 7, Andrew wrote, "Today our minister, Paulson, left us to go to stay with Jons Nilsons for a while."

Edward Nelson became a member of the Scandia Baptist Church after his baptism by the minister, Adolph Paulson, on Sunday, September 13, 1896.

Successive diary entries revealed that the Petersons and their children, Josephine and Carl, often visited the Nelsons, sometimes together, sometimes separately. After the student preacher, Nels E. Valerius, moved from the Peterson home (for the second time that summer), he lived with the Nelsons. Andrew and Elsa also stayed overnight at the Nelsons'. The following day, on October 21, 1897, Peterson wrote, "This morning Mama and I left Jons Nilson's place and went to Hjelm's place where I pruned back more grape vines."

The relationship between these families was strong and close, and continued even after Andrew Peterson died. Elsa, John, and Benedicta all survived Andrew.

Albertina and Inez Nelson

The Nelson home.

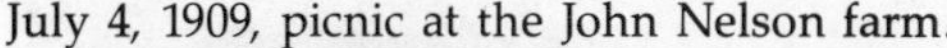
July 4, 1909, picnic at the John Nelson farm.

John and Gesina Holtmeier's grown children visited this abandoned duplex–the log dwelling where several of them had been born. From left: John and Mary (Mrs. C.H. Fairchild), William and Gisena (Holtmeier), Sam and Anna (Mrs. August Lueck), with Herman and Christina (the second wife of Christ Fink who had been married to sister Carrie before her death).

CHAPTER 15

The Moravian Brethren

A close working relationship developed between members of the Scandia Baptist Church and their neighbors, the Moravian Brethren. The Moravian families lived east of Scandia, on the shore of Lake Auburn. Since 1415, many of the Protestants from Central Europe had been members of the Unitas Fratrum, also known in Germany as *Bruederkirche* or "The Church of the Brethren."[1] When these persecuted people, who had the same Eastern European origins as the Russians and the Poles, fled from their Austrian homes in Bohemia and Moravia, many of them settled as refugees on Count Nicholas Ludwig von Zinzendorf's estate in Germany. Since the first settlers in Germany had been from Moravia, the name Moravians stayed with them, although later emigrants were from their Bohemian capital of Prague, which was the center of the Unitas Fratrum movement.

Two Moravian planned communities still exist, one in Bethlehem, Pennsylvania, and the other in Winston-Salem, North Carolina. Some of the Brethren moved west to Minnesota, and settled on the east side of Lake Auburn, at Chaska, and at Zoar, a rural area between Chaska and Waconia.

After John Salter established his claim in the early 1850s on land that is now within the city of Victoria *(map 55)*, he sent letters to friends and Brethren in Ohio, urging them to join him.[2] In 1854, the families of John Holtmeier and his brother-in-law, Henry Gerdsen, responded to this call and also moved to Carver County. They chose a quarter-section of land close to Salter's claim and built a two-story log house in a duplex style, which both families occupied. While Holtmeier developed and farmed the land, Gerdsen, a machinist, worked in St. Paul and provided financial support for their combined interests.

Because these families who had settled in this vicinity were concerned about spiritual matters, they invited the Reverend Martin Erdman, a Ger-

1. The Unitas Fratrum, also called "The Church of the Brethren's Unity," trace their origin to John Huss, a peasant's son who was born in Hussinetz, a village located in southern Bohemia. He received his Master of Arts degree from the University at Prague and became a preacher. While Huss supported the English Reformer John Wycliff's thinking, he and a friend named "Jerome" preached against the practice of indulgences. Huss was burned at the stake for his religious beliefs on July 6, 1415, at Constance in Germany.

During the years of the Counter Reformation, his followers were almost extinguished. The hidden seed managed to survive through help from Count Nicholas Ludwig von Zinzendorf. Zinzendorf provided sanctuary for the Brethren on his estate in Saxony. He dedicated his possessions and entire being to Christian service. From this beginning, a town called *Herrnhut*, (meaning a place that God watches over) was founded and the central feature of Moravian doctrine was expressed–devotion to Jesus Christ and salvation. The Brethren pledged themselves to worldwide missionary service. (Except for the Waldenses founded by Peter Waldo, a merchant of Lyons, France, about 1170, the Moravian Church is the oldest Protestant Church.)

Music, education, and good workmanship have always been an important part of Moravian life, which holds to those teachings known as Evangelical.

2. Heirs of the Salter family donated part of their original homestead, a wooded area, to the city of Victoria for recreational use by its citizens. Today, this property in the southwesterly section of Victoria is known as Salter's Park.

man-speaking pastor from the Moravian Church in Chaska, to minister to them even though some of them were Lutherans. During this time, community meetings and Sunday worship services were held in the large dwelling occupied by the families of John Holtmeier and Henry Gerdsen. On October 31, 1858, "Heinrich and Maria Gerdsen, Johann and Gesime Holtmeier, Friedrich and Margarete Goldschmidt, and Christine Zoerb, Mathias and Magdalene Hueser, Johann and Therese Piltz [Peltz] and Johann and Fredrich Salter," were received into the membership of the Chaska Moravian congregation–a fellowship of believers which was subsequently divided into three districts. Then, "The region around Lake Auburn was called the second district and under the care of Brother Henry Gerdsen." Their log church was built in 1863. "Brother Jakob Hoyler, received the call to become the first resident pastor of this congregation" in 1873. By that time, there were eighty-four names on the church records. These included communicants, noncommunicants, and children.

John Holtmeier and his wife Gesina (Gerdsen) raised nine offspring–Carrie, Mary, Gesina, Anna, Christina, John, William, Sam, and Herman. After the 221 acres of land had been divided into two farms, Holtmeier cleared over forty acres and built his home near three lakes *(map 29)*. During this time, he served as an officer in the church and participated in local politics and school affairs.

Henry and Mary (Wulfeck) Gerdsen built their home in the vicinity of Lake Auburn *(map 30)*, where they raised their children, Herman, Emma, Henry, William, Albert, and Mary. Henry helped develop the public schools and served as the first teacher at District 16, or the "Gerdsen School." School records show that he also taught in Scandia for a short time.

Henry was a civic-minded man. He served a term as justice of the peace in Laketown Township. While holding this office, he recorded in the Laketown Record Book "A" on June 1, 1860, that John Erickson was to act as the Reverend F. O. Nilsson's power of attorney in all matters regarding rent or sale of his land. (The legal papers designating one-half acre of Nilsson's homestead for school use in Scandia were certified by Gerdsen.) Gerdsen also served as a school trustee, then began a thirty-two-year tenure as township clerk.

The Gerdsen and Holtmeier families were frequently mentioned in Peterson's diaries. Gerdsen bought apple grafts and seed wheat from him. Andrew's son Sture helped Gerdsen remodel his home. Andrew noted that Gerdsen was "counting Census," and also recorded an occasion when he passed Gerdsen and Holtmeier on the road. He wrote of attending John Holtmeier's funeral on July 10, 1890. Other diary entries indicated that some of the young people from Scandia shared similar interests with those of the young Moravians, because they visited and socialized back and forth. Andrew's March 6, 1892, entry is one of many that illustrates this fact. "Sunday. The young folks of H. Hjortson's [Peterson's spelling of the name Gerdsen] family visited with us in the afternoon."

Land had been donated to the Brethren for church and cemetery use (by the Gerdsen and Holtmeier families), and in 1887 the Moravians replaced their log church with the present brick structure. In 1928, after the Synod of the Moravian Church accepted a proposal to build a home for the elderly, the Lake Auburn Home for the Aged was built and dedicated, opening with accommodations for eighteen residents. This haven, a place of peace and comfort, is on the very site of the two-story log dwelling where the first church services were held. Located on the shore of Lake Auburn, across the road from the Moravian Church and parsonage, the home celebrated its fiftieth anniversary in 1978, and it still serves its original purpose.

The Gerdsen home, in close proximity to the historic Wendelin Grimm Farm and also within the boundaries of the Hennepin County Park Reserve, still stands. The inside walls are stripped of covering, exposing the large basswood logs of the original building. Tentative plans have been made to use this structure as a picnic shelter or ranger station.

Henry Rietz, another well-known Moravian and respected area resident came to the United States from New Bavaria, Germany, with his parents, and grew up in a Moravian settlement in Tuscarawas County, Ohio. On his move westward in 1862, he married Caroline Bachman, the daughter of the Reverend Henry C. Bachman, pastor of the Moravian Church at Hope, Indiana. After their marriage and move to Carver County, Henry purchased 160 acres of land from Herbert Wey in Laketown Township *(map 56)* and started farming on his place with eighteen acres of cleared meadow, a small shanty, and a straw-covered stable. He enlarged the scope of his farming opera-

The Gerdsen family in about 1897. *Back* (from left): Ruth and husband, the Reverend Herman Gerdsen, pastor of the Moravian Church, Lancaster, Pennsylvania, with Mary and Emma. *Center:* Albert, Henry, and Mary holding Henry's daughter Marguerite. *Front:* William, who worked at the patent office in Washington, D.C., Henry's son Rueben, his wife Anna, and Henry, a piano salesman in Minneapolis.

Henry Gerdsen's family, November, 1900. From left: son William, Henry, and wife Mary, and daughters Emma and Mary. Their son Albert is standing by the hired man, Herbert Sauter.

tion in 1869, after he purchased the former Jonas Peter Johnson homestead *(map 45)*.

Caroline Rietz practiced homeopathic medicine. Although Albertina Nelson *(map 10)* often treated the Peterson family, Caroline also "dosed" them on a number of occasions.

According to an 1868 record book, Rietz was hired to teach in Scandia on October 13, 1870. His term started November 7, at $40 per month. Diary entries show Peterson helped Rietz haul boards in 1873, and he helped thresh while Elsa helped cook for Rietz's threshing crew in 1874. The day following Peterson's entry on October 9, 1877–"Ida is working for Rietz"–Peterson said they attended the funeral of Albert Rietz, three-year-old son of Henry and Caroline. Eighteen years later, "Axel went to Rietz's house to the funeral of their daughter, Mary." Mary, a teacher in the Carver County schools, was twenty-three years old when she became the victim of typhoid fever.

Along with numerous farm-related activities, there were references made of visits to see Henry Rietz for professional services. In 1884, Peterson "went to Rietz's office and had three bonds made out for $200.00 each." (These certificates were given to Ida, Sture, and Axel.) Then, in 1886, he "went over to Rietz's house and had a contract made out which I am to send to Norberg in Chippewa County."

Rietz, an employee of the Laketown Mutual Fire Insurance Company incorporated in 1888, was its secretary for four years. He worked as a public official on the town board for twenty-six years and served as an elder in the Lake Auburn Moravian Church.

The surviving children of Henry and Caroline were all sons, Elmer, Henry, Edwin, John, Charles, Alfred, and Oliver. Elmer, a carpenter, was the youngest. He and his wife Elizabeth continued to farm the land after his parents retired and moved to a rural home between Waconia and Scandia *(map 64)*. Elmer and Elizabeth raised daughters Jane and Dorothy on this homestead where Elmer's parents had built a brick-faced home. The original 18- by 36-foot log cabin forms part of that home and stands almost unaltered today. Although heirs of the Rietz family still own the farm, renters presently live there.

Another member of the Brethren, Tobias Ottinger, raised livestock on his homestead on the shore of a small lake which, in later years, was called Pierson's Lake. His farm was situated in the vicinity of Scandia *(map 67)*, close to the Moravian Church at Zoar in Laketown Township.

Born near Munich, Germany, in 1824, Ottinger arrived in the United States in 1848 and accummulated $700 peddling wares through the southern states. En route to stake a claim in Minnesota Territory, he met Catherina Baeser in St. Louis. She was escorting several orphan children to their relatives, and they were all on the same Mississippi riverboat. Tobias was impressed with her. He thought she would make an ideal wife because she provided excellent care for the children. While on the journey, Catherina accepted his proposal, and the couple was married by the boat captain. They arrived in Laketown Township in 1852 and were among the first settlers in the county.

Andrew Peterson recorded the trips he made with his cows where Ottinger's bull was used for breeding services. Peterson sold nursery stock to to him, and on January 2, 1883, he said, "Sture and I together with Ottinger and his son went to Gale's house in San Francisco Town and bought from him a pure bred shorthorn bull." There were social visits, too. On January 27, 1891, he wrote, "In the evening our family, together with the school teacher, Miss Bardwell, were visiting at Ottinger's house." Several months later, on March 23, 1891, "Ottinger and his son, George, were here this afternoon and got Bluestem seed wheat. Sture is in bed. I went around and visited with Ottinger, so I did no work."Three years later, on October 30, 1893, he wrote, "Axel and Frank were at Tobias Ottinger's funeral."

There were six Ottinger children, Theodore, George, Peter, Louise, Emma, and Carrie. George and his wife, the former Emma Bender, inherited the home place after his parents' deaths, and they in turn passed it on to their son Arthur. In time, the operating capacity of the farm expanded through an additional purchase of land. George's brother Theodore moved to an adjoining site, and Peter traveled west to North Dakota. The Ottinger daughters also left the farm. Louise married Chris Bender and Emma Ottinger married Chris's brother Louis. With Emma Bender, George's wife, three adults in the Ottinger clan had married three members of the Bender family. Carrie became a trained nurse and never married.

Today, members of the Holtmeier family still worship at the Lake Auburn Moravian Church (now on the National Register of Historic Places) and Mabel Hoyler, a grandchild of the Gerdsen pioneers, is a frequent visitor at the church.[3] Elizabeth Rietz lived at the Lake Auburn Moravian Home until moving to Arizona to be near her daughter, Dorothy (Mrs. Arthur Smith).

Other Moravian churches in Waconia and Chaska still flourish, and the old Zoar Church, built in 1863, has also been placed on the National Register of Historic Places. This landmark is presently maintained by the Waconia Moravian Church. Although the sanctuary is not open for services on a regular basis, it is still used by the local Moravian congregations for vesper services, Easter sunrise services, and homecoming festivities, which often feature "lovefeasts." The Moravians reinstituted the apostolic practice of lovefeasts in 1828, and this tradition still serves as a means of celebrating commemorative events at Moravian churches in Carver County and throughout the world. The lovefeast is a special celebration of the Moravian Church involving a musical service, during which time hymns and anthems are played and sung. Special sweet rolls and hot or cold beverages are served to the participants. This event gives celebrants an opportunity to partake in a meaningful experience of sharing—a demonstration of Christian love between Brethren.

3. The Lake Auburn Moravian Church congregation observed its 125th anniversary on October 29-30, 1983.

Fiftieth anniversary celebration of Caroline and Henry Rietz in 1912.
Standing (from left): Henry, Edwin, Charles, John, and Oliver.
Seated (from left): Alfred, Caroline, Henry, and Elmer.

Simon Peltz checking his stacks in the field. On October 22, 1862, Peterson made this evaluation of his own harvest: "All the grain was cut too close to the ground so the straw was too long, also the grain stack had leaked. Another year I must be more careful in the stacking and put all the heads to the inside also make a steeper slant."

CHAPTER 16

The "50"

Scandia families refer to the most northerly part of the original F. O. Nilsson homestead *(map 41)*, which is bordered by the Andrew Peterson and John Zieman farms, as the "50."

This fifty-acre tract, a hillside that gently slopes north, was initially purchased in 1861 by Andrew Hakanson through John Erickson *(map 33)*, the Scandia minister and neighbor who served as the Reverend Nilsson's power of attorney.

Even before Hakanson possessed the property, he performed a variety of farm tasks in cooperation with Andrew Peterson and other settlers. Andrew wrote in 1860, "Hewed logs for the corn crib and had Per Daniel and Andrew Hakanson to help." In that year, Hakanson and his family—wife Hanna, thirty years old; John, five; Hanna, three (both children were born in Sweden); and Albert (who was born in Illinois)—stayed with Per Daniel, wife Caroline, and infant daughter Anna Louise.

Although living conditions were crowded in the Anderson log cabin, the outlook was promising for Per Daniel and Caroline, for workers were building their new home.

On February 9, 1861, Peterson wrote, "In the morning Hakanson and I stepped out the line between our lands." During the next few years, Peterson helped Hakanson prepare building materials and complete the family's two-story log dwelling. They also continued to share their grueling work in the fields.

Without forewarning regarding health or emotional problems, Peterson wrote on October 21, 1867, "I was over at Andrew Hakanson's house all day to take care of his wife, who has lost her mind."

Peterson did not give details of family reaction or how her husband was able to cope with Hanna's illness. Six days later, on October 27, Peterson wrote, "Sunday. Took care of Hakanson's wife."

Perhaps Elna Swenson *(map 47, 47A)* and Caroline Anderson helped Andrew Hakanson with household chores and care of the children. Peterson may have contributed to this effort in Elsa's place, as she was in her last month of pregnancy with their fifth child, Frank.

Hakanson's vocation was first revealed when Peterson wrote, on May 15, 1869, "In the afternoon I went to the meeting in Per Daniel's home when A. Hakanson preached." Also mentioned frequently was Olaf Hakanson, whose name appeared in comments related to the Hakanson family and was presumably Andrew Hakanson's brother.

On June 30, 1870, Peterson said: "Today Olaf Hakanson went from here to Minneapolis. I sent $108.00 with him. He is to get a draft for that in Minneapolis and then send the draft to Johnson in Kansas." This reference may have been related to the sale of Jonas P. Johnson's property *(map 45)* or missionary support sent to him by members of the local church.

The book, *A Brief History of the Scandia Swedish Baptist Church*, published during the diamond jubilee celebration, said of Olaf Hakanson (who was also known as Okerson):

The term of Ola Okerson was brief though he seems to have lived here for a period of three years and in 1865 he became the Home Missionary society's worker. A man of physical strength and endurance who could withstand the rigours of Minnesota winters, he possessed exceptional qualities for his new calling. A will to work, a voice of thunder, a restless spirit, we follow him from Scandia to Lake City, Houston, Cokato, Swede Grove, Willmar, etc., and finally to Oregon. Truly and rightly he has been called the "break plow" of the Swedish Baptists in Minnesota. . . . From this center there radiated the gospel influence and ministry to the salvation of men and women and to the organization of churches . . . .In more ways than can here be recounted the Little Church on the Hillside by the shores of Clearwater has been a power to the spread of the Kingdom of God.

Hanna Hakanson's condition during the four years following her breakdown was never brought up again, although a communion service was held, probably for her benefit, in her home. She died June 27, 1871, and Peterson wrote that John Nelson was at his—Peterson's—home to make Hanna's casket.

Following their mother's death, Hakanson's sons, John and Albert, assisted the Peterson family in the fields. They planted and husked corn, but Peterson says little more about them until September 8, 1871, when he wrote, "We threshed for A. Hakanson. Elsa was there and cooked for the men." He noted that Andrew Hakanson preached in Scandia one year later, on August 24, 1872.

A new neighbor's name appeared in 1873 in Andrew's diary—that of Peter J. Freed, who less than a year later would buy the Hakanson property. Peterson wrote on June 14, 1873, "Today Freed is here laying the stone foundation to the porch." The entry suggests that the Freed family had been living with the Hakansons after Hanna's death.

Freed arrived in Laketown Township from Åhus in the Swedish province of Kristianstad *län* some time between 1871 and 1874, accompanied by his wife, Hanna Swenson Freed, and a son, Swan, who was born November 14, 1870.

It appears Hanna Freed and Nicholas Swenson were related, so the Freeds may have known about Hanna Hakanson's condition before her subsequent death. The Swensons' farm *(map 47, 47A)* which was part of the Nilsson homestead, bordered the 50. Andrew Hakanson's departure from Scandia made it possible for Freed, with money borrowed from his German neighbor Gottfried Lobitz *(map 38)*, to buy Hakanson's property on April 20, 1874.

Freed helped Peterson in other ways in 1873, besides working on the porch foundation. Freed nailed shingles on the woodshed roof, hauled manure, worked on the stone foundation for the barn, stacked wheat in the meadow, and threshed with Andrew.

Although Peterson's diary entry for Sunday, June 13, 1875, did not mention activities at church that day, membership records prove Peter and Hanna Freed were among twenty-six converts who were baptized that particular weekend.

Freed and his family worked hard on their farm, but they still experienced financial difficulty because their acreage was not sufficient in size to maintain the needs of their growing family.

Peterson helped Freed financially. On August 19, 1879, he wrote: "Freed and I went to Chaska when I let Freed borrow $700.00 of that which I inherited from my brother, Carl. I took out a mortgage on Freed's land for the loan."

For years, the only access road to the 50 crossed neighboring fields, and in 1886 Peterson gave Freed a one-rod strip of land for a driveway on the line between his property and that of John Zieman's. This opening provided access to the township road which still goes through Peterson's land and connects to the main road, which is now State Highway 5. The road is presently called Parley Lake Road.[1]

After fourteen years, the Freeds purchased a farm in Watertown Township but managed to keep close ties in Scandia until the end of their lives. Freed, a Republican who often supported the Prohibition Party, and his wife Hanna maintained their membership in the Scandia Baptist Church and were buried in the church cemetery along with several of their children. Their oldest son Swan married Anna Oberg and the two of them had a farm near Oak Lake in Watertown. Daughter Nellie married A. J. Lindgren and moved to Chippewa County. Son Oscar became a physician, Frank stayed on the home place, and the twin sisters, Emma and Anna, taught school in Carver,

1. The Parley Lake Road passes the old homestead properties of John Zieman and Simon Peltz, Per Daniel Anderson, Frederick Schwichtenberg, the Reverend John Anderson, and Herman Lobitz. It looks much the same today as it did when the pioneers were still living. This gravel-surfaced lane joins County Road 30, an asphalt-covered thoroughfare heading north and south—north where it branches off to the opposite shore of the lake before following through to St. Bonifacius, and south to Waconia.

Hennepin, and Chippewa counties.

The new owners of the 50 were John and Therese Peltz, a couple who had left Vienna, Austria, in 1858, and arrived in the United States with their young son Simon. Having lost their savings in a counterfeit money exchange, they worked in New York for four years before they could push on as far as Elkhart, Indiana. Then they worked in Indiana for three more years before they were financially able to complete their journey to Minnesota. After a riverboat ride to Carver, they settled in the woods *(map 21, 25, 26)* on the east side of Parley Lake.[2] When John and Therese heard about Freed's decision to leave Scandia, they seized this opportunity to buy the 50. They purchased Freed's farm on May 25, 1886.

Their son Simon had been working as a hired hand for John Zieman *(map 34)* and had married Ida Zieman, one of six daughters. Simon and Ida Peltz lived with her parents, and they gradually assumed responsibility for the entire operation of the Zieman farm which bordered the 50.

John and Therese farmed the 50, and as previously agreed, John and his son worked their fields together. The Peltzes lived in the two-story dwelling for about twenty-five years. Originally built of log by Andrew Hakanson, the exterior had eventually been faced with wood siding. The farm had a few sheds and a 35- by 26-foot barn whose foundation was built into the side of the hill. It housed about a dozen head of cattle and stood close to Peterson's property line.

Peterson only mentioned these neighboring families during threshing season. Occasionally, however, he took it upon himself to settle disputes between neighbors. For example, on September 23, 1886, he wrote, "I went over to Per Daniel's house to make a settlement between Sieman *[sic]* and him because Sieman's dog seriously injured Per Daniel's pigs."

Most of the time amiable relations existed between these families, who were associated through their church. The Peltzes (who were Moravian) sometimes joined the Ziemans when they attended baptism services at the church in Scandia. Eventually they, too, joined the Ziemans and others of their own nationality at the Baptist church in Minnetrista. The Minnetrista Baptist Church (now within the boundaries of St. Bonifacius) still serves local Baptist families.

On April 28, 1887, Peterson commented, "In the afternoon Axel and Carl hauled cord wood out of the forest from the strip along the north line where Peltz is to have his road." Peterson was referring to the sliver of land he had given to Freed. On May 16, he followed up with this, "In the morning Axel and Carl set fence posts in the north line along Peltz' private road."

Simon and Ida Peltz's children, Minnie, Arnes, Lillian, Ida, Mabel, Albert, John, and William ("Bill") had the advantage of daily companionship with their maternal grandparents, John and Ida Zieman, and were within easy walking distance of the 50 and their paternal grandparents, John and Therese Peltz.[3]

Andrew Peterson wrote on April 3, 1890, that "Mama, Frank and I went to a funeral in the German Baptist Church. Old Mr. John Sieman *[sic]* was buried." Bill Peltz, born July 9, 1890, was three when his widowed grandmother also passed away, and Andrew wrote on May 11, 1893, "Today Mama and I went to Mrs. Sieman's funeral."

Bill Peltz recalled wandering off through the stands of timber during his search for berries while visiting Grandmother and Grandfather Peltz. These trips often took him into Peterson's woods. Even as a very young child, Bill preferred being with grownups, frequently watching as the Petersons dug wells for livestock, a subject often repeated in the diaries. The bucket Peterson made and used as a carrier still exists. It is of oak and reinforced with iron straps. A rope was channeled in place around the grooved handle and was used to raise and lower dirt, bricks, or workers into and out of a well.

Bill remembered the Peterson horses once stomping their hooves because the watering trough, a hollowed-out log in the yard, was empty.

2. After the Indian uprising, the Peltzes frequently encountered Indians roaming the area searching for ginseng, cranberries, and wild game. On one occasion, Therese was startled when several Indian men rushed into her cabin and took a ham which had been boiling in the fireplace kettle. The fragrance was apparently the immediate precipitant of their actions. The family was later surprised to find a half-carcass of venison which had been left by their door.

Other Indians stopped from time to time and were given food. If Therese was baking, she gave them bits of dough to touch and handle. Although they could not understand each other's language, the delight of the Indians was evident as they playfully manipulated the pliable substance.

3. John Zieman and his family had been living adjacent to the 50 for seven years when Alexander Johnson, the former property owner, reappeared in Scandia. He asked to buy his homestead back from the Ziemans, but they were satisfied with farming and content in Scandia. Johnson's eventual destination was not known.

Bill could not understand Peterson's command to his son, but he never forgot the words: "Axel, Axel, vattna du hästarna!" ("Axel, Axel, water the horses!")

In those days, Peterson's cows still fed from a central manger, and the barn was covered with a roof of straw. During Bill's youth, it was common to see basement shelves filled with containers of cooled milk; to watch cream being skimmed and churned into butter, some of which was packed for sale in assorted-sized crocks; and to use handmade egg baskets with oats protecting the fragile contents. Bill also saw newspapers wrapped around fur coats which were stuffed into heating stoves during summer months— a good, safe place away from rodents. Cellars smelled of smoked sausages and meats while large crocks of lard preserved a supply of cooked meatballs or pork chops. The hot summer sun dried apple slices under their covering of cheesecloth, and apple peels released a pleasing fragrance when left to shrivel on hot kitchen stove tops.

In later years, Bill became acquainted with his uncle, Christian Peltz. Christian, a former chef at the St. Paul Hotel, retired to care for his parents during the last few years of their lives. Skillful as a cook and baker, he was known to toss his bread dough into the slop can if the consistency was not just right.

John Peltz died on May 4, 1910, and Therese died on February 23, 1912. After their deaths, Christian sometimes indulged his Sunday social moods. Before leaving for church in the morning, he would fill the cattle manger, expecting the extra ration to last the animals for the rest of the day. But by the time he returned, the cattle were restless and uncomfortable because it was well beyond their usual milking time. Nor did they recognize him as he hurried through chores still wearing his Sunday clothes.

Christian decided he did not want his life regulated by farm animals and moved to Buffalo Lake. The buildings stood empty for several years until Bill's father, Simon Peltz, demolished the house and barns. From that time on, Simon Peltz cultivated the entire 50 as well as the adjacent fields.

Hannah and Peter Freed

Ida Zieman and Simon Peltz

Christian Peltz abandoned this home on the "50."

Andrew Peterson wrote on August 26, 1896, "At 11 o'clock Prof. Green and a photographer, McIntosh, from Hamline came here. They took pictures of several of the apple trees, the large white ash and also our family."

Minnesota Historical Society

CHAPTER 17

Horticultural Beginnings

As early as the 1850s, volunteer agricultural, horticultural, and livestock societies in Ramsey, Benton, and Hennepin counties had been responsible for a concentrated effort designed to promote farming interests in Minnesota. Their major objective was to dispel the belief that the climate in Minnesota was not suitable for agriculture. In order to prove their claim, volunteers promoted public expositions of farm products and featured these exhibits during the Territorial Fair held October 20, 1854. This series of annual events became the forerunner of the State Fair, which was first held in 1859.

In 1860, the State Agricultural Society began encouraging diversification of fair displays, and it called attention to household arts and crafts, farm machinery, and manufactured products.

Diversification of interests also became the objective of the Carver County Agricultural Society, which held its first fair on October 10, 1868, at Chaska.

Society members publicized this event by printing posters which were distributed within the farming villages. Notices also appeared in the local newspapers. The prize money was raised through $1 membership dues combined with a small appropriation of state funds. The society, however, imposed some restrictions on proposed displays, which was stated in a provision that read, "No articles can be entered for competition by any person other than a member of the society."

Theodore Bost, a horticultural pioneer in Minnesota, helped develop the Carver County Fair. He was then vice-president of the county society and was familiar with the Scandia settlement. Bost wrote a letter to his parents on October 25, 1868, in which he said that the fair was not as well-organized as he hoped it would be the following year.

Although the local newspaper, the *Weekly Valley Herald* (Chaska), reported cash prizes were awarded for individual livestock entries, the reporter for the paper also stated, "The display was not as extensive as it should have been, owing probably to the threatening aspect of the weather and bad condition of the roads on the morning of fair day. And owing also to the oversight of the directors in not offering premiums on fruits, manufactures, vegetables and domestic articles."

Some of the featured items were fine specimens of potatoes (which were described as being better than those displayed at the State Fair), cauliflower, squash, and carrots that measured 6 inches in diameter and 16 inches in length.

During the beginning years when Peterson was engrossed with horticultural projects on his own farm, Colonel Daniel A. Robertson, the first professor in the Department of Agriculture at the University of Minnesota, with help from John S. Harris, an orchardist from La Crescent, helped establish the Minnesota Fruit Growers Association, which was later renamed the Minnesota State Horticultural Society. The first meeting was held in 1866. Members shared ideas and gave reports about their individual experiences. Their need for continuing horticultural information eventually led to the establishment of experimental research stations. By the early 1870s, Robertson had traveled extensively and given countless lectures. He also wrote many articles for publication and distributed imported seeds from the best varieties of Russian apple trees to Minnesota fruit growers.

While the network of Minnesota horticulturists grew, Peterson enlarged his own orchard and on September 30, 1871, reported he had received an award for his apples at the Carver County Fair.

In March, 1873, he summarized a season's work in his diary: "This winter I have grafted 404 apple trees, 13 pear trees, 30 plum trees, and 12 cherry trees."

By 1874, Peterson had expanded his interests and joined an organization called the Patrons of Husbandry, a national fellowship of farmers commonly known as the Grange. This program was founded in 1867 by Oliver H. Kelley, a Minnesota orchardist, and six associates. (Kelley also started the Agricultural Society in Benton County in 1852.)

Although the Grange was not a political party, it did take stands on issues, advocating specific legislation affecting farmers, such as reasonable railroad rates and regulation of railroads. Its prime objective was to educate farmers on agricultural matters and to provide social and cultural opportunities for isolated farm families through club meetings. With help from Colonel Robertson, founder of the Minnesota Horticultural Society, Kelley and his supporters also established the North Star Grange in 1868. Its objectives included protection of its members from corporations, and a plan for cooperative buying and selling.

Forty of the forty-nine Granges formed in the United States were in Minnesota, and by the end of 1869 a federation known as the Minnesota State Grange was organized. Five years later, the state had 538 Granges. The Scandia chapter was one of them.

Governor Horace Austin, a Republican, paid serious attention to the Grange movement and its recommendations for legislation to establish reasonable railroad rates through state law. The governor also supported proposals and concerns over freight and elevator charges described as "unjustifiable, extortionate and oppressive." In 1871, the Republicans and Democrats both included platforms supporting state control of railroads, and the state imposed ceilings on fares and freight rates. Also in 1871, an office of railroad commission was established to regulate the railroads. The Grangers publicized the principle that railroads and other corporations that were "clothed with public interest" were justifiably subject to public regulations.

Peterson mentioned its first meeting in Laketown Township on February 3, 1874. He contributed to the creature comfort of the members by hauling six chairs and wood to the hall, building a wood box for the stove, and plastering the chimney.

Not until 1875 did Peterson make it a point to attend one of the meetings held by the local group of Carver County Agricultural Society members. The following year, on May 27, 1876, he explained, "Went to Carver to the agricultural meeting. We voted on whether the fair should be held in Carver or Waconia. Carver won so the fair will be held there next fall."

By this time, the State Agricultural Society and the Stock Breeders Association promoted the State Fair as a joint effort. This alliance turned out to be a dynamic force in developing a wide range of farming interests affecting local fair objectives as well.

Peterson does not explain why the Scandia chapter of the Grange was short-lived. On March 18, 1878, he reported, "In the afternoon we had our last grange meeting, and then sold our grange hall to Malmborg."

Peterson's contacts with other local fruit growers were frequent and profitable. At one time he sold as many as 200 seedlings to August Krause, a farmer in nearby Watertown Township who was also a well-known nurseryman in Carver County. Throughout the years, Peterson mentioned his trips to Excelsior to purchase apple trees and seeds from F. G. Gould. On at least two occasions, he visited Peter Gideon to purchase grapevine cuttings and raspberry canes. Gideon was also a pioneer horticulturist, who had established himself on the south shore of Lake Minnetonka in 1853. He had arrived in Minnesota with thirty varieties of apple seedlings, pear, cherry, and plum trees, one peck of peach seeds, and a bushel of apple seeds.

Gideon suffered devastating losses in his orchard as the result of the severe winters. He used his last $8 to purchase apple seeds from Bangor, Maine. Although badly in need of a winter coat, he patched some old clothes together and used this piecemeal attire to keep himself warm. But Gideon finally achieved success by this makeshift means. By 1869, he had developed the Wealthy apple (named for his wife), which became one of the most famous apples of the north country. He also proved conclusively that apples could be grown in Minnesota's harsh climate.

Peterson was especially diligent in following through with his horticultural routine. Every fall, after the trees were dormant, he dug up the ones to be sold or moved in the spring and "heeled them in" for the winter. Preservation consisted of layering nursery stock in well-drained trenches, which were dug in an east and west direction. Dormant plants were placed against the slope or south side of the excavation. Their roots were lower, or up against the north side, which was vertical. Each layer of stock was covered with sifted soil (almost to the top) and left this way until spring.

Peterson also grafted scions from plum, cherry, and apple trees on hawthorne roots. He did not delegate this highly specialized work to his sons, but cut the scions and prepared the grafts himself. He grafted grapes, planted cuttings, and installed trellises to support the plants in his vineyard. The grapes he harvested and later exhibited at the fairs included Isabella, Concord, Delaware, Iona, and Rogers #15. He sold vine cuttings, pruned back vines, and also heeled them in during the fall. Occasionally (as on October 3, 1877) he "pressed the grapes for wine."

During this period, Peter Gideon's orchard brought statewide attention to the Minnetonka region and his pioneer experiment station. The University of Minnesota and the Horticultural Society persuaded the state legislature in 1878 to help promote fruit culture. The University Board of Regents was authorized to purchase land close to Gideon's farm near Minnetonka and to designate it as an experimental fruit farm. Gideon was appointed superintendent.

Although the work of testing went forward from 1878 to 1889, those years were also marked by "minor storms" resulting from Gideon's personality. He was a religious, somewhat eccentric man whose quirks of character were overshadowed by his horticultural achievements, especially after he developed the Wealthy apple. Gideon has since assumed his rightful place in history, and one agricultural historian, William H. Alderman, professor emeritus and former head of the Department of Horticulture at the University of Minnesota Institute of Agriculture, has called him the "father of fruit breeding in the Northern Great Plains."

Andrew Peterson's work first came to the official attention of the Minnesota Horticultural Society on August 28, 1883, when Oliver Gibbs, a Lake City resident and secretary of the society, visited the Peterson farm. He was searching for apples to be exhibited at the large meeting of the American Pomological Society in Philadelphia. Peterson's Russian apple trees were a great surprise. "The fruit was not ripe, but it was even then very large and handsome," Gibbs later reported to the society. "They were the first root-grafted Russians I had seen—and the first winter keeping Russians I had heard of in the state." Peterson packed seven varieties of the apples to be shipped to Philadelphia.

Hardly daring to trust his own judgment as to the hardiness and quality of Peterson's apples, Gibbs returned to the Peterson farm in November with F. G. Gould, a neighboring fruit grower and member of the society's executive committee. Gibbs's enthusiasm was matched by Gould's: "Some of these trees are the hardiest I have seen in Minnesota. . . . They are not all absolutely perfect, as Mr. Peterson states himself, but there are sorts among them that are, and I believe we have got something here that cares nothing for our cold winters or our hot summers."

Peterson himself appeared at the 1884 meeting at which Gibbs and Gould gave their reports, and his own remarks bore out their enthusiasm:

> It was in the year 1857 that I began to plant fruit trees in Carver County, and I have planted more or less, nearly every year since that time, but without much success until I began with the Russian varieties, which seem hardy enough for Minnesota climate. Of the seventy other varieties I have tried, all blighted or sun-scalded more or less when they commenced to bear. Of the apples, the Duchess stood best against blighting; and of the crabs, the Maiden Bush. When the blighting commenced I had the trees heavily mulched. I did not like the mulching, because it drew the roots up toward the surface of the ground, and even into the mulching. I remember an old farmer in Sweden used to say: 'Plant a stone with the apple tree and then you will have a healthy tree.' I have also observed several times in the nursery rows, a stone close to the tree. Those trees looked healthier and did not blight. As we know that the stone keeps the ground cool, I wonder if the low temperature prevents the sap from rising too early. I should like to know if anybody has tried this or had any experience in it. I will try it myself next spring.

A few days before he spoke at the meeting, Peterson had completed a painstaking task. A number of Russian apple trees were growing on the P. H. Terlinden farm in western Carver County, but most of them were unidentified since their labels had fallen off. The former owner of the farm gave Peterson the original plat of the orchard, and Peterson labeled the trees according to the plat and identified those that appeared to be of value.

During the summer of 1884, Peterson pruned Terlinden's trees and worked with a new variety of Russian apple trees which he had received from Professor J. L. Budd of Ames, Iowa. He requested and received an order of cherry seeds from his brother, Johannes Rydell, in Sweden, and a shipment of 200 apple, pear, plum, and cherry scions from Captain C. J. Liljehöök. In September, 1884, he delivered apples to Gould to be shipped to the World's Industrial Exposition in New Orleans.

Although Peterson's diaries reveal evidence he interacted with many local farmers interested in horticulture, his most frequent contacts included Carver County Agricultural Society Officers Theodore Bost and Charles Luedloff. All of these pioneers were beginning to make Minnesota a productive fruit area, according to the information recorded in the 1884 Annual Report of the State Horticultural Society:

> Carver County is one of the "Big Woods" counties, one of the richest in the State, and is one of the best fruit regions in the Northwest. In 1884 there were over 20,000 apple trees in the county, producing liberally. It was the superb fruit of this county that made it possible for our State Horticultural Society to make so fine an exhibit at the meeting of the American Pomological Society, at Philadelphia, in 1883, where our apples were awarded the highest prize (the Wilder medal), in competition with every other state in the Union.

The 1884 *Annual Report* also described Luedloff as a thrifty German, well-versed in American and German agricultural and horticultural literature. He was said to be the owner of a large and beautiful orchard, and conducted experiments on a scale more intensive than any other experimentalist in the state.

The following January, Peterson attended the annual session of the Minnesota Horticultural Society in St. Paul, bringing apples that Elsa had packed in a box he had made for this purpose. With increasing frequency he was sending letters, reports, and shipments of stock to a fruit grower named Patten in Charles City, Iowa. During the winter of 1885, he also noted that he had finished making more than 400 Peerless apple grafts for O. F. Brand in Faribault.

Peterson wrote about a sudden windstorm on July 27, 1886, and nine bushels of apples that fell that day. He also told about his visitors on September 10, 1886: "At noon J. S. Harris from La Crescent, A. W. Sias from Rochester, G. W. Fuller from Litchfield and Luedloff from Carver came here and looked over the different varieties of fruit trees in my orchard."

Following seven days of work on the same project, he reported on February 11, 1887, "I finished making apple grafts. I have made close to a thousand grafts."

Andrew Peterson's experimental work was formally recognized at the January, 1888, annual meeting of the Minnesota Horticultural Society when he was awarded an honorary life membership. Before the question was put to a vote, Peterson asked to speak. "Mr. President, I am old," he said. "It is not much more that I can do for horticulture. Mr. President, I guess you better draw that motion back." But the motion was put up and adopted unanimously. Peterson then thanked the society for what he saw as an undeserved honor. He added that his Swedish neighbors would benefit from the society's publications, which he hoped to distribute, and that they would cooperate with the society and its future work.

The honor was both timely and well-deserved. Because Andrew Peterson was an early settler in Minnesota, his orchard was by that time well-established. The Hibernal apple trees which he had obtained from Russia had stood the test of time on his Scandia farm. Other Russian varieties that through his patient experimentation he had proven suited to Minnesota's rigorous climate included Anisim, Charlamoff, Cross, and Christmas. Professor Samuel Bowdlear Green summarized Peterson's contribution:

> His work, in fact, amounted to his carrying on at his own expense and in a most careful way for more than a quarter of a century what amounted to a private experiment station. He proved to the people of Minnesota that apples could be profitably grown in this section; that some varieties imported from Russia were especially adapted to this section and could be depended upon. He also showed that many of them were worthless, and his labor of sifting the good from the bad Russian varieties of apples has been very helpful and valuable.

Peterson wrote in 1889 of going "to Luedloff's place after apple trees and gooseberry bushes," which was straight south in Dahlgren Township, a distance of seven and one-half miles from his farm. Later, he wrote of purchasing seed potatoes and scions from Luedloff for Charles Hawkinson, a friend who was in the nursery business in Minneapolis.

Theodore Bost lived eight miles east of Scandia.[1] Although Bost and his wife Sophie farmed and lived in primitive conditions on their homestead in Carver County, they came from backgrounds of culture.

Peterson mentioned Theodore's presence in Scandia throughout the years. Besides engaging in an exchange of apple seedlings, there were frequent sales of stock. Other visits by Bost and his son or his wife included several tours to inspect Peterson's Russian apple trees and a trip to hunt rabbits at Peterson's farm.

After harvesting fruit in 1890, Peterson reported, "This morning mama and I went to Waconia and sold apples." Then he "went to Waconia and sold apples and did some errands." He also "finished the fence around the barn yard, and then took 8 bu. apples to Kugler's store in Waconia." Later he wrote, "The women folks and I packed down apples and grapes that are to be taken to the county fair in Carver."

Throughout the years, Peterson's source of income from prizes increased considerably. His September 11, 1890, entry revealed: "Mama and I went down to the state fair in Minneapolis. I had previously sent down 30 varieties of apples which Hawkinson from Rose Hill entered for me – 80 plates in Lot 1; 28 varieties. They took second prize, $20.00. Lot 2 took second prize, $10.00. Best collection of Russian apples: For plate, took first prize, $10.00; for Antonovka took first prize, $2.00; for Charlamoff took first prize, $2.00; for Hibernal, second prize, $1.00. Altogether $45.00."

1. Theodore Bost emigrated from France in 1851 at the age of 17. The son of Jenny and Ami Bost, he was one of thirteen children. His father was a Protestant theologian who had been educated in the schools of the Moravians. After reaching America, he spent brief periods of time with family friends in New York and New Jersey, then traveled west. He worked as a farmhand and taught French classes in a school at a settlement called La Grande Ligne near Montreal, Canada, was baptized at this Swiss-run Baptist mission, and then taught school in New England. Following his arrival in St. Paul, he worked for William B. Dodd, a road contractor and builder who died during the Indian uprising at New Ulm.

Theodore and Sophie Bost's dwelling still stands. Since the vacated farm happens to be located within the grounds at the University of Minnesota Landscape Arboretum, proposals seem to favor preservation of the home which is to be situated in the midst of an old-fashioned herb garden setting.

Andrew Peterson's farm was well-managed and prosperous. Although fruit was his most important money crop, he harvested a wide variety of vegetables and grains, including rutabagas, turnips, corn, potatoes, sugar beets, alfalfa, wheat, oats, barley, and sugar cane. He raised cattle, sheep, pigs, and poultry, and he sold eggs, milk, cream, butter, and cordwood.

As Peterson continued to expand his horticultural objectives, he used true scientific methods to find the stock that would withstand the severe Minnesota climate. Besides planting, grafting, working with scions, and packing stock to ship to his customers, he recorded other kinds of work: hoeing around his fruit trees, picking caterpillars off the trees, and smearing the stems of young trees with pieces of liver to repel the rabbits.

Peterson also planted cedar, arbor vitae, spruce, and pine seedlings he had received from Charles Luedloff. He sold cuttings from Russian poplars, willows, and box elders, and sent some of these seedlings to his sons to plant on their farms near Maynard. His close friends and neighbors, Frank Lundsten and Andrew Swanson, both purchased evergreens from him.

Peterson subscribed to several horticultural publications in Swedish and English. In an 1891 diary entry, he noted, "I sent a letter and $.50 for Green's Fruit Grower and the same for Orchard and Garden and also for Farm, Stock and Home." An earlier 1891 entry shows his practical, inventive turn of mind: "I finished making a machine in which I can twist hay into rope. I want to use the rope to wind around the apple trees."

At one time he had 200 varieties of apples growing on his premises, and on a number of occasions he was host to leading horticultural experts from neighboring states and from as far away as Ottawa, Canada, who came to inspect his orchard.

After Samuel Bowdlear Green, professor at the University of Minnesota, and Wyman Elliott, president of the Minnesota Horticultural Society, saw Peterson's orchard on an August 25, 1891, stopover, Green wrote a long account of his visit that read in part: "His whole farm shows systematic care and intelligent management. It was the orchard, however, that we were most interested in and came to see. Mr. Peterson showed us every attention and spent several hours with us in his orchard. In whatever he told us, we were impressed with his impartiality, discrimination and thorough knowledge of the subject." Green then recorded his notes of Peterson's comments about various kinds of apples.

Peterson's orchard soon became one of fifteen experimental research stations in Minnesota. The chief station was in St. Anthony Park. Established by the Minnesota Horticultural Society to conduct controlled experiments with seedlings and to develop new varieties of fruit trees, vegetables, and ornamentals, it was headed by Professor Green.

Peterson mentioned fruit-breeding experimentation on his farm on May 31, 1892, when he wrote, "Today Prof. Green from St. Anthony Park came to hybridize the apple blossoms. He and his farm hand worked with that all day, and I helped every once in a while." Green stayed overnight, then Peterson said, "This morning Prof. Green and his farm hand returned home by way of the north line. I crossed a few flowers and then pruned apple trees." On June 30, Green returned and put mosquito netting over the hybridized flowers.

In addition to the experimental fruit farm (near Peter Gideon's orchard in Minnetonka) the state legislature authorized financial assistance in 1907 for the development of the University of Minnesota Fruit Breeding Farm which is located about six miles east of Peterson's homestead. This local effort was promoted simultaneously with the professional experimental work carried on in Owatonna from 1887 to 1925 under the supervision of Edward H. S. Dartt and his successor, Thomas E. Cashman.

Both the Horticultural Society and Professor Green can take credit for the establishment of the University of Minnesota Fruit Breeding Farm in Carver County, and experimental work by Charles Haralson, then under the supervision of William H. Alderman. Alderman served as superintendent of this station for thirty years after his appointment in 1923.

Today this experimental farm, now called the University of Minnesota Horticultural Research Center, has about 5,000 seedlings on the farms it operates between Victoria and Chanhassen.[2] According to Dr. Harold Pellett, director of research, the current practice of selling excess fruit helps to defray some of the development cost at the center.

2. The University of Minnesota Horticultural Research Center continues to place its emphasis on fruits in their crop program while its affiliate—the University of Minnesota Landscape Arboretum (located a few miles east of the center)—researches ornamentals.

CHAPTER 18

The Good Templars

One organization in which the Peterson children had a good deal of interest was the Good Templars, a local chapter of young people in the Scandia area that favored prohibition on a nationwide basis. They studied and supported the issues, despite general opposition of the prohibition movement by those who felt taxation justified the manufacture and sale of alcoholic beverages in the United States.

The Democratic Party openly opposed prohibition while the Republicans ignored the subject. Intertwined within this complex issue was the fact the country depended on liquor revenue to complete restoration work in those states laid desolate by the Civil War.

Alcoholism and problems from excessive drinking caused family disturbances in Carver County, but even so the brewery business flourished, partly as a result of the strong influence of the German culture, and indeed, the Scandinavian heritage. "Zahler and Metz" (as they were identified in the *Compendium*) ran a small brewery in Waconia from 1865 to about twelve years thereafter. The Berthold Hertz Brewery, which was located in Carver, was known to deliver their finished product to threshing crews as well as saloons. Beer made locally by other breweries provided an adequate supply to all of the near-by taverns, and the trade was brisk. Even today, the strong influence of German culture endures, and one brewery, the Beyrer Brewery in Chaska, stands although it is no longer in operation. Until 1980, the huge copper vats, cooling system, and kegs still stood in the old frame structure.

Peterson's January 1, 1880, remark, "In the morning a few of us went over to Nicholas's house and tried to get him reconciled to his wife because we heard that he had hit her," describes neighborhood concern regarding the influence of strong beverages. This incident was also discussed two weeks later, during a business meeting held at the church, although Peterson did not elaborate on the particulars or the outcome of this case.

It was common, however, to hear stories from the past relating to members of families in Waconia and in the surrounding area who were forced to spend the night locked in haybarns in order to escape abuse when drunkenness occurred.

Although the Good Templar lodges had their origin in the United States (through the Masonic Order) and were some 400,000 members strong by 1868, it does not appear that intense local interest developed until neighborhood young people became active in the program.

On January 11, 1888, Peterson reported, "In the evening the boys went to Hjortson's [Gerdsen's] school house for a temperance meeting," and on February 13, 1888, he said, "In the evening we had a contest to dispute about the righteousness of the cause of the prohibition party. There were 10 of the young people that delivered the speeches." During the month of March, Peterson also wrote: "Frank and Oscar Norman went to Norwood to a prohibition contest," and they returned to Scandia at ten the following evening. Several entries in April revealed Gerdsen's son had been selected the prohibitionists' gold medal contest winner, and "Editor Lind from Minneapolis" spoke during prohibition meetings held in Scandia.

Of the statements written by Peterson on August 1, 1888, "Today the prohibitionists had a subscription festival and steamboat rides on Clearwater Lake. Our people were all there." Carlton Qualey observes, "Peterson apparently felt no conflict of interest between this activity and the annual supply of wine produced from his grapes."

When "Mr. and Mrs. Bailey" (from Elk River) were in Scandia, they promoted support for prohibition through the spoken word and song during meetings held on October 20, 21, and 22. The Baileys, as well as Editor Lind, were guests in Peterson's home. On November 6, 1888, Peterson asserted his position on the matter. He said, "In the morning Axel, Carl, Frank and I went to the election. We voted for the national ticket this year. The boys and I cast our votes for the prohibition party."

Diary entries in 1889 and 1890 confirm continued interest in prohibition activities. The young people met to discuss issues of health and morals as they related to drinking, and continued to promote abstinence and the prohibition of liquor traffic. They also distributed tracts called *Prohibition Bombs,* published weekly by the National Prohibition Bureau.

When Henry Gerdsen's son, Albert, ran for state representative as the Prohibition Party candidate from Carver County, his campaign cards stated: "The protection of the home is the first concern of government." He supported the same platform chosen during the national convention in Chicago in 1869, but omitted equal suffrage, which the national organization favored.

Although his campaign met with defeat, Gerdsen and fellow club members continued to endorse the merits of abstinence and identified themselves by wearing Good Templar lapel pins as a sign of their stand on the issue. In time, after Andrew Peterson's death, some of these same temperance members became staunch supporters of the Scandia Literary Society and local farmers' club.

The Templars. *Back* (from left): William Gerdsen, Frank Peterson, Dan Walter, Albert Gerdsen, George Bray, and Herman Klatt. *Center:* John William Broberg, Amanda Broberg, Mary Gerdsen, Emma Zoerb, and Newton Bray in front.

Carver County Historical Society

This portrait of Andrew's sister Gustava (Petersdotter) Johnson suggests it was taken during her visit with Andrew and Elsa in 1869. The photographer's imprint is S.T. Bryan, Young America.

CHAPTER 19

Family Legacies

Andrew Peterson wrote most often to his family in Sweden, especially to his brother Johannes Rydell. Rydell lived on a small farm in the province of Småland, by the shore of Lake Bellen and next to the church at Bellö. His life was centered on his work as music director and church organist as well as on his family—his wife, Anna Carin Samuelsdotter and their only child, Anna Lovisa.

Peterson told of receiving photographs from Sweden and, although he did not identify them, he did say he received another single picture from his brother Carl, who was serving in the Civil War. Peterson also mentioned writing to his sister, Anna Charlotta, on February 27, 1867. Anna Charlotta was twenty-two years old and married to Peder Norman at this time. After several discussions of financial matters, Peterson said on March 24, 1868, "I went to Shakopee and bought a draft for $125.00 that I sent to Chicago to buy two tickets to send to Sweden."

Without explanation or reference to his sister Anna's arrival in the United States, he wrote on July 6, 1868, "Sent the letter to Sweden to tell them sister Anna was dead." He did not refer to the cause of death, her husband, or their children, Charlotte, Charles, and Oscar.

Rydell's granddaughter Linnéa later wrote of Anna's death, her husband, Peder Norman, and their five children. She said "Cousin Amy [Charlotte's daughter and Linnéa's second cousin] writes about the terrible happenings when her grandmother came to America. Two children died during the trip. . . . She also had a baby on her arrival."

One year later, on August 24, 1869, Andrew's sister Gustava (Mrs. Louis Johnson, who traveled with him during his ocean voyage and married while she was in Iowa) arrived in Scandia from Illinois. The following day Peterson said, "Did nothing but visit with my sister Gustafva." Perhaps they reached decisions about Anna's youngest child, because a later diary entry refers to Gustava's husband and adopted son Oscar Norman visiting in Scandia.

Meanwhile, in Sweden, life at Bellö had taken on an air of excitement for Johannes Rydell and Anna Carin. Preparations were being arranged in 1869 for the marriage of their daughter Anna Lovisa to Karl Gustav Widéen, a young teacher and organist at Järsnäs, a parish located in the province of Småland.[1] Anna Lovisa was described as an attractive, witty, young woman with a spirtual nature and a lively temperament. Ivar, Frithiof, and Linnéa were born in 1871, 1873, and 1877 respectively. Then Anna Lovisa began to have health problems.

Ten years had passed after sister Anna's arrival and subsequent death when Peterson disclosed on January 7, 1878, "Wrote a letter to brother Rydell in Sweden and also wrote and sent in the letter a receipt to him, because he had paid me his debt for the immigration tickets."

1. Järsnäs is about twenty-five to thirty miles from Västra Ryd. Although Västra Ryd is in Östergötland, it is not far from the border of Småland.

Peterson also wrote to his brother Carl in Colorado and his sister Gustava in Illinois on January 9 and 10, 1878. One week later, he received word that Carl had died on January 10, 1878. Soon afterward, he heard from Gustava about Carl's burial in Kirkwood, Illinois, and relayed the information to the relatives in Sweden. Carl visited in Scandia in 1876. At that time, Peterson wrote that he had not seen his brother for over twenty-one years.

Five months later, on June 8, 1878, Andrew Peterson traveled to Albert Lea, where he met his brother-in-law John and sister Maria Christina Anderson. The three of them went on to Kirkwood to see Andrew and Maria Christina's sister Gustava and her family and to view Carl's final resting place. Carl's marker at the Kirkwood Cemetery identified him as a private in the Civil War with Company G, the First Cavalry. The visitors stayed about ten days, stopping in Burlington en route home to visit Andrew's former employer, the orchardist, Neally.

After Carl's death, Peterson told of being at the mill in Watertown with a load of rye and stopping at a studio to have his picture taken. He also ordered six reproductions of the only picture he had of Carl. Later that month Elsa was photographed. Then on September 25, 1878, he wrote, "Today I mailed the letter to Sweden and enclosed brother Carl's, Elsa's and my pictures."

On March 19, 1879, Peterson received a telegram telling him that his sister Gustava had died suddenly on the afternoon of March 17. "It was a terrible shock to me," he said. "I wrote at once to Kirkwood, Ill. that I did not dare attempt the trip to the funeral as I am not well enough. I also [wrote] to Johannes and 'Majastina' [John and Maria Christina] in Minneapolis, and in the afternoon I sent Sture down to Chaska to mail the letters."

Carl had had a financial interest in a silver mine at an undisclosed location in the Southwest. One year after his death, Andrew wrote to Johannes and Anna Carin asking permission to use $112.23 from their joint legacy (including other family members) to pay for Carl's monument and to send sister Gustava's son-in-law, Gustav William Norman, to Colorado. Estate matters included dealings with several men in Elizabeth Town and Willow Gulch, New Mexico, and in Cuckera and Leadville, Colorado, where their family representative or power of attorney, a man named "Hedberg," was located. Although acceptance of a $5,000 offer was made for the Saxony mine on January 20, 1879, Andrew Peterson's paperwork continued from March 26, 1881, with his letter to A. J. Rowth in New Mexico, on through his February 27, 1882, correspondence to Hedberg.

Johannes Rydell, his wife Anna Karin, and the relatives in America suffered another shocking loss when Peterson's brother Samuel died. He drowned in Lake Solgen after his team of horses and wagon broke through the ice. Johannes and Anna Karin were the first to hear about his death. Although they were suffering themselves, their first concern was for their daughter Anna Lovisa. They tried to ease the expected pain associated with the news because she was suffering from a serious heart condition. After Johannes Rydell notified Stina-Kari, a neighbor and family friend, about his brother's death, she traveled by train to "Nässjö," and walked the remainder of the way—a distance of about twelve to thirteen miles—to Järsnäs to personally deliver the tragic message to Anna Lovisa from her parents at Bellö.

Two years later, on March 8, 1882, Peterson said, "In the forenoon I painted the old wagon and at noon I received a letter from my brother Rydell in Sweden that he was dying. I wrote to him at once and also wrote to my brother-in-law, Johannes and sister, 'Maja Stina' and a letter to my brother-in-law, Johanson [Gustava's husband], in Kirkwood, Illinois."

Rydell, who was asthmatic, did not die, however. Although his condition was a constant source of discomfort, he lived another fifteen years. When his asthma became unbearable (especially during the night), he would often leave his bed to play the klaveret because he found it easier to breathe sitting up.

Three years after Samuel's death, Peterson wrote on June 20, 1883, "In the morning I went to the Waconia post office to get a registered letter. It was from Sweden and contained $571.42. This is our share of the inheritance after my brother, Samuel. This inheritance is to be divided among the heirs in [the] United States. I mailed a letter containing a receipt to Sweden."

Anna Lovisa was thirty-eight years old when she died in 1885 at her home in Järsnäs. Her children, Ivar, Frithiof, and Linnéa were fourteen, twelve, and eight years old, respectively, at the time. Sensing her death was at hand, she wrote a moving letter to her parents, Johannes and Anna Carin, at Bellö, telling them about the tender care she received from their grandson, Ivar. She said it was difficult to believe the manner in which he assumed the responsibility of helping the family and caring for her. Ivar's attention to the household was said to be so much more than anyone could have expected from one so young. She told of her diminished strength. She closed her letter with these words, "I shall see our Lord's goodness in the land of the living. Our Lord's peace be with you!"

Anna Lovisa's husband, Karl Gustav Widéen, remarried, but the situation at home was not always pleasant for the children. In later life, Ivar, Frithiof, and Linnéa learned that their stepmother's behavior was the result of the beginnings of an emotional illness. Circumstances were such at Järsnäs that their grandparents decided to take the grandchildren to live with them at Bellö.

Although the memories of their mother's death and burial at Bellö were dark and depressing, the youngsters were now comforted and secure. Ivar developed an intense interest in music at Bellö and studied with his grandfather, Johannes Rydell. He continued his lessons in Stockholm at Svenska Akademien (the Swedish Academy). Membership includes writers, musicians, artists, and other talented students in related fields—men and women who are carefully screened before being accepted in the academy's classes. Ivar graduated with highest honors.

Even when Anna Lovisa was still alive, the grandchildren frequently visited Bellö, where Grandfather Johannes Rydell was especially good to Linnéa and her brothers. Bellö was paradise for the children. Their heritage included their grandfather's love of music as well as his fondness for animals. Mase the cat and Nellie the dog were special pets, though the horse Piro, the sheep, and the pigs all received their share of attention, as did the ever-present litter of kittens to be lovingly cared for. Most of Grandmother Anna Carin's free hours were spent knitting stockings or weaving cloth for clothing.

At the close of the day in Bellö, the soft toll of the church bells echoed beyond the lake and throughout the countryside. To Linnéa, Bellö was always filled with the fragrance of sweet perfume from her grandmother's herb and flower garden. After meals (memorable ones included spinach and smoked ham), Linnéa, Frithiof, and Ivar concluded their daylight hours by saying the Lord's Prayer in unison with Anna Carin.

Andrew Peterson received a third inheritance from Samuel's estate in Sweden, this one for $129.87. Then, in two separate letters to Sweden, he described in 1887 the deaths of Maria Christina and her husband, the Reverend John Anderson.

Charles ("Carl"), Andrew's brother, who died out West in the United States.

Hardly had the children, Ivar, Frithiof, and Linnéa, settled at Bellö and adjusted themselves to the security provided there than Anna Carin Rydell was taken from her loved ones. Linnéa wrote a letter to Helen Wettstein in later years: "Grandmother died [in] 1892, the same year I was confirmed. Then *everything* got black for me. But Ivar promised as soon as he got a position, I could be with him and we would have a home together."

After Anna Carin's death, Johannes Rydell remarried. This was not a particularly happy time in his life. When his second wife died of tuberculosis, he contracted a third marriage, this one of convenience. He received nursing care, and his wife received financial security. She attended to his needs throughout his life and inherited his pension after his death, as they had agreed.

On October 12, 1897, Peterson received the message that his brother Johannes had died. His journal entry was, "As I received a letter yesterday from my brother Rydell's grandson, Ivar Widien *[sic]* from Laholm, Sweden, that my brother, Johannes Rydell, died the 21st of September, 1897, I wrote an answer to the above mentioned *[Widéen]* in Laholm today."

Peterson did not tell in his diary about his response on October 29, 1897, to a letter he had received from his niece, Maria Christina's daughter Ruth (Mrs. Fred Johnson). She had written to tell him that she had read an article about Johannes's death in a Swedish newspaper. His letter to her is as follows (spellings are as Peterson wrote them):

> I recieved a letter from Rydell's daughter's oldest son Ivar Wideen, the eleventh of Oct. telling of Rydell's death. Ivar Wideen is Musik-direktär in Låholm, Hällen's Lån Sweden....The week after I recieved the letter I recieved the paper from Eksjo-Tidninges, and the piece about Rydell was very long and all the offices that he had was mentioned there and also mentiond that he got the medal from the king of Sweden and I spose I'll have another paper from Eksjo telling about the funeral which should be the 29 of Sept. in Bellö Church. And last Ivar Wideen says I have done my duty in writing to you because that was what Grandfather Rydell wished.
>
> As it is very hard for me to write Josephine + I have transilated it as best we could, but it is far from correct. Please let Charlotte Johnson + Chas. Norman [Peterson's deceased sister–Anna's children] read this letter because they are the only ones that knew him in person.

Andrew Peterson confided that he expected the Lord would come to take him soon. He was the oldest of eight children–the only one left. Before he closed his letter to his niece he said, "The 20th of this month I was 79 yr. old, nearly two yr's older than Rydell. A long journey."

Petter Jonasson **m** **Ingrid Samuelsdotter**
August 4, 1785—July 11, 1846 **January 9, 1795—April 25, 1853**

Both born in Västra Ryd parish

Henceforth Petter's sons (except Johannes) used the name Peterson

---

Andrew
1818-1898
m
Elsa Anderson
Ida
Emma
Anna
Josephine *m* Nels Carlson
(without children)
John/Axel
Charles/Carl
Frank
Oscar
George/Sture *m* Ada Taplan
(without children)

Johannes Rydell
1820-1897
m
Anna Carin ?
Anna Lovisa m Karl Gustav Widéen
Ivar m Augusta ?
Anna Lisa
Brita
Harald
Linnéa m Olaf Andrén
Björn
Tor
Rolf
Frithiof

Maja Stina/Maria Christina
1826-1887
m
John Anderson (The Reverend)
John *m* Jennie Fredine*
Lilah
Clinton
Wenona
Henry *m* Hulda Fredine*
Terrell
Dale
Gaylord
Lillian
Ruth *m* Fred Johnson†
Oma
Ora
Forest
Westel
Hazel
Julie *m* Bennett Melin
Blanche
Emmeline
Bert
Russell
Verna
Earl
Grace *m* Stephen Booth
Gladys
Helen
Frances *m* Stephen Herrick
(without children)
Andrew Ludwik (died at 3 years of age)

Anna
1828-1829

Johannes Rydell, Andrew's musician brother, who remained in Sweden.

Samuel Peterson, brother of Andrew, who stayed in Sweden.

Karl Gustav Widéen, the father of Linnéa, Frithiof, and Ivar.

Gustava
1829-1879
m
Louis Johnson

Anna Martha *m* Gustav Wm Norman
- Maude
- Helen
- Berniece
- Neil
- Robert
- Louis
- Gerald

Fred *m* Ruth Anderson†

Edward *m* Mollie Ackerman
- Minnie
- Helen
- Ruth
- Byron
- Raymond (twin)
- Robert (twin)

Charles *m* ? Snook
- Marion
- Waverly
- Phyllis
- Joyce
- Virginia
- John

Samuel
1831-1880

Anna Charlotta
1834-1868
m
Peder Norman

Charlotte *m* Andrew Johnson
- Amy**
- Lilly
- Edwin
- Luke

Charles *m* Alice Anderson‡
- Maude
- Wave
- Florence
- LeRoy
- Floyd
- Clifford

Oscar

Carl
1837-1878

* Sisters
** Amy married Per Daniel Anderson's son Fritchof
† Cousins
‡ Alice was Per Daniel Anderson's daughter.

Nicholas Swenson is shown with the first page of his letter telling Peterson's relatives in Sweden about his death. The original correspondence is located at the Emigrant Institute, Växjö, Sweden.

Wäcoma den 18 April 1898

Som jag Nicolaus Swenson är namnar-
nabbo till till Andrew Petterson hade han
På Sitt Sista bett om jag ville Skrifva
till Eder när han dog. Som orsak för hans
barn Skrifva engelska, så kunde ni
få trabbel att läsat, jag kan nu På
familjens vägnar delgifva eder att eder
moderfaders Broder Andres Petterson Sluta
Sin vandring Den 31 marts Kl. 11 ak han
Somnade i Stillhet ak frid Hän var uppe
ak Stvälta Sig ak Hade familj aftonbön
kl half 9. ak gick till Sängs ak låg ak
talade med Sin Hustru ak Kl. 11 var hans
Ande fri från tidens vidervärdigheter.
Han blef af många vänner ak trös
fränder, följd till Sitt Sista hvilorum
begrafnings texten var den 15 v. af
Psalmen 17 af David. Der var en stor
Skara Samlad 8 barn 5 Söner ak 3

CHAPTER 20

The Last Letter Home

Peterson was unaccustomed to the role of an observer, but his remarks during the late 1880s reveal that his health was deteriorating, preventing him from taking responsibility for and engaging in heavy farm labor. He told of his son Frank's going to Minneapolis to hire a farmhand in 1892, and of his (Andrew's) exemption from jury duty on September 16, 1895, because of his age.

Although he was now seventy-nine years old and his strength was limited, Peterson continued working in his orchard and neighboring vineyards during the final year of his life. He also maintained an avid interest in his family as well as others in the community. In the late summer of 1897, he sent fruit to the state fair as usual. According to the diary entry for August 25, he shipped thirty-three varieties of apples.

On October 20, he wrote, "Mama and I went over to Lobit's place [Herman Lobitz, *map 38]* and [I] pruned back grape vines then to Andrew Swanson's place *[map 11]* and pruned his grape vines. In the evening we went to Jons Nilson's house *[map 10]*. We stayed overnight with them."

He made cuttings from the Beta grape for Samuel B. Green. It was a local product, developed by Louis Suelter of Carver and named for Suelter's wife, Beta. This prolific, flavorful grape can still be obtained in nurseries. Green reciprocated by sending Peterson grafting roots, which the latter noted on November 22 were "frozen hard as rocks."

He also wrote that his sons had begun to build an addition to the barn, with help from Frank Lundsten and Andrew Anderson. Then on March 7, 1898, he said that "Axel, Frank, Emma and Josephine went to Herman Labit's [Lobitz] funeral."

Four days later, he wrote, "I worked a little in the shop. Beautiful weather. In the evening Pettijohn, that has taught our school this [year], had an entertainment in the schoolhouse. The children provided the music and the songs." In the days that followed, he reported that Frank and Josephine went to a young people's Baptist church conference in Minneapolis. He also said he set teeth in the harrow and applied a second coat of paint to it, set seed wheat out to sprout, "made mortar in order to set the evaporation pans on the outdoor stove at the syrup camp," and cleaned the stoves. While Peterson worked on projects he alone could handle, Frank hauled milk to Waconia for Nicholas Swenson, and he and Axel fanned old wheat to use for seed wheat and hauled sap troughs out to the forest. Frank also helped Peterman shingle his barn, then hauled milk and sap and cooked syrup.

Ingrid and Swan Swanson *(map 65,* parents of the lumber dealer John Swanson in St. Bonifacius) were the last visitors Andrew Peterson saw. On March 24, he wrote, "In the afternoon Swen Svanson and his wife, Ingrid Christina, and Beata Carlson were here visiting. I was in bed." On March 26, Peterson wrote, "I became so very ill they had to carry me to bed." From his bed, Peterson continued to write in his diary until March 29. In these few days, he noted an all-day snowfall and that outdoor conditions were suitable for sleighing. His last written words, were, "It is clear weather, but not mild weather."

Peterson's conversation with his neighbor and request that he, Nicholas Swenson, write a letter to his relatives in Sweden after his death reveals that Elsa, like most women of that generation, was illiterate. Although Swenson's correspondence was sent to Johannes Rydell's grandson, Ivar Widéen, it was written without a salutation. It turned out to be the last letter home.

Ivar Widéen safely kept this letter from Scandia, the last letter home to Sweden, with other belongings of his grandfather. When Vilhelm Moberg's literary talent was being recognized through Swedish newspaper and magazine articles in the 1950s, Ivar remembered the letter he had received about Peterson's death. After reading one story about the novelist and his American research, Widéen realized that the diarist Moberg had referred to in an interview was his great-uncle, Andrew Peterson. Widéen sent Moberg a copy of the last letter home. For the first time, Moberg learned that Peterson was not from Småland, but from the province of Östergötland.

The December 28, 1961, issue of the *Smålands-Tidningen* included an article about Moberg's works and the link between Andrew Peterson, Ivar Widéen, and Linnéa Widéen Andrén. It said in part, in this translation:

> Now it is apparent that Anders Peterson, the oldest brother of Linnéa's grandfather, who was Bellö parish choir director, Johannes Rydell, is the true model for Karl-Oskar Nilsson in Vilhelm Moberg's great emigrant epic which has been so widely read in Sweden. . . .
>
> Norman [Neil F. Norman, Peterson's sister Gustava's grandson from Galesburg, Illinois] relates that as a seven-year-old boy he visited Andrew's farm, and understandably he has great admiration for this remarkable farmer from Sweden and the work he left behind. Norman does not doubt that Moberg is a great author but believes that Uncle Andrew was nonetheless a bit sharper. That Andrew's diary, kept for forty-four years from 1854-1898, is a classic of the most fascinating kind, Norman holds unshakeably. . . .

The revolutionary events of the move to America were probably responsible for prompting Andrew to begin his massive enterprise, a folk journal which seems to have no counterpart in Sweden. Andrew is considered to be an exception, too, among the Swedish emigrants. The majority of them, growing up as they did before the advent of public schools in 1842, could not even write their names, and thus had no presumptions about being able to tell what they experienced in the foreign land. What they needed to survive in that wild land of pioneers was in the first place not pens and words but the capability to break ground, build houses, and make shoes, clothes, and all manner of useful equipment.

Andrew Peterson was what the Småland common-folk call a "maker of sundries" (or what Americans call "a jack-of-all-trades"). He seems to have been able to do everything, and when it comes to his diary entries, one must agree with Neil Norman that as an author Andrew excells. His ability to observe could not have been keener; life on the farm is registered in language that is lean and precise. Even when describing the most important events in life, Andrew holds to his spare style–the most crucial task for him to note the events, not to comment on them.

Karl-Oskar [the Americanized version of his name was Charles O. Nelson] has been given most of Andrew Peterson's qualities: the versatility, the leadership ability, the piety, the stubborness *[sic]*. Andrew's daily entries on tasks, weather, births and deaths of people and animals, church services, journeys to town, and all the rest that made up the way of life in the pioneer colony in Minnesota–all this has been a gold mine for Vilhelm Moberg who has said the diary gives a complete picture of a pioneer's and farmer's life in Minnesota during the late 1880s.

Perhaps nowhere is the link to the diaries more precisely illustrated than through the letter written by Nicholas Swenson in behalf of the Peterson family. Moberg clearly used Swenson's original letter as a basis for his *Last Letter Home*, the book that concluded the four-volume immigrant series, *The Emigrants, Unto a Good Land, The Settlers,* and the *Last Letter Home.* Moberg's version of the letter (paperback books differ slightly) as well as the entire message Nicholas Swenson sent to Ivar Widéen (without a salutation) have been included in this chapter.[1]

1. Quoted from *Last Letter Home* by Vilhelm Moberg, book four of *The Emigrants' Saga* by Vilhelm Moberg (c) 1978 by the Estate of Vilhelm Moberg. English translation copyright (c) 1961, 1978 by Gustaf Lannestock. With permission of the publisher, Popular Library.

Foreign Rights–Albert Bonniers Förlag AB, Sveavägen 56, Box 3159, 10363 Stockholm 3. (Bound volume-pages 382-383.)

I, Nicholas Swenson, am the closest neighbor to Andrew Peterson. He asked me shortly before he died to write to you, when he wasn't with us any more, and tell you about his death.

His children write only English so he thought you would have trouble reading a letter from them. On behalf of the family I now must tell you, that your grandfather's brother, Andrew Peterson, died March 31 at 11-o'clock in the evening. He died quietly and peacefully. He was out of bed in the evening for awhile, washed himself and took part in Evening Prayers with the family about 8:30 in the evening. Afterwords he went to bed and he talked to his wife for awhile after they were both in bed. At 11 o'clock his spirit was free from the difficulties of this world.

Many friends and Church members paid him respect at the Funeral. Also present were 8 children (5 sons and 3 daughters) and many other relatives from near and far. Davids Psalm 17, Verse 15, was read at the Funeral.

Andrew Peterson was born October 20, 1818 and his age was 79 years, 5 months and 11 days when he died.

I was with him when he received your letter some time ago, and he then said, "I am the oldest in the family and all of my sisters and brothers are already on the other side of the 'Jordan River' and I am left to the last." I did not think at the time that he was to go so soon.

Andrew Peterson had lived in this community since 1855, and we have been neighbors for 37 years – since 1861. He and his wife had been married for 40 years and they were blessed with 9 children. Only 8 are still living. One daughter died young. He is mourned by his family and a lot of friends and neighbors. He was a true Christian in every way and he is going to be missed in the Church, because he has been a very good member and leader in the Church. He was a very god-fearing man and did his duties accurately and with good sense. He was a quiet man with an honest and good character, and nobody had any reason to complain about the way he took care of things.

He had laid down his sins at the foot of the cross and so he received strength to live his life after the words of the Bible and to praise the Lords name. Now he has finished his life in this world and has gone to meet his Lord and Master and from Him receive the "Crown of Life." I now pray that Gods grace and peace will be with us so we all will meet again in Heaven where we will never have to part.

From us, all kind and cordial greetings to you. If you would be so kind and write to us we will certainly answer your letters. Let us know if you read English. In that case it would be easier for us to write to you.

In haste: Your affectionate relatives

Address Frank Peterson
P.O. Box 84
Waconia Minnesota

Peterson sent a letter to you October 13, (1897 ?) but did no[t] receive an answer. It is possible it was lost so you never received it.

Chisago Lake Settlement
Center City Minnesota
December 20, 1890

Missis Lydia Karlsson
Åkerby in Ljuder Parish
Sweden

Your Brother Charles on several occasions asked me to write to his Sister in Sweden and let her know when he died. I am an old neighbor, and no one else could do this for the reason that your Brother's children have forgotten Swedish and write English and this might cause trouble for his relatives to read. Therefore I promised to write.

Speaking for his Children I wish to advise you that your Brother Charles O. Nelson came to the end of his life the 7th of the month in the Evening. At half past eight he was up and took his supper and washed Himself. Then he went to bed and at eleven o'clock his soul was liberated. He went to sleep peacefully, no one expected his time to be so near.

Your Brother's Birthday was October 31. His life lasted 67 years, 1 month and 7 days. He had lived on this place since 1850. Exactly 40 years ago he came from Sweden and I was his neighbor since 1872.

Your Brother was brought to his last resting place the 15th of December. Many were gathered, 6 children, 4 Sons and 2 Daughters and Sons-in-Law and Daughters-in-Law and Grandchildren and Neighbors were also there. The Funeral text was David, Psalm 15, the verse that says "He that walketh uprightly, and worketh righteousness and speaketh the truth in his heart, he shall never be moved in Eternity."

Nelson is mourned and greatly missed because he was a Man of Order, and Just. He had much concern for his Children and Grandchildren. He has also fulfilled his obligations and no one can step forth with any blame of him. I visited with him the evening before he left. He had told me many times that he was ready to Die.

With these lines I have fulfilled my Promise to my neighbor while he was in Life, that I would write and notify his Sister. Your Brother often spoke of you. I send the letter to the Address he gave me.

I apologize that my writing is so poor and disjointed. I am full of years and my hands tremble so it is hard to write. I am the oldest of 10 Brothers and Sisters. All except me have crossed the River Jordan, 3 rest in Swedish ground, 6 in America's. I was the oldest and now I have been left to the last. I will be 80 next March if the Lord lets me live that long, I am ready when He wants to call me home to Him.

Your Brother Nelson's family who are close blood relations to you all send their heartfelt greetings to you. I am an unknown Stranger in North America writing these Lines to you. I extend my hand to you in Friendship and Wish you Well.

Over my Old Native Land I call down the Lord God's Blessing and Eternal Peace.

Written down with Respect by

Axel J. Andersson

Aerial view of Andrew Peterson's farm, about 1930.

CHAPTER 21

The Promised Land

While the obituary notice in the April 7, 1898, *Weekly Valley Herald* in Chaska briefly mentioned Andrew Peterson as "an old and respected citizen of this county," Professor Samuel Bowdlear Green wrote a more personal tribute in a report published by the Minnesota Horticultural Society. Green praised Peterson as "a man of sterling integrity and a lover of everything that he believed worked for the building up of Christian character. He loved truth, he was patient, thorough, persistent, careful and enterprising. In his very successful efforts to better Minnesota Horticulture, all these features of his character were prominent. 'For his heart was in his work, and the heart giveth grace unto every art.' "

The eldest and the youngest of the Peterson daughters died within a few years of each other after Andrew's death. Ida, the oldest, died in 1900, and Josephine, the youngest, died in 1908. After Frank's passing, in 1921, Charles left the farm they called Fairview in Maynard (where he had lived for thirty years) and returned home to take charge of the farm in Scandia. Emma, too, left the farm in Maynard and returned to help Elsa and her brothers. She would also serve the Scandia Baptist Church as organist and treasurer for the next eighteen years.

For Elsa Peterson, the memories of her log cabin beginnings had long ago been dimmed by time. Although she joined friends and relatives in pleasant social gatherings in the decades following Andrew's death, she must have endured a very real sense of loss. The lives of the younger people she knew were changing rapidly, while the men and women who had settled in Scandia–her contemporaries–were all being "called home" in death. She was one of the few left.

Elsa died on March 8, 1922, and the *Waconia Patriot* on March 16 expressed a community's gratitude to all members of her generation by writing the following in her obituary:

> With the passing of Mrs. Andrew Peterson, the last representative of that wonderful race of men and women that challenged the wilderness in the fifties has passed from our circle. . . . That generation accepted the call into the wilderness. Undaunted and unafraid they took up the task of making that wilderness the abode of civilized man.[1]

Until four years after their mother passed away, Emma, Oscar, John ("Axel"), and Charles Peterson continued to care for the farm their parents had carved out of the wilderness in Laketown Township. By then, age prevented them from managing the place by themselves, and they hired Simon Peltz's son, John, to work for them.

John and his wife Louise lived as tenant farmers in a small home especially built for his family close to the Peterson home. They worked the farm, shared the profits, and raised their ten children–Alice-Mae, Ralph, Karl, Mary, Roy, Grace, the

1. Elsa Peterson's obituary referred to her birthplace in Sweden as the province of Skåne.

twins Harold and Herbert, Kermit, and Albert—who all experienced a warm relationship with the Petersons.

Mary and Harold Peltz were especially sociable, and at this time they were old enough to visit Emma on their own.[2] If they stayed to play dominoes with Charlie, Oscar was quick to express concern if his brother kept winning. He felt that the children would become discouraged and might not want to come back to visit with them again. Sometimes Emma played the piano (it is not known when the organ was replaced). By now Oscar had developed a severe arthritic condition and could no longer accompany her on the violin as he used to do.[3]

The years passed quickly. Sture lived in Maynard at the time of his death in 1928. His passing was followed by that of Axel on March 6, 1930.

In 1940, Mary Peltz, who was then a teenager, became interested in reading the transcripts of Peterson's journals. She could relate to the information in a personal way because the pages were sprinkled with references to her grandparents. Mary thought about the settlers in Scandia and had poignant reminders about survival as she worked in Emma's kitchen. If her hostess was not feeling well, she often stayed to prepare the evening meal.

It was sad for the Peltz family to witness the decline and eventual death of Oscar on July 24, 1941, and three months later that of Charles. Charles was then president of the Scandia Baptist Cemetery Association and served as a member of the Midway Hospital Association Board in St. Paul. He passed away at the Midway Hospital on October 30, 1941, at the age of seventy-five. John Peltz served as a pallbearer for his funeral.

As Emma grew older, Sarah, the daughter of neighbor Selby Peterson, looked after her. Although Sarah and Emma bore the same family name, they were not related. Josephine Peterson was briefly married to Sarah's uncle, Nels Carlson, before Josephine's death on October 18, 1908. Although Emma's family relationship with Sarah was brought about indirectly through marriage, they had always been close neighbors and very good friends. In addition, they shared a common religious heritage. When Emma's eyesight failed to the point where she needed continuous care, she moved in with the Selby Peterson family in the home her brother Frank formerly owned *(map 48)*.[4]

After Emma's death on May 17, 1943, the Reverend G. Arvid Hagstrom wrote a memorial tribute which was a fitting farewell to Emma and the entire Peterson family:

> Emma R. Peterson, a member of the Scandia church, was gathered to her fathers. By the death of Miss Emma R. Peterson, the last member of the Andrew Peterson family has been called home.
>
> The Scandia Baptist church was organized in the log cabin of this family on August 1, 1855, with a membership of nine. Emma was the last of nine children to go. She was born in this early home in Laketown Township April 11, 1870, and died May 17, [1943] at the home of Mr. and Mrs. S. E. Peterson. She spent most of her life on the farm home.
>
> On July 5, 1885, after being converted, she was baptized by the Rev. Magnus Larson who was serving the Scandia church as student pastor. Fifteen years of her life were spent in Maynard, Minnesota where she kept house for her brother Charles J. While there she was an active member of the Leenthrop Baptist church, serving as organist for many years, and devoting much time to the Women's Temperance Union of which she was secretary for some time.
>
> In 1908, upon the death of her sister Josephine, she returned to Scandia to take charge of the family home. She then served as treasurer of the Scandia church for 18 years, taking the place of her brother Frank after he passed away. She gave much help and financial aid to the Mission Circle. She gave liberally of her means to world-wide missionary enterprises, to Klingberg's Children's Home, and other benevolent causes. She donated a Christian flag and U.S. flag to the Scandia church.
>
> Her death is a distinct loss to the church of which she was a faithful and devoted member, as well as to the community where she was highly respected and well known. Her life was beautified by Christian virtues of patience, quietude and humility. Never did she employ her tongue to speak unkindly of anyone, but rather for that which was uplifting, wholesome, and Christlike. In her Bible was found one of her favorite prayers, which reads, 'Endow us,

2. After Harold's younger brother Roy had been told "not to go begging," Roy returned home with an apple in hand and said, "I found it rolling in the snow!"

3. Oscar's arthritic condition stiffened him to the point where even the simplest chores became a burden. He would let Emma pile his outstretched arms with wood from the shed, and upon reaching the kitchen, he would bend slightly at the waist and let the chopped pieces roll from his arms into the wood box.

4. The Selby Peterson family *(map 48)*, tenants on Frank Peterson's farm, eventually purchased the claim once owned by George Mattson. There they raised their children—Myra, Sarah, Ruth, and Milo—on the farm next to the Scandia Baptist Church.

we pray Thee, with strength greater than our mortal own, that through the indwelling of Thy Spirit, we may be fortified by that power which is Thine alone.' She was fully fortified in death as well as in life by that power. . . . She passed away at the age of 73 years, one month, and six days. Thus is closed the human history of another family of the charter members who originally composed this oldest Baptist church in the North Star state. Peace be to her memory!

Because Sarah Peterson had provided the loving care and nursing service that Emma needed, Emma willed the Andrew Peterson homestead to her.[5]

By then, having met their commitment to the farm's original owners, the Peltzes were ready to leave the small home built for them on the Peterson estate. It was time to take over their own family homestead, the adjacent Simon Peltz farm.

The Andrew Peterson home was then occupied by the Carver County farm agent, George A. King, and his family during Emma's absence from the farm and following her death.

After King's passing, his family left the farm and Sarah Peterson moved there. She managed the place with hired help as long as she could, but finally decided to sell it. An auction was held on March 22, 1969, and the property was purchased by a private corporation that intended to develop the acreage for residential purposes. The idea was abandoned, however, and the entire farm was later sold to Ward and Georgene Holasek.

The Andrew Peterson home still stands, with only minor changes made by Sarah Peterson. She installed plumbing for the kitchen and bathroom facilities and added an enclosed back porch.

5. Sarah (who was thirty-one years old at the time Emma died in 1943) said Emma received a great deal of attention from a gentleman who courted her while she lived at Fairview. Although she cherished the gold watch and chain she received from him, Emma declined to tell Sarah why she avoided a serious relationship with him.

Elsa Peterson and Lillie Larson during a Fourth of July celebration in Scandia.

The Scandia Baptist Church or meeting house as it looked after the 1904 tornado.

CHAPTER 22

Disaster in Scandia

Lillie Remembers

Andrew Anderson, one of Caroline's and Per Daniel's four sons, was born in Scandia on June 13, 1873. He lived on the family farm near Parley Lake until he became a carpenter at the age of twenty-one. He worked at his trade in Minneapolis until 1902. Then he returned to Scandia and purchased the lakeshore farm (*map 50*) homesteaded by Andrew Bergquist on Clearwater or Waconia Lake.[1] The following year he married Beda Peterson. She was a native of Sweden, and lived in Isanti County before her marriage to Andrew.

While watching storm clouds gather on the afternoon of August 20, 1904, Beda expressed concern because Andrew was not back from his construction job in Minnetonka. That particular day, Andrew Peterson's son Frank, and Arvid Hagstrom, a seminary student who was married to Per Daniel's daughter Carolina, had been working as members of Anderson's construction crew. Meanwhile, Beda's sister from Minneapolis, Louise Larson, and her children were spending the weekend at his farmhouse.

At the same time, Louise Larson's daughter Lillie was vacationing for several weeks at the Andrew Peterson farm. Lillie had not joined her mother and sisters who were swimming and relaxing on the beach in front of her Uncle Andrew Anderson's home because she had never been fond of water. It was hot and humid. It was the kind of Minnesota day that frequently ends in a storm, and by late afternoon the dark clouds were gathering. As the overcast sky became more threatening, Lillie was in the Peterson home with Elsa, Oscar, and Josephine. Their supper was ready, and they were waiting for Frank to be dropped off by her uncle Andrew.

Lillie was bewildered as she watched from the house and saw Andrew urging his team to move faster into the farmyard, and wondered why he headed his horses into Peterson's shed. She saw Frank's hat whirl away into the air as he and his brother Axel (who had been at work in the barn), Andrew Anderson, and Arvid Hagstrom rushed into the house.

Meanwhile her father, Oscar Erick Larson, had only moments before stepped off the Minneapolis train at the Coney Island Depot.[2] He walked the short distance from the station located on the lakeshore and joined his family at Anderson's home. Other passengers—visitors and vacationers from Minneapolis, St. Paul, and even the far eastern seaboard states—were then being

1. The Bergquist home and post office was situated directly across the township road and in line with the entry road into the churchyard of the Scandia Baptist Church.

2. The Minneapolis and St. Louis Railroad (formerly the Minnesota Railroad Company) was built from Minneapolis through Victoria, Waconia, Young America, Norwood, and Hamburg. Although depots were established at each village, most of the travelers arrived at the M. & St. L. or Coney Island Depot (merely a shelter—a roof set over posts) near the Cedar Lake Ice House on the shore of Waconia Lake. From there the passengers were transported to town or to the island for their vacation retreat. The line continued a distance of twenty-seven miles to Merriam Junction and on to Albert Lea and Iowa.

transported into town by omnibuses or by boat to their destination at one of the cottages or three hotels on the island.

When Larson arrived at the farm, Beda decided not to wait supper. Almost immediately, only seconds after they were seated at the table, the meal was interrupted by a deafening roar. Alarmed by the sound and simultaneous rocking of the house, they rushed into the cellar.

By this time, Beda's husband and the men had already found shelter in Peterson's house, and before Lillie knew what was happening she had been ushered into the basement. As she listened to voices and footsteps of concerned adults walking about on the floor above her, she recalled her feeling of terror. She cried out, "Uncle Arvid [Hagstrom], save me, save me!"

Without waiting for the storm to subside, Andrew Anderson returned to the shed where only moments before the roof had been torn away. The yard was strewn with shingles from the roof of Elsa Peterson's house. Anderson climbed into the wagon and was pulled by the horses through the wind, rain, and hail, past the twisted windmill and broken trees. As he was approaching his farm, his wife Beda, the farmhand, and her sister's family were in a state of shock. On reaching a place of safety under the stairway, they looked up and saw the turbulent sky! The entire house was gone. There was nothing left.

Andrew was horrified as he advanced closer to the exposed cellar of his home, but felt relief when he heard familiar voices. Although safe, the survivors were drenched and dirty. They had been covered with dust and soot from the ashes Beda had been collecting to make her soap.

Andrew's first thought was for the safety of his parents, Per Daniel and Caroline Anderson *(map 35)*. After Andrew assembled his wife, his farmhand and guests, they traveled toward Parley Lake and Per Daniel's farm. The streaks of lightning that guided them also revealed that the meeting house was still standing in its familiar setting on the hill *(map 49)*.

On reaching the farm of Per Daniel and Caroline, the family could see only minor damage to the roof and chimney of the home. They were thankful to be united and safe.

During the inspection tour of Andrew's farm the following day, the families found one of the kitchen chairs out in the middle of the field. Larson had placed his coat and vest on the back of it before sitting down at the table, and now they could be seen hanging exactly as he had left them, but quite some distance from the house.[3] Even the pocket watch and papers were all safe in the pocket of Larson's coat. When the news of this oddity reached some of the neighboring farm families, Ida Peltz told her son William to hitch up Dick, their horse, to the buggy. She was determined to see this strange happening for herself.

The hired man who was at the table with Beda Anderson and Larson's family remembered that he was still holding an ear of corn when he reached the cellar. Some time after the storm, he presented Beda with her diamond ring, which he had found in the grass. Beda's trunk, which has a hole in it made by the tornado, is still a cherished possession of the Andrew Anderson family.

Andrew Anderson's dog may have found safety in some unknown sheltered spot at the church. For as long as he lived thereafter, he waited out each storm seated on the church steps.

The Lake Is Coming to Get Us!

August Nelson, son of John and Benedicta Nelson, was forty-one years old when he met Karin ("Carrie") Olson Englund, a widow. She had been born in Burnsberg, in Värmland, Sweden, and married Nels Englund after emigrating to Minnesota. The couple settled in Minneapolis, where they attended Elim Baptist Church. Before and after her husband's death in 1893, Carrie frequently visited Lena Person. Lena, formerly Mrs. George B. Nilson and a resident of Scandia, also had lost her husband in 1893. Carrie met August Nelson during a church service in Scandia, and they were married on March 3, 1897. A few weeks later, on March 27, Andrew Peterson wrote, "In the afternoon August Nilson and his wife, Karin, also Albertina Nilson were here visiting."

The Nelsons lived for a short time in Maynard and then in Cambridge, Minnesota. In 1902, they returned to Scandia with their children—Edna, born in 1898; Ruth, in 1900; and Amy in 1902. They purchased property *(map 62)* bordering the farms of Andrew Anderson and Theodore Broberg on the south side of the lake. August established himself as a dairy farmer and carpenter at the same time the recreational advantages of the surrounding area were being proclaimed. Nelson's dairy business began to benefit from his milk sales to the hotels on Coney Island.

3. Oscar Erick Larson was the proprietor of the O. E. Larson Mortuary. The business is in existence today as the O. E. Larson-Osborne Chapel.

A story in the May 6, 1904, edition of the *Waconia Patriot* reported "Reinhold Zeglin and family have returned to Coney Island for the season and are busily engaged in putting their grounds into first class shape before any of their guests arrive. The Hotels *[sic]* will open on Saturday, May 28th." On May 27, the paper reported, "The Minneapolis Market Gardener's Association will hold its 7th annual picnic here on Wednesday, June 15. They expect to bring out between 1000 and 1200 people on their excursion."

Amy Nelson (Mrs. Earl Lyford) remembered the stories of her older sister Edna's frightful experience during the 1904 tornado that leveled the Nelson farm. Outdoors in the farmyard, Edna had looked up to see an ominous formation approaching from a westerly direction, above and across the water and the southwest edge of the island. During the split second when it seemed the whirling mass and the water were one, she screamed, "The lake is coming to get us!" There was a rushing roar like that of a speeding train and it was over.

The family miraculously survived. The house and all the barns were demolished. Carrie's trunk was perched up in a tree and their clothing lay scattered about in the woods at the Andrew Anderson farm.

The August Nelson family stayed with their neighbors, Theodore and Johanna Broberg, until they moved into the upstairs room at Rudolph Hilk's farm *(map 6)*. Their temporary residence was located close to August's family home on the northwest shore of Waconia Lake.

Flora's Strange Situation

Theodore Broberg's marriage to Johanna Gustafson on February 28, 1899, began the second generation on the Broberg homestead. Theodore and Johanna raised grain crops and a large herd of dairy cows with help from hired men. Later, their children–Elwell, Gustaf, Gordon, Theodore, Waldo, Catherine, and Margaret–did their share of the work as well.

Church-related socials and Broberg family gatherings usually included the Lundstens. Cousin

August and Karin Nelson

Rhoda Lundsten stayed as an overnight guest during student days at the Waconia High School, when drifting snow blocked the roads home.

When the tornado devastated the settlement in 1904, the large sturdy oaks were uprooted all around the Broberg home. Although the house itself, which had replaced the log cabin in 1877, received only minor damage from mud blown in through broken windows, the barn and farm animals were all destroyed with the exception of one mare.

When the storm was over, members of the Broberg family heard the whinny of a horse. After following the sound to its source, they stared in disbelief. Flora, the horse, had been lifted thirty feet into the air and dropped into an open space in the roof of the Cedar Lake Ice House. She had been set inside the building between the wall and tons of cakes of ice and sawdust. After a barrier of ice was torn away, she was released. She lived out the rest of her days pulling the family buggy. In the front yard of the farm, a depression that indicates Flora's grave still remains.

At Rest in the Hog Yard

Albert Schwichtenberg (*map 36*), son of Herman and Anna, said that when he was born, the first family shanty was no longer standing, but had been replaced by a large family dwelling. He spoke fondly about his brothers and sisters as he told of their experiences when the tornado struck: "The kids were still in the barn with the animals when suddenly without warning the cupola and doors were jerked and twisted off the barn. They blew away!" The family observed the scene and saw that none of the shingles remained on the house. The shed was gone. The windmill had been toppled by the whirling wind, which was blowing in two different directions!

The Schwichtenbergs, as well as every youngster within the settlement continued to receive their schooling, even though the Scandia school was destroyed. Although the minutes of the Scandia School District make only a brief reference to the tornado, a faded photograph of the demolished building, taken after the storm, confirms the story related by William Peltz. The school was lifted off its foundation and dropped about 150 feet away into the Lindenberg hog yard! The corner of the school caught the dirt and dug a deep furrow in the ground before it came to rest on its side. Although most of the building collapsed, not one fragile window or lantern had been broken.

After the storm, the school board met on September 13 at the school grounds to decide what to do. Frank Lundsten called the meeting to order, and Andrew Schraan served as moderator. It was decided to sell the damaged building to the highest bidder and rebuild on the old foundation. Frank Lundsten purchased the wrecked building for $35. According to William Peltz, Lundsten used the windows from the school to replace those broken in the church.

It is curious that even though the widespread swath of the storm leveled several adjacent farms located in the vicinity of the school, Scandia Baptist Church escaped serious harm. Trees were stripped bare of leaves and windows were broken, but otherwise the church was not damaged.

For a short time, school sessions and school board meetings were held in the church. A new school was built, and later, when the existing road was straightened, the building was removed from its foundation and moved to a location closer to the new road.

Extent of Damage

While Minneapolis, St. Paul, St. Louis Park, Stillwater, Hutchinson, and other communities throughout Minnesota, as well as places in other states, reported the extent of damage wrought by the tornado, the bold headlines of the August 24, 1904, edition of the *Waconia Patriot* screamed: "Waconia is Devastated. Half of the village in ruins. Deadly tornado strikes our little village on Saturday evening, destroys four lives in town and one in the country nearby; injures a score of others; and damages $500,000 worth of property." The report continued:

> At about 6 p.m. the sky began to darken and it became imminent that we would have a heavy rainstorm but no one dreamt what its result or termination would mean to our inhabitants. The first intimation anyone had of the real nature of the storm came at about 7:30 when the sky became illuminated with an electric storm, such as had never before been witnessed here-abouts and then without a seconds warning, the holocaust was among us....Mrs. E. Amblard's cottage, Villa Marie was literally buried in a mass of fallen trees....The pavilion and summer house was tumbled and wrecked....The lower end of the island where is situated Monsieur Amblard's elegant cottage, Villa Emile, is a scene of carnage and desolation. Monster trees are strewn about so that it is almost impossible to pass through.

Other than the destruction of a small cottage

owned by Reinhold Zeglin, and a number of trees, the island hotels and other buildings were spared.

Just before the tornado hit, Beda Anderson's brother-in-law, O. E. Larson, walked to her lakeshore home from the M. & St. L. (also known as the Coney Island) Depot. Meanwhile, a large group of passengers boarded omnibuses for rides to Waconia. Of those waiting for the carriers to return for a second pickup trip, A. C. Klanke reported later to the *Waconia Patriot*, "There were in the depot about twenty or thirty people. There was little rain just then, and after waiting about five minutes or so, Louis Krueger and myself started for town at a rapid walk, but the rain came down in torrents . . . . Clear Water *[sic)* Lake presented a sight I shall never forget. Lightning played about and the thunder was terrific and it seemed as if Satan was holding high carnival." Klanke was later guided into town by, "A lantern at a distance carried by one looking for unfortunates."

By September 2, the *Waconia Patriot* explained that the work of rebuilding churches, business places, and homes was in progress. Several photographs featured the wreckage of buildings as well as a street "where not a single structure remains and in which seventeen homes were swept away."

Although the paper reported that, "The M. & St. L. railroad company has broken ground for its large new depot [in Waconia] which will be 64 x 58 and strictly modern," the articles did not include information about the passengers who were left stranded at the Coney Island Depot that evening.

These neighborhood scenes reveal all that remained on August and Carrie Nelson's farm as well as the school in Scandia.

At the John Zieman/Simon Peltz farm. From left: William Peltz, Otto Schwichtenberg, William Klatt, and Hank ("Happy") Hawiller, who was Fritchof Anderson's hired man.

CHAPTER 23

The Changing Scenes

A New Beginning

After the tornado, the demolished buildings on the Andrew Anderson farm were eventually replaced through Andrew's effort as a building contractor. He supplemented the income that supported his family–wife Beda and five children, Donald, Benjamin, Virginia, and twins Lucille and Leonard–by selling milk products from his large dairy herd. In later years, he managed a business known as the Waconia Creamery Association and served as its president.

Andrew's father, Per Daniel Anderson, was one of many who lived to witness the tribute local people bestowed upon their Civil War veterans. The citizens of Carver County showed their appreciation to them by dedicating a memorial statue of a soldier after it had been set in place at the Waconia City Park. It stands today with 588 inscriptions, chiseled on four sides of the base, recording the name of every soldier from Carver County who fought in the war. Fifty-six of these men were from Laketown Township. The words on the inscription are: "To the memory of the defenders of the Union, 1861-1865. Erected by the citizens in Carver County in 1892."

Per Daniel Anderson was seventy-eight years old when he passed away January 10, 1906. Caroline was also seventy-eight when she died February 10, 1913.

Although Beda Anderson died in 1923 at the age of forty-seven, leaving a young family, Andrew Anderson lived until he was seventy-five years old. He passed away August 15, 1948. On July 4, the month before his death, the Swedish author, Vilhelm Moberg, visited him. Moberg was seeking answers to questions about incidents referred to in the Peterson diaries, perhaps making decisions about locations or the background setting for the books he intended to write. Andrew's daughter, Virginia, a schoolteacher home from St. Paul during the summer vacation, remembered the visit. Unfortunately, her father, who was very ill, no longer had the strength to speak. She told Moberg that her sister and brothers were gathered with other relatives that very afternoon for a celebration at the Lundsten's Sunny Hill Farm *(map 42)*, and suggested that he visit there to speak to them. Although it is doubtful that he did so, it is known that Moberg spent a brief period of time at the Scandia Baptist Church. One of his private photographs shows him walking on the grounds in front of the historic building.

The Andrew Anderson home faces Waconia Lake to the west, and is approximately 300 yards from the corner where County Road 30 and the township road meet. Even in Peterson's time, the property was bordered by these roads. Today, children of Andrew and Beda Anderson–Lucille, a widow and a former nurse; Virginia, a retired schoolteacher; and Donald, a farmer who never married–still live in the dwelling which was rebuilt after the tornado. (Among the family's cherished possessions are several pieces of their mother's mirror, broken during the tornado; a wall clock; a pair of wooden shoes; a chest of drawers made for Per Daniel by John Nelson; and one of

This photograph of the Andrew Anderson family was taken during the flu epidemic of 1912. It was arranged by Beda because of her concern over the possibility of losing a family member. Back (from left): Virginia, Donald, and Ben. Front: Beda, the twins Lucille and Leonard, and Andrew. (No one became ill.)

the rope beds from their grandparents' home.)

Brothers Leonard and Benjamin both married and are grandparents. Leonard lives in Minneapolis and Benjamin in Chaska.

Andrew and Beda Anderson's neighbors, August and Carrie Nelson, rebuilt their home and barns and added another daughter, Adeline, born May 3, 1906, to their family. August continued to increase the size of his dairy herd while selling milk in ten-gallon cans at $.85 a can to the hotels on Coney Island. These containers were loaded on Zeglin's launch, which also transported crowds of people from the train at the Coney Island Depot.

At that time, Edna, Ruth, and Amy Nelson attended school in Waconia.[1] They traveled to town with their father when he made his daily milk deliveries to the nearby creamery. After it became apparent that their younger sister Adeline was not happy with her teacher, she was allowed to attend the Scandia School instead, while her sisters continued in Waconia.

The children liked to watch the steamers, "Coney Island," the "Chief," and the "Klondike," loaded with passengers for moonlight cruises and day excursions on the lake. Their grandparents, John and Benedicta Nelson, sometimes provided lodging for guests who disembarked from the Great Northern train depot *(map 12)* on their side of the lake.

Even though Andrew Schultz's double-decked carrier "Niagra" could accommodate up to 300 passengers, and the "Chief" and "Klondike" each carried fifty people, there were days when everything that would float was pressed into service on the lake.

John and Benedicta Nelson also provided housing for Lillie Larson, Per Daniel and Caroline Anderson's granddaughter and frequent houseguest of the Petersons, during her teaching assignment in District 42 *(map 9)*, at the school next to Nelson's farm. Lillie taught school at Pipestone, Minnesota, before she moved to the Scandia area. She continued to live with the Nelsons even after Benedicta passed away in 1908 at the age of seventy-four. Albertina kept house for the family until her father's death, May 25, 1912, at the age of eighty-five. The household broke up after both

1. When Edna came of age, she married Oscar Cutkosky, the superintendent of schools in Clarkfield, Minnesota. During a transition period in her husband's career, Edna lived with Andrew Peterson's daughter Emma while Edna taught school in Scandia.

CONEY ISLAND HOTELS, EMIL KRUEGER, Propr.

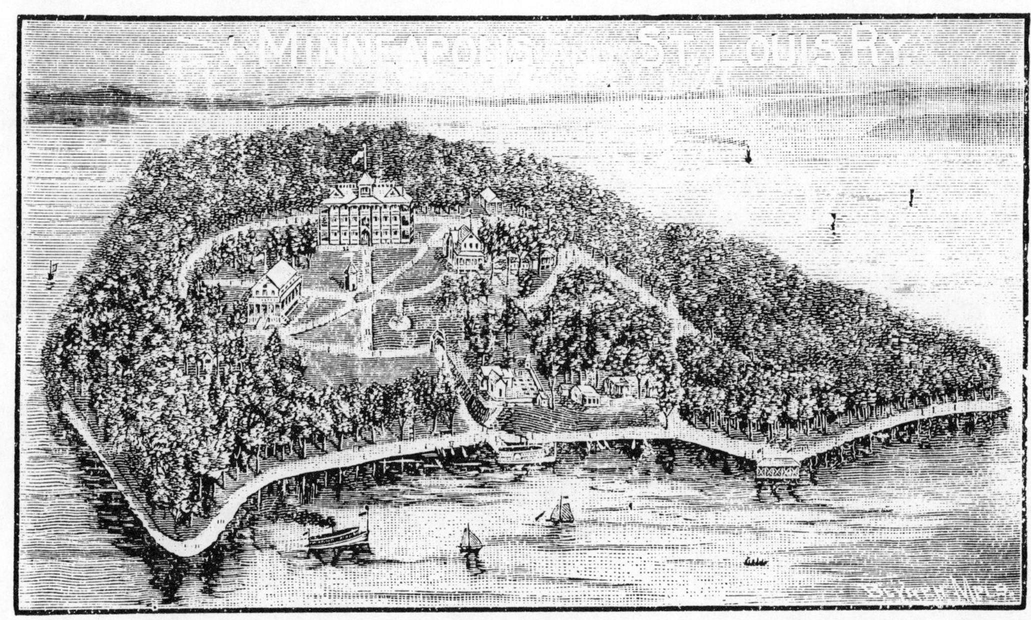

Coney Island Hotels, Situated on the Beautiful Coney Island, in Carver County, Minnesota, 30 Miles West of the Twin Cities, Steamboat Connections with the M. & St. L. R. R. and at Request also with the Great Northern Railroad.

The Healthiest Place on Earth. The Hotels Open from June 1st Until October 1st.

RATES MODERATE.

Waconia, Minn., ... *189*

parents were gone. Then Lillie moved in with a family named Meuftels who also lived in the vicinity of the school. Albertina and Inez traveled to Seattle, Washington, where they lived out their lives. Edward and Solomon remained at home, but neither married. Edward lived to be seventy-eight and Solomon eighty-five. August, the oldest of the family, was the only one of eight brothers and sisters to have children of his own. He died in 1935, and Karin followed in 1943. Both are buried at the Scandia cemetery.

For Amy Nelson Lyford and those of her generation, picnics in the surrounding farmyards, in the glow of flickering flares and campfires, are vague memories, as is the memory of the male quartet in which Andrew Anderson's sons, Ben and Donald, sang. The games, "Last Couple Out," "Prince of Paris Lost His Hat," and "Old Mrs. Mulligan Died Last Night," always accompanied by peals of joyous laughter, were among the social activities that strengthened their friendships. Even today, certain church activities bring Amy and others of her generation back to the place of their birth in Scandia.[2]

While Lillie Larson taught school at District 42, she observed the gradual changes taking place in the community life of Scandia. After grandmother Caroline Anderson passed away in 1913, her uncle, Fritchof Anderson, and his bride Amy remained on the farm for only a brief period of time. Then he purchased a larger place not far from Scandia, on the Scandia road. After the Andersons moved, William Goethke and his family lived there.

A succession of dry years with poor crop yield followed soon after the Goethkes' arrival. When the triple-walled wood silo blew down in a windstorm, it had to be replaced. Such adverse situations made it increasingly impossible for the Goethkes to meet their mortgage payments. Then came even more disaster. Spontaneous combus-

2. Amy Nelson Lyford inherited the family organ (which was said to be in excellent condition) from her grandfather John Nelson. She donated it to Bethel College when the Scandia Baptist Church was relocated on the campus grounds.

tion caused a tremendous explosion in the hayloft of the barn. Shingles flew into the air. Soon the entire barn, including the new silo, was engulfed in flames which quickly spread to the hog house, the machine shed, and the granary. In less than an hour it was over. The roof of the house burned in four places, and the twelve doors on the new cement silo were completely burned out. The only building left without damage was the chicken barn.

Not long after the fire, this property became part of a large tract of farmland purchased as an addition to the Jesuit College Campus; it is now the St. Paul Bible College.

Today the site of the farm can be identified by the windmill. Although it is no longer used, this tower still overlooks the cultivated farm fields as it did yesterday.

Of the second generation of neighbors living near the families of Andrew Anderson and August Nelson on the shore of Waconia Lake, Theodore Broberg was laid to rest in 1947. His wife Johanna was also buried in Scandia the following year, and the farm *(map 61)* passed on to Elwell and his wife Anna. Elwell died on July 13, 1974, but since then Anna is seldom by herself. Her sons James, Thomas, Philip, and their families are frequent visitors to their 1877 dwelling.

Although most of the smaller sheds are gone now, the barn still stands, though deteriorated and empty. The remaining fields continue to yield a harvest of crops for neighboring farmers who rent and work the land.

About six acres of farmland on the west side of John Broberg's homestead were sold recently to the Christian Missionary Alliance Church in Waconia, and the members have already started the first step in a three-phase building program.

The Gypsy Camp in Scandia

During the late 1800s, Charles Klatt, a mason's apprentice, left his uncle Henry Pintz's home in Carver to marry Annie Zieman, one of John and Ida Zieman's six daughters. The Klatts first made their home in Waconia, but moved to Scandia after they purchased the Nilsson homestead *(map 47, 47A)* from Nicholas Swenson's son Hans on November 18, 1904.[3]

3. Although Nicholas Swenson's cemetery marker establishes the date of his death as 1903, little is known about his family and their departure from the settlement the following year.

The tornado had damaged this property, too, so Charles had to reshingle the roof on the house and replace the windmill as well as part of the L-shaped barn. Even so, as he viewed the surrounding farms after the tornado, he realized he was better off than most people. Adam Fisher's home *(map 40)* had been twisted on its foundation. All of his barns had been damaged. Fisher also lost a horse and seven head of cattle.

The five Klatt children were born in Waconia; the three eldest, Charles, Fred, and Minnie, were no longer living at home when their parents moved to Scandia. But for the other two, William and John, the move to the country resulted in a drastic change in lifestyle. Living on a farm meant a great deal of responsibility, and, to make matters worse, the children found that their work was never done! Their young cousins, the Peltzes and Petermans, were equally busy on the neighboring farms—and equally full of complaints.

Each day, just before milking time, the children listened for the distant sound of cowbells, determined the direction of the grazing cows, and then chased them across the meadows and into the barn. In later years, the Klatt nephews and nieces confessed to riding the cows bareback all the way home and tying the tails of certain heifers to the stanchions before milking them.

Charles Klatt and his family soon discovered that their farm attracted Gypsy caravans traveling through Scandia. These visitors frequently hobbled their horses to nearby trees (close to the site of the first log school—*map 47A)*, where they were content to graze while the Gypsies occupied the surrounding area with their wagons. Apparently it did not occur to them they were camping on private property in this shady grove. These trespassers sometimes begged for food and allowed their children to roam from place to place. Farm families often complained that eggs, chickens, and garden produce were missing following their stay. These intrusions finally ceased after John received permission from his parents to remove the trees. He labored on weekends as well as after his daily chores and eventually turned the entire grove into firewood.

During one of the last conversations John Klatt and his cousin Bill Peltz would have together (on November 18, 1977), John explained his reason for remembering a particular late fall when the weather was so mild and dry that his father plowed his field on December 24, and could have continued till late afternoon. Instead, he decided

Annie (Zieman) Klatt and Charles with Minnie, Fred, and Charles, Jr.

to rest the horses so they could make the trip to church in Waconia that Christmas Eve. On the way, he noticed the beginning flakes of snow and how quickly the temperature had been dropping ever since sundown. When the children's part in the Christmas program was over, for reasons he could not even explain, he quickly ushered the family out of the church and headed for home. It was already becoming difficult to maneuver the horses through darkness and gathering drifts of snow, and by the time they reached home they were in the midst of a raging blizzard.

Although John Klatt did not recall the date of that Christmas storm, he did remember his shock when he awoke on Christmas day and saw huge drifts of snow. One drift was so high it entirely blocked the view of the barn from the house and stayed that way until it melted in the spring.

John also commented that numerous bushels of apples were harvested from trees originally started from seedlings in Peterson's orchard. They were a favorite family treat. The Russian greening, the Wealthy, and a hard sour apple, a winter keeper that turned sweet in the spring, were their favorites.

John was also in the cattle barn during the time his father discovered that wooden shoes left behind by the Swensons were good for use in the barnyard but could cause problems if misused. In a moment of frustration, Charles Klatt kicked at a cow, sending the shoe hurtling into the air and against a kerosene lantern suspended from a beam in the barn. The lamp fell and ignited the straw. Although there was a brief moment of panic, John and Charles quickly brought the fire under control.

John Klatt, who eventually married Julie Krenz, fought in World War I. He owned and operated a filling station in St. Bonifacius, but lived in Waconia until his death on December 17, 1978.

When Charles and Annie Klatt's son William married, he and his bride Lilly moved in with the elder Klatts. Charles's grandson Karl inherited the farm. He and his wife Marjorie built another home on the land and sold most of the original Nilsson property, including the brick dwelling in which his parents, his grandparents, and Nicholas Swenson had all lived. He reserved acreage west of the farm, and the Klatts moved into their new residence. The barns, situated between their new place and the old, still stand. Although extensively remodeled, the original farm home remains on the property bordered by the 50.

An Attraction at Isabelle's Home

John Swanson lived with his parents, Swan and Ingrid *(map 65)*. He owned and managed the St. Boni Lumberyard in St. Bonifacius, but also had other profitable interests. He was one of the original shareholders in the Minnetonka Creamery Company in that village and a financial investor in the Waconia Creamery Association.

John was fifty-three years old when his parents died within months of each other. That same year, on December 27, 1911, he married Per Daniel and Caroline Anderson's daughter Isabelle.

After moving into a smaller guest cottage located on the farm, John had the original home and barn placed on rollers and had horses pull the house to its present location on East First Street in Waconia, and the barn to the former Andrew Bergquist homestead. There, John's brother-in-law, Andrew Anderson, used it to house his growing herd of dairy cattle. The barn, which has since been painted white, is still used on the Anderson farm.

Isabelle and John Swanson built a new home on the hill overlooking Waconia Lake, said to be the first modern residence in the vicinity. The indoor plumbing was a feature of special interest, especially for the children. Since the house was near a lake, Isabelle was all too often left to clean up a

Isabelle Anderson Swanson

trail of sand from the beach to the bathroom after visiting nieces and nephews returned to their homes.

The Swansons frequently cruised the lake from their launch. But they did not live very long to enjoy their lives together or their new lake home. They passed away only a few years after their marriage. John died on December 9, 1918, and Isabelle on April 8, 1919. Isabelle's sister Louise (Mrs. O. E. Larson) and her family from Minneapolis used the home as a summer place until they sold the property.

Today, the outward appearance of the home remains much the same as it did when John and Isabelle built it, except that a wing was added to the east side of the house. Out in front and beyond the yard, across the road dividing it from the beach area, five family dwellings sit all in a row. Each commands a private view of power boats and sailboats being navigated for pleasure, as well as of regattas and Fourth of July fireworks displays from Coney Island.

Things To Do, Show, and Share

After John Lundsten's death in 1894, his widow, Maja Lisa, spent her final years at Sunny Hill Farm *(map 42)* with son Frank's family. Until health problems prevented her from sharing the work, Maja Lisa assisted Mary (her daughter-in-law) with household and kitchen chores. The house was often filled with the enticing aroma of hot rye bread, cinnamon rolls, biscuits, and kringles baking in the old kitchen range. The coffee pot was always at hand, ready to provide instant refreshment for visitors and peddlers, who were expected to share in eating the treats.

Birthdays and holidays were special occasions for celebrations, and Maja Lisa seemed to enjoy an extra measure of contentment on those days. She was constantly surrounded by her grandchildren, because her house was the natural gathering place. Before those occasions and the arrival of aunts, uncles, and cousins, there were chores such as scrubbing, washing, and much baking to do.

The excitement started well before Uncle Otto Lundsten's shiny-topped buggy, pulled by Nellie, the horse, and the team from his livery stable, were first sighted as they traveled along the road to the farmhouse. The galloping horses bringing other relatives were thrilling sights for Frank and Mary's children, who were eager for the arrival of their cousins. There were things to do, show, and share. There were corn ears and crooked-necked squash to use for their dolls, garlands of wild flowers to be made, currants and gooseberries to pick, empty corn cribs to play in, willow swamps to roam, kittens to search for in the hayloft, piglets to fondle, and new calves to pet.

The Fourth of July was also a memorable day. Families and friends waved flags and sang the "Battle Hymn of the Republic" as their buggies were pulled along country lanes or on the lakeshore road. Celebrants gathered at church or at their chosen farmyard for annual picnics, fun, and frolic.

Maja Lisa Lundsten, Caroline Anderson, and Elsa Peterson were close friends and neighbors who had been privileged to share these relationships with their families. Of the matrons who had survived those harsh pioneer years, Caroline Anderson was the first to die, February 10, 1913, and Maja Lisa was the second to leave her circle of loved ones in death, only a month later, on March 27, 1913. She was buried beside her husband John and several children in the cemetery *(map 51)* across the road from the Scandia Baptist Church.

The Lundstens' homestead is gone now, but children and grandchildren still have happy memories of Sunny Hill Farm. They remember watching John, and later Frank, carpentering in the barn, and writing their names and initials on the barn doors. They remember rows of peonies in Grandma's garden, the little round kerosene stove in the upstairs room, the old windup phonograph, the noise of the milking machine that replaced the rhythmic sound of milk being squirted by hand into pails at milking time, frequent trips down the hill at night to "read the catalog" by candlelight in the outhouse, late evening walks in Buelows' pasture, spearing pickerel in the creek, watching the sky for ducks flying south, tobogganing in the moonlight, and skating on the pond called Pig's Eye.

John's and Maja Lisa's devotion to their religious beliefs and the time they took to nurture their children provided their grandson, John Everett Lundsten, reason to express his gratitude by saying:

I cannot thank God enough for the fact that I was born in a Christian home. Our God-fearing and church-going grandparents first established the home, and then continued by our dear parents and being continued by the third, fourth and fifth generations. All down the line we are trying to follow in the steps of our ancestors' and family beliefs.

The farm where "the horses floundered through deep snow drifts when dad [Frank] took us to the little old school a mile and a half away," and other land adjoining it have been incorporated into the grounds that now belong to the Hennepin County Park Reserve. The buildings were removed, and the land, once painstakingly grubbed free of trees, is returning to its natural state. Pig's Eye is no longer just a pond. A dam has been built at the

Lundsten family in 1901. *Front* (from left): Rhoda, Mary with Hazel, Mabel, Frank, Everett, and Esther. *Back* (from left): Amy, Clarence, and Frances. (Uncles of the children are shown below.)

John George Lundsten

Joseph Oscar Lundsten

Otto Wilhelm Lundsten

The Scandia Literary Society in 1910. *Back or first row* (from left): Amy Lundsten, Edward Molnau, John Klatt, Arnes Peltz, William Klatt, Tillie Molnau, Frank Peterson. *Second row:* Anton Zahler, Jean Wendt, Walter Schwichtenberg, Minnie Groth, Fritchof Anderson, William Peltz. *Third row:* Amy Lindenberg, John Peltz, Annie Zahler, George Zahler, Dora Schwichtenberg, Anton Pofahl. *Front row:* Amelia Lietzau (lived with grandmother Brethorst) and Frances Zahler.

inlet to Parley Lake, and the water from Sunny Brook is backed up and spreads itself throughout the lowland. Current maps refer to this body of water as Lundsten's Lake.[4]

Although most of the reserve is a woodland at rest, a refuge for wildlife, some of the trails in the park are used for recreational purposes.

Community Clubs

In the early part of the twentieth century, community clubs played a strong role in rural life, and those in Scandia were no exception. Milo J. Peterson, professor emeritus at the University of Minnesota School of Agriculture, grew up in Scandia and belonged to some of its clubs. He described an organization known as the Literary Society and told of its influence upon young people in the community from about 1909 until January, 1918. Members voted to buy a copy of *Robert's Rules of Order*, and it is apparent from the minutes of these meetings that parliamentary procedure was part of the entertainment. Some of the motions were obviously facetious, most likely made so they could be amended, tabled, or voted down.

A program always followed the business meeting. It featured group singing or other musical entertainment, readings, debates, spelldowns, and "minute" speeches. One such debate, "Resolved: that Cattle Raising is more Profitable than Hog Raising," was decided in favor of the hogs. Other

4. This wetland which is part of the watershed contributing to the flow of water into Lake Minnetonka eventually finds its way to Minnehaha Falls and beyond to the Mississippi River.

Club members and drama participants, William Klatt, William Peltz, and John Peterman.

topics were "Local Buying vs, Mail Order" and "That Women be Allowed to Vote," in which the affirmatives won. Speeches limited to one minute were popular and topics ranged from "Should Congress Revise the Tariff?" to "Should Paris Fashions be Abolished in the U.S.?"

Usually someone gave local news or current news or events as part of the program. The society also promoted special activities from time to time. Basket and ice cream socials were popular. Meetings were held in the school, where the main expense was oil for the lamps. (Two lamp chimneys and some oil came to $.35.) Officers included a sergeant-at-arms whose duty seems to have been to light and care for the lamps, and a "critic" who assessed the speeches and debates. The "minute" speeches and the participants on May 24, 1912, were as follows:

Bread Making	Malinda Pofahl
Art of Dressmaking	Amy Lundsten
Outlook for the Crop	John Klatt
Skill of Painting	Ted Lobitz
Automobiling	Otto Schwichtenberg
Married Life	Ed Molnau
Physical Culture Methods	John Peterman

The Farmers' Club soon took precedence over the older literary society while continuing many of its functions. Such clubs met the social needs of the community, and they were educational in that day of limited opportunities. They provided training in conducting meetings and transacting business, and their members gained confidence in their ability to get to their feet to speak on a topic of the day. The members who were skilled at playing an instrument or singing had frequent opportunities to perform.

Of the Farmers' Club, Milo Peterson said:

> The hired hands on the farms of the community are always present at meetings and functions of the club. For the hired men to miss a meeting is a rare occurrence in Lakeside.
>
> Because of the beautiful lake there is always a family or two of summer residents from Minneapolis or St. Paul. When asked what they found in the Farmers' Club that brought them to meetings the young ladies blushed slightly, the young men admitted a weakness for country lassies, the boys mentioned the lunch, while the parents frankly stated that they enjoyed it far more than their own bridge clubs at home because 'the people are so interested,

natural, and friendly.' Whatever the reason it is evident that they found something worthwhile in it.

In 1914, the Smith-Lever Act provided federal support for "extension" programs and the county agent movement. Nearly every county in the state eventually formed a local farm bureau. County agents provided guidance and informational services to support farming interests. In compliance with his responsibilities as county agent, George A. King initiated the local 4-H movement which stands for "Head, Heart, Hands, and Health," and started the Future Farmers of America organization in the local public schools. These organizations phased the old Farmers' Club out of existence. In Waconia, Etta Goemenpott, the home economics teacher, also promoted local interest in the 4-H. Other 4-H groups were started with the help of King's secretary, Mrs. Melvin Mulhern (Florence Lobitz), who was familiar with the program. She had been a member of the Scandia (or Lakeside) Farmers' Club, and had her own beginnings in 4-H work under Etta Goemenpott. Mulhern then became the group leader of the Lakeside 4-H and spent thirty-two years working with young people interested in the program.

With the help of others such as Mrs. Art Krause, a twenty-one-year veteran leader for the neighboring Pleasant Valley 4-H, and Mr. and Mrs. Henry Wrase, for thirty-five years leaders of the Chaska (or Sugar City) 4-H, the dream of a 4-H building on the Carver County fair grounds became a reality. The frame structure was called the "King Building" in honor of George A. King for his promotion of farming and related activities in Carver County.

The Blazing Inferno

Twenty-one years after the tornado there was another Scandia school disaster. This time fire destroyed it! In 1925, Albert Schwichtenberg, a former student and later a school board member, was helping the Pofahl family *(map 37)* with their early winter butchering when he heard the Waconia fire bell. Through leafless trees he saw the school engulfed in flames. The school minutes do not mention the fire, but they do discuss plans for rebuilding.

Of two Carver County women who held similar positions in office as superintendent of schools, it was Estella L. Elke who met with community residents in the Scandia Baptist Church.[5] On that day, February 26, 1926, an election was held to determine whether to rebuild the school immediately or to adjourn classes for several months. Twenty-two people were in favor of rebuilding, eleven were not. Meanwhile, some students met in the Scandia Baptist Church; others were transported to nearby schools. On January 31, 1927, school board member Schwichtenberg called a meeting to present proposals and plans for a new building. Committee building members appointed at this meeting were Carl Lobitz, Frank Lundsten, Sr., and Otto C. Peterman. This committee drew up specifications for a new school, estimated at a cost of $4,000, which were accepted on March 14. Work on the school started almost immediately.

For as long as the children in the surrounding countryside attended the Scandia school, its familiar name helped keep the name of the settlement alive, especially after the post office was discontinued. After the school consolidated with Waconia School District 44 (now District 110), the building which had served as a gathering place for community activities was no longer used for school functions. The building itself was converted into a private dwelling and is still used for this purpose.

William Peltz, or "Bill" as his friends respectfully called him, gave unselfishly of his time in public service. He served thirty-eight years as the clerk on the board of the Laketown School District 17. He also served as treasurer of Laketown Township for thirty-seven years, during which time he supervised the expenditure of over $750,000 in township funds.[6]

District 17 had been started by the pioneers in 1858 and closed one hundred years later with a financial summary by Peltz, clerk of the Laketown School District 17, on July 1, 1958.

5. After the state law was passed in 1876 (granting females the right to hold school office) Matilda ("Tillie") Ochs, a schoolteacher from Chaska, served as superintendent of schools in 1899 and for several years thereafter. At that time a teaching certificate, good character references and a stable personality were the only prerequisites for that office. Tillie Ochs' and Estella Elke's achievements were considerable in that era before and immediately after women had the vote. (In 1920, the nineteenth amendment to the United States Constitution allowed women throughout the United States the right to vote during general elections and for all purposes.)

6. William Peltz also served as a board member and past president of the Waconia Creamery Association and a board member of the Laketown Fire Insurance Company. Up until a few years before his death in 1978, he campaigned actively for Republican Party candidates.

The Cooperative Creamery

Hubert and Regina (Kirsch) Lohmar, both natives of Germany, met in Illinois, were married, and in 1857 traveled to Minnesota Territory where they purchased a wild, undeveloped tract (*map 59*) close to Waconia Lake. They moved into the small cabin which had been built by the squatter who sold them the land. In time, they enlarged the half-acre clearing and had forty-five acres under cultivation. Their sons, John, Jacob, and Hubert, Jr., helped them on the farm.

Eventually John went to Minneapolis to work as a merchant, and Jacob farmed his own place in Watertown Township. Hubert, Jr. married Alma Weise (whose sister was the wife of Herman Schwichtenberg) and brought her to live with his aging parents.

Regina Lohmar died in 1903. The next year, the tornado killed Hubert, Sr. and wrecked the entire farm. Hubert, Jr. and Alma were unhurt, even though they were also in the house.[7] After the elder Lohmar's death, Hubert and Alma cleared away the wreckage, rebuilt the house and barns, and maintained a large dairy herd.

Theophilus Haecker, often called the "Father of Dairying in Minnesota," was brought from Wisconsin to start the dairying school at the University of Minnesota's College of Agriculture. Haecker, a strong advocate of scientific dairying principles and of cooperation, apparently influenced Lohmar. Haecker wrote a bulletin in 1894 called "Organizing Co-operative Creameries," and also spoke, traveled, wrote, and visited farmers to promote cooperatives. He had support from the Farmers' Alliance and Grangers as well as a number of Carver County farmers.

In 1908, Hubert, Andrew Peterson's son Frank, and Andrew Anderson, the son of Per Daniel and Caroline, paid $4,000 for a small creamery located on the lakeshore close to the old sawmill in Waconia. They operated it as a cooperative. Members delivered milk to the creamery and then shared in the profits, which were based on the amount of milk each person contributed. Called the Lakeshore Creamery, it specialized in making butter and processing other milk products.

Albert Schwichtenberg recalled the rickety dock at the creamery where he used to unload milk cans. August Gomoll and his wife had been the owners of the business. Now old, they found it difficult to maintain the creamery. The building was run down. The volume of the business (never a threat to Peterman's Creamery operation in Waconia) was low because the Gomolls failed to keep up with promotional work and necessary building repairs.

The new cooperative business soon outgrew the old building and so, about 1914, Lohmar, Peterson, and Anderson moved into a large cement block building constructed at South Elm Street in Waconia.

Lohmar also built a large, two-story duplex next to the cooperative creamery to provide living space for the families of the buttermaker and the manager. He matched the same brown-toned cement blocks used during the construction of the creamery and used it as facing on the house exterior.

Production at the new building increased until the equipment could no longer handle the volume. Eventually, the cooperative negotiated a purchase price and bought out the enlarged creamery Henry Peterman had started. Following its move into Peterman's building, the cooperative stepped up production and incorporated the process of making casein, a phosphoprotein which is the principal ingredient of cheese. By 1927, newspaper reports stated that local creamery patrons received nearly $3 million annually from this and other creameries located throughout Carver County. The county's total farm production was valued at $7 million.

Hubert Lohmar served as the secretary for the Waconia Creamery Association until his sudden death in 1917 from an apparent heart attack. On the afternoon of April 19, when it was reported his three-year-old son Kermit was missing, Hubert, remembering it was about time for the 6:00 train, ran in the direction of the track. Soon after the train passed through to the Coney Island Depot, the child returned home, telling his mother that daddy had "gone to sleep" in the pasture.

Mrs. Lohmar struggled with the work on the farm until she could no longer carry on. Eventually she moved with her three children—Alfred, Leona, and Kermit—into the duplex next to the vacant creamery building in town.

In 1939, the St. Paul Bank of Cooperatives sent Arnold Westphal, an expert on dairy products manufacturing, to help the Waconia Creamery Association resolve a $100,000 debt brought on by

7. The Lohmars lived with Alma's sister Anna and her husband Herman Schwichtenberg (*map 36*) while they were building their new home. Their nephew, Albert Schwichtenberg, was eight years old at this time.

overexpansion. After installing an elaborate stainless steel, milk-drying equipment system, the cooperative suddenly found the volume of product it received from its patrons was not adequate to carry on the operation of the expanded plant. To make it worse, farmers were holding back on deliveries, fearing they would not get paid.

Westphal was appointed general manager of the creamery. Although this six-week assignment to save the cooperative from bankruptcy turned into a major challenge, he managed to restore the farmers' faith, in part through a series of public meetings.

The creamery business went on as usual while Westphal attempted to implement his idea of using the milk-drying equipment to dry eggs. It was not until World War II that he was given the opportunity to prove the merits of the plan. Not satisfied with using frozen eggs for army consumption, the government negotiated an arrangement whereby a truck with a stainless steel bulk tank was filled with eggs at a plant on Nicollet Island in Minneapolis. The eggs were then transported to Waconia for drying. The operation paid off the creamery's entire debt and accumulated interest. Westphal's process of drying eggs was also used successfully at several other plants in Ripon and Colfax, Wisconsin.

After the war, patronage at the creamery increased to the point where egg drying was phased out. However, the plant had reached its peak. As farmers supporting the cooperative in Waconia retired, more and more acreage was taken out of production. In Laketown Township, thousands of acres of farmland had been purchased for seminary use as well as for preserve and park purposes. As the remaining farms grew smaller, their dairy herds also decreased.

With competition from twenty nearby creameries, all but two of which were cooperatives, it was no longer profitable to transport milk to Waconia from outside the county. In 1966, the largest creamery in Carver County (also known as the Farmers' or Waconia Cooperative) phased out the dairy products line. Although the creamery itself is no longer in existence, the Waconia Farm Supply–one of the association's diversified business interests–continues to provide local families with a large selection of farm and home supplies.

At the Church

In a booklet prepared for the seventy-fifth anniversary of the Scandia Baptist Church in 1930, the Reverend Carl G. Tideman said of the early years:

> In a primitive pioneer community where law procedure as laid down by established courts was not always in easy reach, we find the church itself serving this purpose . . . . The record states no case shall be taken to court until it first had been brought to the church . . . . All things considered it must be conceded that the church succeeded beyond expectations in this pioneer settlement. Discipline was carried out with a Puritan severity.

On a day-to-day basis, the church continued to be a strong influence in the lives of its members. The structure itself served as a meeting house, drawing many church-related families back to Scandia. The congregation officially opened its centennial celebration with a Sunday service on July 31, 1955. An all-day schedule of events came the following week. Many of the visitors who returned to celebrate the event August 7 had grown up in the community and had established their church ties in Scandia.

After morning worship, the celebrants socialized during an outdoor picnic and attended an afternoon service. The Reverend Paul S. Meyer concluded the anniversary tribute at the cemetery.

An undated newspaper clipping from the *Waconia Patriot* reported that sunny skies and cooler weather created a pleasant situation for those who sat outdoors and listened to the services broadcast over loudspeakers, as well as for those who attended the gathering at the cemetery. "O. W. [Otto Wilhelm] Lundsten, now in his 90th year, of Excelsior presented an ornamental archway to the cemetery association on behalf of himself and his twin sister, the late Mrs. Alice Linder." Visitors had traveled from great distances–Seattle, Washington; Oakland, California; Gary, Indiana; Tempe, Arizona; Des Moines, Iowa; Kansas City, Missouri; Portland, Oregon; and Fargo, North Dakota.

Because the size of the Scandia Baptist Church building limited its potential growth, the congregation decided to build another place of worship. On October 16, 1973, members watched with mixed emotions as this link to the past, their meeting house, was taken from its foundation and lifted to a waiting carrier which transported it to the Bethel College Campus in St. Paul.

The Reverend Carl Tideman served as the minister of the Scandia Baptist Church during the years 1905, 1910, 1913, 1916, 1918, 1919, 1926, 1929, and 1930. He married John Lundsten's daughter Esther Marion, on June 17, 1919. He is buried in the Scandia cemetery.

The site where the church once stood has since become part of a golf course outside the Waconia city limits, within Laketown Township. The new church building was built in a woodland setting close to the original site and the Scandia cemetery. The present church faces State Highway 5, and is bordered by the farm Per Daniel Anderson's grandson, Donald Anderson, now owns.

An English instructor at Bethel, Ms. Jeannine Bohlmeyer, noted the arrival of the church in the December 1, 1973, biweekly publication of *The Standard*, a denominational magazine of the Baptist General Conference. In her memorial tribute entitled, "Lines Written on the Occasion of the Coming of Historic Scandia Church to Bethel," she wrote:

A church board, chopped in northern forest, hauled
Through zero-hardened snow, the heavy horse
Pulling the log-piled sledge to orders bawled
By shrill-voiced lumbermen. Severed from source
Of life and root, a tree no more, but wood
Shaped by screaming sawmill, grooved and planed
By careful craftsman's strong, gnarled hands for good
Tight joining of the neighbor board, and stained
To let the beauty of smooth wood glow
If any trampling feet had eyes to see.
Worn by the years, but sturdy still to show
The steps of servants, saints bound to be free.
One journey more—tree, board, a pilgrim, still,
Telling tomorrow yesterday sought God's will.

Students, faculty members, and visitors have reason to be reverent as they enter the portal of the Scandia Church at Bethel. Prayer services and campus weddings are often held in this pioneer church. The communion set was the gift of Philip and Josephine Johnson (who, many years earlier, had been married by the Reverend F. O. Nilsson). This beautiful possession is kept with the pulpit Andrew Peterson told of hauling to the church in 1876. These items exist with other original furnishings.

Although church work among Roman Catholics was not described in this account portraying the establishment of Protestant churches in the Swedish settlement areas, the work of the Benedictines, Franciscans, and Catholic priests was very much in evidence during the time the Swedish people were establishing their churches.

Local church directories printed in the newspapers identify thirty-four established churches in the area. In addition, at least six Protestant churches are not always listed in the directories. There are seven Catholic churches, three Moravian churches, two Baptist churches, and one each of the Missionary Alliance, Presbyterian, and Methodist churches. The remainder of the denominations represent various branches and synods of the Lutheran church.

Today, the public school system has increased competition from the Catholic and Lutheran parochial schools throughout Carver County as parents seek to create a Christian environment for their children.

Migration from the Twin Cities has infiltrated the predominantly German and Swedish congregations in varying degrees. The Waconia Baptist Church is rural and draws new families from a wide area as well as students from the nearby St. Paul Bible College Campus. The recently formed Baptist church in Chaska draws from the newer residential areas. Although the Minnetrista Baptist Church in St. Bonifacius is predominantly German, it is becoming more mixed. The Trinity Lutheran Church in Watertown (formerly called the *Swedish Evangelical Lutheran Götaholm Congregation, Carver, Minnesota*) is predominantly Swedish and German. It remains rural as does the predominantly Swedish church at West Union.[8]

8. Those who trace their origin to the church at Oscar's Settlement paid tribute to these pioneers and their beginnings by publishing books commemorating their 125th anniversaries in 1983. The East and West Union congregations also held special services on June 19 and during the weekend of August 13 and 14, respectively. The Trinity Lutheran Church at Watertown celebrated with special meetings during the first Sunday of each month (January to November), and also conducted a separate memorial service at the site of the first church.

East Union is no longer only a farming community, and many of the members of the East Union Church work in the city and live in the country. Although still strongly rural, both it and the former Scandia Baptist Church are becoming cosmopolitan.

Of the splinter groups which were once part of the East and West Union congregations, the church brochure entitled, "Welcome to East Union Lutheran Church," noted that the Salem church dissolved its congregation in 1952 and members rejoined the church at East Union. Their church bell replaced the cracked bell at East Union, and the original was placed on a base set close to the entrance road leading into the grounds at the East Union Church.

Although the building once used by the Gotha congregation no longer exists, the Methodist Episcopal Church still stands. Today the building is used as a barn, and the original East and West Union churches currently serve the several generations of families still living there.[9] In 1978, these churches and a complex of buildings (including St. Ansgar's Academy) were placed on the National Register of Historic Places. They are picturesque landmarks in a peaceful country setting.

Making a Home for Leslie

Bill Peltz lived on the homestead bordering the hillside known as the "50" and Andrew Peterson's farm for all but one year of his eighty-eight years. He married Ludmilla Reinitz on August 7, 1932, then built a home close to the Peterson property line, on part of the same land where he was born *(map 34)*. After grandparents John and Therese Peltz died, and his Uncle Christian moved to Buffalo Lake, his father Simon removed the buildings from the 50 *(map 41)*. While these structures were being demolished Bill salvaged the boards from the roof of his grandparents' log home and used the material for the roof on his garage.

Ludmilla Peltz died on November 5, 1942. Although Bill was left with his young son Leslie, he never remarried. Bill's second cousin Harold (the son of Otto and Alma Peterman) and his wife Lillian made their home with Bill to care for Leslie.

Bill sold the entire family complex to the Jesuits in 1958, but the agreement allowed Bill to remain on the property as long as he paid the taxes. Six years later the Petermans moved into a new home built on the northeast corner of Henry and Amelia Peterman's original homestead.

Bill continued to farm, keeping about 80 acres—including the 50—under cultivation until he was eighty-five years old. Leslie, who had married and moved to Excelsior, helped his father whenever he could.

Bill moved to the Lake Auburn Home for the Aged before the sale of his household and farming possesions at an auction held on June 22, 1977.[10] He lived at the Lake Auburn Home until he suffered a stroke on July 1, 1978, was briefly hospitalized, and passed away at the Excelsior Nursing Home on July 22, 1978.

Renters occupied the Zieman and Peltz farms until the Jesuits liquidated their holdings in 1980. Today the Lindley Deardorff family lives on the old John Zieman homestead inherited by Bill's parents, Ida and Simon Peltz. Most buildings still stand. Bill Peltz's farm home is rented.

Until 1980, the rod of land Andrew Peterson gave to Freed for an access road existed as a machine road leading up a slightly rutted incline to the hill and field still referred to as the 50. After the present property owners of the Andrew Peterson farm, Mr. and Mrs. Ward Holasek, purchased the 50, the road, by now abandoned, was plowed under and became part of the fields.

The Holaseks run a small business as hay and sleigh ride operators, and they often take their riders across the fields to the summit of the 50. From this spot, where the home of Hanna and Andrew Hakanson once stood, passengers marvel as they gaze out across the beauty of the fields merging with the St. Paul Bible College Campus (formerly Jesuit property) and view the town of St. Bonifacius off in the distance.

9. The Methodist Episcopal Church located on the farm belonging to Mr. and Mrs. Hillard Berg at 17205 Homestead Road (Section 10 in San Francisco Township) is no longer recognizable as a place of worship. The steeple and windows were removed and the exterior has been faced with steel siding.

10. When the simple wooden benches were sold during this auction, few people realized that they were from the original log school, and that Bill Peltz had carefully preserved them.

The Lakeside Farmers' Club at the Andrew Peterson farm in 1928. Of Andrew and Elsa Peterson's grown children Oscar can be seen wearing the light colored sweater (far left). Charles is standing in the back row (second from right), and Emma is seated to the right of Beatrice Mayer—the girl wearing the bib overalls. John Peltz (tenant farmer) is shown in the center front row with son Roy on his lap. Fifteen years later, Sarah Peterson (shown wearing dark sweater at far right) inherited the Andrew Peterson homestead.

Sjungen med stort bifall av Smålands Sångarförbund vid den stora Olympiska Sångarfesten 1912.

Till Smålands Sångarförbund.

Smålandssången
"Röd lyser stugan"

ord av **Linnéa Andrén** född Widéen

komponerad för manskör av

Ivar Widéen

1. För manskör .... Kr. —40
2. Arr. för en röst och piano ... » 1.80
3. Arr. för piano med bifog. text » 1.80

Stockholm
Abr. Lundquist, Musikförlag

CHAPTER 24

The Song of Småland

An enormously popular Swedish song, "Smålandssången: 'Röd Lyser Stugan' " – "The Song of Småland: 'Red Shines the Cabin' " – became the instrument by which the granddaughters of Andrew Peterson's sister, Maria Christina Anderson, made contact with the granddaughter of Andrew's brother, Johannes Rydell, in Sweden. The relatives, living in different countries and speaking different languages, did not know of each other's existence until 1961.

When Ivar Widéen – grandson of Andrew Peterson's brother, Johannes Rydell – an organist and composer of considerable reputation, was commissioned to write a commemorative song for the 1912 Olympic games, he asked his sister Linnéa to write the words. Their combined talent produced the beautiful composition entitled "The Song of Småland," a song that has remained popular in Sweden, especially in the province of Småland. Linnéa drew inspiration from childhood memories, the home or red cabin belonging to her grandparents, Johannes and Anna Carin Rydell, at Bellö. It was here that she and her brothers, Ivar and Frithiof, found refuge following the untimely death of their mother, Anna Lovisa. The song begins: "Red shines the cabin behind the veil of weeping birch." The composition includes a reference to the "rosy Linnéa," a small pink flower named after Karl von Linńe, the famous Swedish botanist who was born in Småland. The piece has been reprinted in a variety of song books. The words and music of the song have been favorites through the years; copies of the sheet music and recordings of the song have been widely sold.

The link between the American and Swedish branches of this family that had its origin in the heavily timbered cottage at Sjöarp, the parish of Västra Ryd in the province of Östergötland, was to be Elsa Carlson. Elsa had been born in Sweden. She taught school there, was familiar with the song, and knew something about Ivar and Linnéa Widéen. Mrs. Carlson later married and moved to Minnesota where she became acquainted with Helen Booth Wettstein and her sister, Gladys Booth, granddaughters of the Reverend John and Maria Christina Anderson. During an afternoon visit, Helen showed Elsa Carlson their collection of family photographs, among which was a picture of three children. Although names (Ivar, Linnéa, and Frithiof) were written on the back of the print, the information did not mean much to Helen and Gladys. But they did to Elsa! Elsa Carlson recognized the name of Ivar Widéen as that of the musician and composer, who, it appeared, could be related to her friends. She encouraged Helen and Gladys to search further through family records to look for additional evidence. Their enthusiasm mounted after discovering a letter written by Andrew Peterson, dated October 29, 1897. It was his response to their Aunt Ruth (Anderson) Johnson, in which he told her he had been notified about his brother's death through Rydell's grandson Ivar Widéen (see page 136). Now it was clear to Helen and Gladys that Johannes Rydell was their great-uncle and grandfather of the children in the photograph!

From that moment on, the women initiated a

search to find out if the children in the picture were still living. Just when they thought they had reached an impasse, Elsa Carlson received several back issues of the *Vetlanda-Posten* from a Wisconsin relative. She stared in disbelief. The answer appeared before her. On the front page of one of the newspapers was a picture of Linnéa Widéen Andrén and a news story about the Fiftieth Jubilee of "Småland's Song." Linnéa, then in her eighties, was the guest of honor at a Småland celebration. A full-page account reported the history of Linnéa and her family. Elsa immediately translated the information for Helen and her sister and helped them write a letter to Linnéa.[1]

Linnéa's June 20, 1961, answer expressed her gratitude and joy. She said:

> I always did believe that the *best* about "Smålandssången" is that God's blessings are with it. We would still be unknown relatives to each other if the 50th Jubilee of Smålandssången had not taken place. . . . It's all so hard for me to understand [that] those simple, naive lines I wrote down February 5, 1911, and my dear brother brought to life with wonderful tones have lived for 50 years and are still going to *live*. If only *everybody* knew how much [meaning] there is *behind* this simple song. The much loved home of my grandparents with tender love and care that had no limit.

Linnéa also explained she had kept house for her brother until she married. He held the position as organist at Skara from 1900 until his death in 1951. Ivar's fame as a composer extended to many other countries. Besides being a member of the Swedish Academy in Stockholm, he was decorated with the Order of the North Star, and had received the medal, "Litteris et artibus," from King Gustaf Adolph of Sweden. There were also many other honors Linnéa felt were too numerous to write about. She also disclosed:

> On what would have been Ivar's ninetieth birthday March 21, 1961, his church choir sang by his grave at Skara's new cemetery. The minister spoke. A Widéen concert was held that evening in the church where he worked for so many years. Ivar was 80 when he passed away. The funeral was held at the same church, which was decorated with, many flags from all parts of Sweden. He was sick only 11 days and died from a heart attack.
>
> My brother Frithiof died in Gränna [when he was] 73 years old. He had a hardware store there. He is buried at Bellö.
>
> Now a little about myself. In 1904, I married Olaf Andrén, a railroad bookkeeper. We had our wedding at Ivar's church. My husband was promoted to inspector of railroad stations and we moved quite a bit. We lived in 9 different cities. We have 3 sons. *Björn*, a businessman in Stockholm, *Rolf*, has a bookstore in Gothenburg, *Tor*, has a position at the factory connected with the air force in Arboga. I have 4 grandchildren and 2 great grandchildren. Their father [this nephew was not named] works for the European Nuclear Commission and they live in Geneva. My husband passed away in 1956 and I have been a widow for 5 years.

After Linnéa's first letter, her American relatives received additional information regarding the jubilee celebration, including other matters of family interest. On May 13, 1961, the *Vetlanda-Posten* displayed a full-page story about the anniversary celebration, with several photographs showing young people at Bellö. A youngster playing a flute was shown sitting in the prow of a boat on the shore of Lake Bellen just as Ivar Widéen loved to do. Other children simply gazed at the home that inspired the famous song.

The May 16, 1961, issue of *Tisdagen den* reported that Linnéa Andrén had left her seacoast home in Halmstad to go to Bellö to help celebrate the fiftieth anniversary of "The Song of Småland." A photograph showed Linnéa standing beside a child who was seated on the rail fence in front of the home where Linnéa's grandparents once lived. The story reported:

> It is not every day one has a chance to hear a lady of eighty-four years old speak and read poetry in front of thousands of people. It happened at the church in Eksjö on the last Sunday evening at the fiftieth anniversary of Smålands Sången [The Song of Småland] with opera star Bernhard Sommerstedt as leader. He had taken time away from his theatrical job at Gothenborg and gave glorious proof of his skill, when he sang several of Ivar Widéen's compositions. Mr. Sommerstedt is the same age as the song (50) and he was born in Småland. . . . Linnéa had been preparing breakfast cereal when she was inspired to write her thoughts. She tore open the empty oatmeal bag she held in her hand, and used that container to write on. In a few minutes the memorable words for the *Song of Småland* had been written. After the music was composed by Ivar this song was heard for the first time in the spring of 1911 at the church located at Eksjö. The song was received

1. Elsa Carlson often remarked that the full meaning and beauty of newspaper articles as well as Linnéa's correspondence was lost in translation.

with applause and cheers during its first church performance as well as at the anniversary celebration.

In another undated newspaper story, it was disclosed that Linnéa Andrén was "discovered" in 1911 as a gifted reciter of fairy tales. She traveled throughout the country lecturing. She made quite a hit during her recitations, especially when she dramatized the fairy tales of Hans Christian Andersen. For this reason she was called "Sagomor från Getapulien," or "The Fairy Tale Mother from Småland."

Linnéa's letters to her American cousins did not give an account of relatives on her father's side of the family, only of her brothers and that of her own and Ivar's family. She explained that Ivar's son Harald was in charge of Gothenburg's Historiska Muset (History Museum), which was concerned with historic preservation of Sweden's old and interesting buildings. Ivar's eldest daughter, Anna Lisa, married Professor Arns Huggert, and the couple lived in Umeå with their five children. His youngest daughter, Brita Westergren, had established herself as a textile artist in Skara. Her only son, Staffan, was a professional photographer.

During the last years of her life, home for Linnéa was the seacoast resort city of Halmstad where, in that summer of 1961, she experienced discomfort brought about by incessant rain, along with sharp, cold Atlantic winds. She confessed, "I would like to move away from this windy place, but I am too old." She also spoke of sympathy for the industrial workers, thousands of whom were taking advantage of their annual three-week holiday to live in tents on the beach while the rain drenched the oceanfront day after day. "The whole west coast has become Sweden's bathtub and the sun is a seldom seen guest. When it does peep out, it is still cold."

Linnéa frequently revealed her concern about world affairs. She discussed the funeral of Dag Hammarskjöld (the second secretary-general of the United Nations who succeeded Trygve Lie in 1953) and how she, along with all of Sweden, mourned his death when he was killed.

Soon after initial contact had been made with Linnéa, Helen Wettstein completed a simple genealogical record (see page 136-137) starting with the Petersons' parents, Petter Jonasson and Ingrid Samuelsdotter, and their offspring. After this family tree had been sent to relatives in Sweden and America, contacts expanded.[2] Other cousins throughout the families of Andrew Peterson's sisters, Maria Christina (Mrs. John Anderson), Anna Charlotta (Mrs. Peder Norman), and Gustava (Mrs. Louis Johnson), also wrote to Linnéa.

Upon learning about Linnéa's American relatives, the editor of *Smålands Tidningen* published an article on the front page of its December 28, 1961, issue. He called the celebrated music "A Unifying Song" and featured information about the contact made as a result of the fiftieth anniversary celebration.

Linnéa's eighty-fifth birthday on February 8, 1962, was celebrated with many visitors who stopped by to see her. This year was special because there were not only the traditional music, speeches, coffee, and refreshments, but flowers and greetings from her American relatives.

Linnéa also received cards on May 13 because it was "Linnéa Day." Scandinavian countries observe name day and, in particular, saints' names, which are listed on church calendars. Sometimes more attention is given to a name day than to a birthday because everyone knows when it occurs.

Relatives of Helen Wettstein's relations, Mr. and Mrs. Carl Youngren from Klamath Falls, Oregon, traveled to Sweden to visit Youngren's brother in Eskjö. There they spoke to a woman shopkeeper in a store in Eksjö and told her of their interest in the Rydells, the Widéens, and Bellö. The storekeeper said she had been on the same bus on which Linnéa Andrén was traveling during the fiftieth anniversary celebration of "The Song of Småland." The entire busload serenaded Linnéa when she was recognized. The Youngrens later wrote to Helen Wettstein to tell her of this coincidence.

In one of her letters, Linnéa enclosed a news clipping describing a fund-raising project for a memorial stone to be placed in honor of her and Ivar Widéen in the churchyard at Bellö. Linnéa modestly said she felt undeserving of so much honor; it was her brother who deserved it.

Linnéa's September 30, 1962, letter was to be her last. She mentioned she was "out of breath," and

2. When Gustava Johnson's grandson Neil Norman was seventy-seven years old, he thought the Swedish branch of the family should have a copy of the English translation of the diaries. With this objective in mind, he typed the entire English translation (from the set of diary transcripts his side of the family had received) and sent three folders consisting of more than 1,000 pages of material to Ivar's son Harald Widéen in Sweden. These copies have remained in the possession of Johannes Rydell's great-grandchildren since 1963, and, most recently, with Linnéa's son Tor Andrén in Arboga.

because of it she was to be confined to the hospital the following day. She expressed her gratitude for the donations being sent from America for the memorial marker. She learned about the contributions in news reports published in *Göteborgs Handels- och Sjöfartstidning*, a Gothenburg newspaper.

A letter from Linnéa's son, Tor, bore the sad news informing Helen and Gladys that Linnéa had passed away on November 5.

"Småland is in Mourning. Linnéa Andrén is Dead." Those words prefaced the beautiful tribute, a memorial published in the Eksjö paper on November 6, 1962. The message said in part:

> Linnéa Andrén has with the song *Röd Lyser Stugan* forever written her name on the people's hearts in Småland. They will remember her with warmth and thankfulness, because it was at Bellö, the beautiful parish a few miles southeast of Eksjö, that Mrs. Andrén received the inspiration for the cherished song. [See music at the end of this chapter.]

Elsa Carlson traveled to Sweden the year following Linnéa's death to visit friends and relatives in Eksjö. When she had first begun to plan her journey, she had hoped to meet Linnéa. However, she attended the special ceremonies in connection with the unveiling of the monument to Ivar and Linnéa instead. This commemorative event took place June 16, 1963, at Bellö. The monument, of reddish-brown granite, is almost six feet tall and is graced with medallions of the faces, in relief, of Linnéa Andrén and Ivar Widéen. The first verse of "The Song of Småland" is also engraved on the stone. Birch trees are planted around the marker because these trees were mentioned in the song. The background fence is made from the tough, pliable branches of juniper trees.

Elsa Carlson did not think Bellö could have honored the memory and accomplishments of Linnéa and Ivar in a better way. The memorial proved how grateful the whole of Småland was for the honor given their province through words and music. Three choirs participated, and nine of Ivar Widéen's compositions were featured during the program.

Kantor Assar Wallin chose a beautiful floral arrangement for the relatives in America. The tribute was made in the shape of a lyre and was adorned with flowers in Småland's colors – red and yellow. As an honored guest, Elsa Carlson was seated with Ivar and Linnéa's relatives during church services and included with them at the refreshment table.

In 1968, Helen Wettstein traveled with Elsa Carlson to Sweden. At long last she had the op-

Linnéa Widéen and her husband, Olaf Andrén.

Ivar Widéen, organist and composer at the church in Skara in 1921.

portunity to see Bellö and to meet the younger generation of relatives. Helen carried her tribute, a scrapbook of news stories, photographs, and letters entitled "Our Linnéa Story" to show relatives. The scrapbook explains the full significance of the fiftieth anniversary news story, "The Song of Småland," and the resulting family contact. For Linnéa, the celebration and publicity had taken on a miraculous aspect, something she never quite ceased marveling over. For Helen, it seemed to be by divine intervention. It had to be. Their contact was made possible only a few months before Linnéa's death. Helen, who currently resides with her sister Gladys in Green Valley, Arizona, continues to correspond with Linnéa's and Ivar's children.[3]

The families, both here and abroad, have all experienced the truth associated with the "unifying song." Throughout the years, it has established an almost sacred chord of love, a spiritual force for good that continues to bind people together. The beautiful words included in Linnéa's last letter, "Just now a pale little September sun ray peeks in my window and dances around my desk," reflected her own inner peace. In quiet acceptance she left all those family members and friends who dearly loved her.

3. In a January 7, 1965, letter to Helen Wettstein, Harald Widéen (Doctor of Philosophy with a Docent degree), projected his thoughts for family heirlooms. He mentioned in particular his plans to display in a "memory chamber" at Bellö the old "Klaver," a music stand, two eighteenth-century chairs, a fine ornamental razing glass, portraits, and poems by Linnéa, as well as books and letters.

After initial contact had been made with Linnéa, Helen Wettstein responded to a request from the Swedish press in 1961 by sending this photograph to Sweden. From left: Elsa Carlson, Gladys Booth, cousin Verna Wilcox, and Helen Wettstein examine the April 1, 1961, edition of the *Vetlanda Posten*.

Memorial stone dedicated to Linnéa Andrén and Ivar Widéen.

Till Smålands Sångarförbund.

Smålandssången.

"Röd lyser stugan".

(Till minnet av Morfars röda stuga vid sjön Bellen.)

sköt - dar som skän - ka åt ål - der - dom ro. Sjö - ar - na glitt - ra i
som - ma - rens da - gar, glitt - ra och blän - ka likt stjär - nor i fall.
Fu - ror - na su - sa i ens - li - ga ha - gar, spri - da sin väl - lukt av
sol - sken och tall. Små - land är nam - net på lan - det det kä - ra,
min - nes du hem - met från barn - do - mens år? Sko - gar - nas doft av lin -
- né - - a den skä - ra, tall - tras - tens to - ner i jub - lan - de vår.

Tor Andrén, Linnéa's son, at home in Arboga, looking at a family copy of the translated diary of Andrew Peterson, his great grand-uncle.

Courtesy of Timo Maijala

CHAPTER 25

Tribute

Several people traveled from Sweden to participate in festivities held at the Andrew Peterson farm on September 23, 1978. They joined local dignitaries in paying tribute to Peterson and others of his generation who labored to develop productive farms and industries in Carver County.

Encouraged by public interest generated through involvement during the Open Forum, site surveys of historic landmarks throughout Carver County, and financial grants, members of the Heritage Committee promoted this celebration of thanksgiving, a Harvest Festival.[1]

To start with, as a way of informing the Swedish families in Lindstrom and throughout Chisago and Washington counties, a letter of invitation was written to the editor of the *Chisago County Press*. The proposal to attend festivities at the Peterson farm was also intended to alert the residents of these Swedish communities that they shared a common interest with Carver County through Vilhelm Moberg and his writings.

Letters were sent to Andrew Peterson's relatives in Sweden, as well as to local descendants who had both direct and indirect relationships to Scandia, outlining celebration plans and requesting their presence. These efforts were successful. Families with Scandia heritage from outside of Carver County came from Albert Lea, Anoka, Crane Lake, Delano, Eagan, Elk River, Excelsior, Faribault, Milaca, Minneapolis, Montevideo, Park Rapids, Roseville, Royalton, St. Cloud, St. Paul, Stanchfield, Wahkon, and White Bear, Minnesota. Others came from Culver City, La Mesa, Los Angeles, and Santa Anna, California, as well as from Sarasota, Florida, and Seattle, Washington. Guests were descended from the Reverend John and Maria Christina Anderson and Per Daniel and Caroline Anderson, the Bergquists (spelled Burgquests today), Brobergs, Buelows, Lobitzes, Lohmars, Lundstens, Nelsons, Nordbergs, Peltzes, Petermans, Selby Petersons, Pofahls, and Schwichtenbergs. There were joyous reunions, embraces, laughter, and tears.[2]

1. After the State Review Board completed its examination of information provided in site survey reports featuring landmarks in Carver County, it nominated fifteen individual sites, 126 additional sites within two historic districts, one archaeological site, and three archaeological districts to the National Register of Historic Places. Shortly thereafter, the Minnesota Historical Society provided financial assistance to publish this book. The society also made it possible to create a two-projector slide-tape show entitled "Andrew Peterson and the Scandia Story" through a second matching grant. This program features a series of vignettes narrated by Mary Peltz Luedke, Bruce Anderson, and Thomas Broberg, descendants of the Scandia pioneers of this story.

2. There was a degree of sadness. Some of the elderly friends who provided resource information, including photographs for survey work, the audio-visual program, and this story were not able to attend. The grandchildren of the Reverend John and Maria Christina Anderson – Helen Booth Wettstein and her sister Gladys – and Per Daniel and Caroline Anderson's granddaughter, Lillie Larson Osborne, received information about the events from other family members. But this was not so for Bill Peltz, who passed away July 22, 1978, several months before the festival. His brother John and cousin John Klatt were confined to bed and believed to be too sick to comprehend. Bill's brother John Peltz passed away October 2, 1978, and John Klatt followed both cousins on December 17, 1978.

Chaska attorney Robert Nicklaus and his farm neighbors transported vintage threshing equipment for display and demonstration to the field where hundreds of fruit trees once grew on the Peterson farm. From the vast expanse of open field, the sound of threshing resounded as the stacks of grain released their treasure.

Along with festive music broadcast throughout the day, there were activity centers and displays everywhere. Posters and pictures related the history of the entire county, and an impressive proclamation, signed by Governor Rudy Perpich and delivered in honor of the occasion by state representative Kenneth J. McDonald, was in prominent view.

Moravian Brethren from the Waconia, Chaska, and Lake Auburn congregations, dressed in traditional clothing, were also there. Several Moravian women served as hostesses, while others demonstrated the wrapping of beeswax candles with the customary red fringe. Others served food and Moravian sugar cake treats. Guests were transported to activity centers in buggies pulled by teams of horses driven by the Brethren, and given hay rides to the site where Hanna Hakanson once lived. From this spot passengers viewed the surrounding countryside from the 50.

Visitors purchased meaningful remembrances: Swedish recordings of songs by Anne Charlotte Harvey, linen wall hangings commemorating the "Song of Småland," and bright wooden apples appropriately stamped "Andrew Peterson 1855-1898 – National Register of Historic Places – 1978." Local artisans featured tole-painted articles, apple-head dolls, stained glass, and straw crafts. Guests watched spinning and weaving demonstrations, a smithy at work, and a two-man saw operation. Youngsters acquainted themselves with a variety of animals in the children's barnyard. Visitors purchased apples, cheese, and cracker snacks and reviewed exhibits from the Minnesota State Horticultural Society, the Minnesota Historical Society, and the American Swedish Institute. An impressive design defining the branches of the tree of life by Mrs. Benjamin Anderson showed the genealogy of Swedish pioneers in Scandia, while Kathy Heidel, Carver Park Reserve interpretative naturalist, told the story of Wendelin Grimm in a display.

Guests viewed the slide shows "Andrew Peterson and the Scandia Story," "The Carver Story," and "Historic Sites in Carver County," as well as a twenty-five-minute film on surveying the state, from the Minnesota Land Surveyors.

Professor Philip Tideman, son of the Reverend Carl Tideman, of St. Cloud State University, was master of ceremonies and introduced George Kulkay, the mayor of Waconia, State Representative Kenneth J. McDonald, and State Senator Robert Schmitz.[3]

Distinguished persons taking part in the afternoon program included Lorraine Nyvall, acting director of the American Swedish Institute, Dr. Francis de Vos, director of the University of Minnesota Landscape Arboretum, Russell W. Fridley, director of the Minnesota Historical Society, Milo Peterson, professor emeritus of the University of Minnesota School of Agriculture (who died October 8, 1981), Glen Ray, executive secretary of the Minnesota State Horticultural Society, and Tage Pousette, Swedish Consulate-General. Susanna Thilquist accepted a Swedish flag from the Consulate-General on behalf of the Heritage Committee.[4]

Friends and relatives from communities in Chisago and Washington counties embraced and greeted Flight Captain Carl-Werner Pettersson, a pilot in Linjeflyg, the international Swedish airlines.[5] As a representative from the Emigrant Institute in Växjö, he came to Carver County to pay tribute. During the program, Pettersson delivered a message which had been prepared by Governor Astrid Kristensson, president of the Institute and Ulf Beijbom, director. The writers said:

> We would like to extend our cordial greetings to the Heritage Committee of the Carver County Historical Society on your Harvest Festival of 1978.

3. A distinguished visitor, Emeroy Johnson – minister, author, and former archivist for the Minnesota Synod of the Lutheran Church in America – also attended the festivities. Thinking that a map might be of historic interest, he thoughtfully presented a copy of a rare sketch – a handwritten outline of the central part of Carver County which was made by the Reverend Peter Carlson for use by Eric Norelius, a well-known and influential traveling missionary-preacher. Unfortunately, the outline itself is too faint to use for reproduction purposes. Norelius served the Swedish Lutheran Church in Minnesota and has been mentioned previously in this book.

4. This flag is in safekeeping at the Carver County Historical Society and is available for short-term use during festivities, particularly those related to Swedish culture.

5. Louis Torres' article, "Searching for Sunrise: A Swedish Saga," appeared in the *Minneapolis Tribune's Picture* magazine, November 20, 1977. While searching for "Papa's Cousin in America," Pettersson joyfully discovered that he had relatives in America – a host of them!

This is indeed a celebration of great historic importance since you honour one of Minnesota's many pioneers from Sweden, the farmer Andrew Peterson.

The Rock Isle Farm of Andrew Peterson stands out as a monument over Swedish-American diligence and interest in the cultivation of Minnesota's rich soil. In his lifetime Andrew Peterson was known for his horticultural interests and skills. Long after his death his unique pioneer diaries written in his native Swedish was read in [the] Minnesota Historical Society by one of Sweden's greatest novelists.

Vilhelm Moberg had come to Minnesota in 1948 to trace the history of his relatives, the emigrants from Småland. Peterson's diary provided him with a long series of data on the life of a Swedish pioneer farmer. Thus Andrew Peterson's notes from day to day were reborn as a piece of world literature some 70 years after the last note was written down.

The Emigrant Institute has many ties with Minnesota and its immigrants from Sweden. Vilhelm Moberg was one of the Institute's strongest supporters. He placed the complete source material to his Emigrant novel in The House of Emigrants, among other things the excerpts from Andrew Peterson's diary. Later we have completed this material with a microfilm of the entire diary and the mourning letter about Peterson's death which served as a model for Moberg's "Last Letter Home." Since 1968 the Emigrant Institute celebrates the world's only Minnesota Day. We have microfilmed most Minnesota church records of Swedish origin and we are frequently represented in your state by our representative, Captain Carl-Werner Peterson *[sic]*.

With this as a background we would like to express our best greetings to the good people who have come together this day in order to celebrate the memory of Andrew Peterson and the heritage he represents.

Pettersson announced that the last letter home, written by Nicholas Swenson to Andrew Peterson's relatives in Sweden informing them about Peterson's death, had been preserved at the Institute with family pictures and papers. Copies of photographs and the last letter, with the postmarked envelope, were also included with the document that was officially signed by the president and director at the Institute and presented to the Heritage Committee.

Anne-Marie Johansson, a young journalist from Sweden, also attended the celebration. She visited the United States on an exchange scholarship funded by Rotary International, traveling as a goodwill ambassador to represent the families of Andrew Peterson's brother, Johannes Rydell. Before Anne-Marie's departure for America, she interviewed Linnéa Andrén's son Tor and his wife Ruth (from Arboga), at which time Timo Maijala took pictures for a feature story which later appeared in the September 1, 1978, edition of the *Arboga Tidning/Bärgslagsbladet*. These photographs, as well as copies of family pictures Andrew Peterson had sent to Johannes Rydell, were featured in the lengthy news story telling about Tor Andrén's relationship to Peterson and Moberg's character Karl Oskar. Copies of this article with glossy prints of Andrén had been included with several gifts Johansson delivered personally to the Heritage Committee in behalf of Peterson's relatives. The package also contained a recording of the "Song of Småland" and small stickers depicting the red cabin of Johannes Rydell. These ornamental seals can be found on many letters and packages being mailed from Småland today.

Dr. Harald Widéen, Ivar's son and Linnéa's nephew, expressed his best wishes in a message sent from Gothenburg. He also said that his father and Vilhelm Moberg were both proud of the fact they were from Småland.

A spectacular bonfire signaled the finale of this day-long event following a festival dinner and screening of *The New Land*, the second film adapted from Moberg's emigrant series of books.[6] Thus the celebration concluded during the evening hours on September 23, 1978.

6. Warner Brothers film studio furnished an assortment of black and white stills from the movie, *The Emigrants*, which were used during the festival. Studio personnel also helped arrange to show the film, *The New Land* (adapted from the book, *Unto a Good Land*, published in 1954).

Although film stars Max von Sydow (Karl Oskar) and Eddie Axberg (Robert) sent written permission to reproduce their photographs in this book, these plans were not implemented because of legal technicalities.

The Heritage Committee is grateful to all of these people, as well as to our local theater manager, Michael Deluhery, who made the showing of the film possible.

This aerial view of Waconia and part of the lake was taken by the *Agricultural Administration* on August 19, 1937.

Courtesy National Archives

CHAPTER 26

Today

The Andrew Peterson homestead is now owned by Ward and Georgene Holasek. They are breeders of Arabian horses. Georgene also is a doctor of veterinary medicine specializing in horses, while Ward cares for a large stock of percherons and supervises the entire family operation called the Rock Isle Farm.

The Holaseks built a new residence and horse barn with office, medical and lab facilities, machine shed, and large utility-party room complex behind the Peterson home and barns. Some of these old landmark buildings provide valuable storage space for essentials used for professional services, as well as a thriving sleigh and hay ride business.

This farm, which is on the National Register of Historic Places, attracts various clubs, church families, and other large visiting groups of people interested in old-fashioned rides, and socials which are held in the party room.

At this writing, Andrew Peterson's orchard is gone. Only a grassy expanse, where mares feed with their young foals, marks the place where the fruit trees and the original log shanty once stood. The 1870 house has been rented. Even though some buildings have been removed (including the home of John Peltz, the tenant farmer), those that remain show the effects of deterioration, but are otherwise largely unchanged from Peterson's time. Although removal of diseased elms has thinned the stand of timber, a large grove of maple trees remains along with the base of the maple sugar cooker which can be found in the high grass.

State and federal matching funds made it possible to begin a restoration program on the Peterson farm. However, progress has been slow.

After restoration of existing buildings has been accomplished, the renters, as live-in caretakers, will eventually manage the historic aspect of the farm. It is expected that the audio-visual slide-tape program, "Andrew Peterson and the Scandia Story," combined with future projects such as exhibits, will provide valuable educational experiences in addition to recreational pleasure.

The part of Laketown Township which was known as Scandia ceased to be a unified settlement after the schools consolidated and the District 17 building was converted for use as a home. For a long time thereafter, the area was called Lakeside, but even that name finally disappeared. Now most of the farms, starting with school District 42 on the north side of Waconia Lake, have been subdivided into residential lakeshore lots. Farther northeast, the Roman Catholic Jesuits purchased and developed a large tract of farmland for seminary purposes. The Jesuits in turn have since sold this campus to the St. Paul Bible College and have released additional parcels to private families. This area includes a golf course as well as the Hennepin County Park Reserve where the Wendelin Grimm farmhouse still stands. Grimm's homestead was the first site nominated to the National Register of Historic Places—even before the countywide survey of historic landmarks had taken place.

In 1924, an association of alfalfa growers attached a bronze plaque to a large boulder in the farmyard about seventy-five feet from the southeast corner of the farmhouse. The inscription reads as follows: "Commemorating Wendelin Grimm, resident of

Minnesota 1857-1891, who originated Grimm Alfalfa on this farm. Erected June 1924 by Grimm Alfalfa Growers Associations." (The date of Grimm's death is incorrect—he died in 1890.)

A group headed by Andrew Fuller (a Minnetonka resident) who call themselves "Friends of the Park Reserve" has provided financial support for a matching grant and a feasibility study. This report outlines future objectives and their estimated costs in a program to complete the restoration and preservation of Grimm's two-story brick dwelling and the reconstruction of other farm buildings. According to the feature article entitled *Profile: Hennepin County,* a supplement which appeared in the *Minneapolis Tribune* on January 28, 1979, the plan is that the farm will eventually be restored as a nineteenth-century working farm.

Today, Wendelin Grimm's wooden trunk (the container carried family possessions as well as a small box filled with alfalfa seed from Germany) is part of a collection of artifacts on display at the Carver County Historical Society museum in Waconia.

The former Schwichtenberg farm (*map 36*) was purchased by Per Daniel Anderson's grandson, Ben, in 1946. Today, Ben's son Bruce occupies the farm and cultivates the land adjacent to the grounds of the college. Until a few years ago, he also rented the same field once cleared and planted by his great-grandparents, Per Daniel and Caroline. The nearby farm of George and Wilhelmina Brethorst (*map 33*) is now located within the Hennepin County Park Reserve, while the former homestead of John Zieman and his son-in-law, Simon Peltz (*map 34*), is once again in private ownership.

To the east of the grounds where the old church once stood are a golf course and a clubhouse near the lake. The church site is a narrow strip of land between the lakeshore road to the west and a crowded assortment of storage sheds. In the cemetery, which is to the south and across the township road from the clubhouse, a single stone with individual foot markers points out the remains of the Peterson family. The bodies of Peterson's children were placed in adjacent cemetery plots, with the exception of Josephine (Mrs. Nels Carlson). Her grave is located just a few rods away. Most of the church pioneers and their families are also buried there.

The old township road, beyond the cemetery and school, has been straightened to follow the lines of Sections 17 and 8. This short stretch (part of the old Yellowstone Trail) is now referred to as the Island View Road and joins Highway 5 almost at the jog in the old road to the right of the school. From there the highway follows the railroad track west, beyond Waconia. Going east, the highway (which is part of the old road) passes through the center of the former Nilsson and Andrew Peterson homesteads, through Victoria, and on through the Twin Cities.

The diagonal road (between 50 and 51 on the map) is the starting point of the Scandia Road. It had its beginning near the corner where the church once stood and actually appears today as a little-used machine road behind the cemetery and through the existing farm field. A sign identifies it as the Scandia Road on the other side of Highway 5. From here, this well-traveled township road crosses the abandoned railroad track, continues to head southeast, and finally intersects with the Airport Road.

Virginia Anderson, granddaughter of Per Daniel and Caroline Anderson, pointed out the location of Andrew Bergquist's first shelter. It is located in the triangular-shaped, grassy piece of ground bordered by the cemetery, the township road, and the farm machine road. This spot can be easily located in front of the ornamental archway over the main gate leading into the Scandia cemetery *(map 51)*. It was here that Andrew Peterson and his brother-in-law, John Anderson, met Bergquist in 1853. On this trip from Iowa, they established their claims, traveled back to Illinois and Iowa, and then returned to Minnesota in 1855.

It is possible the cabin left standing on the former John Anderson farm (*map 37*), which was dismantled by Arlo Hasse in the late 1960s, was the first dwelling used by the pioneers in this story. Upon hearing that this cabin was scheduled for destruction, Hasse received permission to salvage the timber. It was dismantled and numbered piece by piece and safely stored away. Hasse hopes that it will some day be reconstructed and the building used for historic purposes.

Not far away are the converted schoolhouse, now a home, and the new but still rural Waconia Baptist Church located at its present address—9030 State Highway 5. Also nearby on the former Henry Peterman farm is a residential development called Rolling Meadows. The cluster of more than fifty dwellings was constructed on single-acre lots east of the existing brick-faced home built by Henry and Amelia Peterman.

The Chaska or Preachers' Road, now called Laketown, was platted through Sections 16 and 21. This cartway was said to have been the main route used by local preachers traveling between the Lake Auburn and Zoar Moravian churches to conduct worship services at both places. It is now a back road to several housing developments and large farms beyond Rolling Meadows. Although it was straightened at the point of entry from Highway 5, it basically remains the same gravel road traveled by the pioneers in this story.

If these ministers, or neighborhood father and son, Frank and John Everett Lundsten, were traveling today, their journey east would be alongside the continuous swish of traffic on the paved highway. They would surely be happy to see the Rietz farm *(map 56)* and the historic church and grounds of the brethren, but they would miss seeing Clara Salter *(map 55)* working in her garden. Although these men would no longer be able to purchase refreshments or sundry items at the inn or board the 10:00 a.m. train, they would be interested to see the changes made in the old creamery—a restored building in Victoria housing a restaurant and a gift and antique shop.

Amy Nelson Lyford recalled stories her family told about Indians who visited the burial mounds located beyond the wooded acreage at the Hilk farm *(map 6)*. Today this area is properly identified within the grounds of Camp Manakiki—a youth camp which is funded and supervised by Pillsbury-Waite Neighborhood Services in Minneapolis. Camping enthusiasts from the metropolitan communities combine rigorous outdoor activities with leisurely walks through the woodland to the tranquil setting once visited by the Indians. Church and civic groups rent the buildings throughout the remainder of the summer and winter months.

Beside the lakeshore but facing Highway 5, there is also a large ballroom called Waconia Lakeside and a business called the Country Store. This marketplace features fresh produce, garden supplies, and nursery stock, as well as floral and gift items. Just a few miles farther west, on the lakeshore, restaurant and marina facilities (308 East Lake Street, Waconia) offer another attraction. Guests in the dining room enjoy the pleasant view of the countryside surrounding the lake with its historic island setting. Although hundreds of visitors and vacationers were attracted to Coney Island of the West during the years from 1884 through 1915, today the abandoned island buildings provide only a ghostly reminder of the glory that once was. They are now part of the overall island complex listed on the National Register of Historic Places. Matching funds provided the money needed for a research and planning study that Miller-Dunwiddie-Architects, Inc., completed November 26, 1979, for the City of Waconia. Even though most of the existing buildings are structurally sound, restoration and preservation efforts are at a standstill.

While the Island View Country Club (9150 Island View Road) maintains an excellent restaurant, they also provide carefully groomed grounds for golfing enthusiasts. In addition to the public beach and picnic grounds (located between the former Andrew Bergquist and John Broberg homesteads), individuals who travel to this popular fishing lake appreciate the advantages provided by the bait and boat rental facilities at the In Towne Marina (8 East Lake Street, Waconia). Other visitors merely browse in the nearby cemeteries, reading on markers and headstones the names of those who made the colorful history of the area.

Descendants of some of the prominent German pioneer families who were included in this history still live in the immediate area. Their ancestors made important contributions to the county and the state and they still make up a strong segment of the population in Carver County.

Although fewer Scandinavians than German immigrants settled in and around Carver County, these people who lived in the four settlement areas of East and West Union, Götaholm, and Scandia, established lasting reminders of their existence in Carver County. While Lutheran congregations in Minnesota look to St. Ansgar's Academy at East Union as the start of Gustavus Adolphus College in St. Peter, the Minnesota Swedish Baptist Conference looks to Scandia for its beginnings.

Even before Vilhelm Moberg discovered Andrew Peterson's diaries, the Reverend Carl Tideman wrote of the families in Scandia, "whatever their weaknesses may have been, [they] were a light that could not be hid, an influence not easily definable but ever present as an irresistable *[sic]* power toward higher ideals of life. . . . They were and are a type of men and women that have so romantically enriched the history of the American frontier."

Courtesy of *Smålandsposten*

Captain Carl-Werner Pettersson presented this wooden "apple" plaque to Governor Astrid Kristensson, president of the Emigrant Institute, Växjö, Sweden. The plaque commemorates the September, 1978, Harvest Festival in Carver County when the Peterson Farm was placed on the National Register. Both the Swedish papers, *Smålandsposten* and *Kronobergaren,* carried news stories of this presentation. The plaque was to be kept on display at the Institute.

CREDITS

The author gratefully acknowledges Ford Johnson Graphics for design and production and the following people for lending private photographs that were used in this book.

Anderson, Terrell
Anderson, Virginia
Andrén, Tor
Berg, Donald
Buelow, Anna
Effertz, Evelyn (Zrust)
Giesen, Gladys (Peterman)
Holtmeier, Ron
Hoyler, Mabel (Gerdsen)
Klatt, Julie (Mrs. John)
Kratzke, Mabel (Peltz)
Lundsten, Everett
Lundsten, Rhoda
Lyford, Amy (Nelson)
Nordberg, Lucy (Mrs. Rueben)
Olson, Florence (Norman)
Orsen, Sue
Peltz, Leslie
Peterson, Sarah
Pofahl, Allegra
Schwichtenberg, Irwin
Smith, Dorothy (Rietz)
Swenson, Robert O.
Watson, Catherine (Broberg)
Wendland, Gladys (Schraan)
Wettstein, Helen (Booth)

Other picture sources:

Arboga Tidning/Bärgslagsbladet and Timo Maijala, photographer

Carver County Historical Society

Centennial Anniversary of the Leenthrop and Maynard Baptist Congregation, 1872-1972 (reproductions)

Diamond Jubilee Celebration and History of the Scandia Baptist Church, 1855-1930 (reproductions)

Emigrant Institute, Växjö, Sweden (letter)

Minnesota Historical Society

National Archives and Records Service

Smålandsposten and Carl-Werner Pettersson

Swedish Information Service

SOURCES, COMMENTS, & RELATED READING

Preface

Eidevall, Gunner, "The Swedes in Moberg's Tetralogy," *The Swedish Pioneer Historical Quarterly,* 29:69-78 (January, 1978).

Golden Valley Post, April 26, 1979, p. 8A, "For Palmers, the world is full of friends."

Minneapolis Star, June 4, 1981, p. 5B, "They [Palmers] rode the train from London to Hong Kong."

Moberg, Vilhelm, "Why I Wrote the Novel About Swedish Emigrants," *The Swedish Pioneer Historical Quarterly,* 17:63-77 (April, 1966).

New Hope-Plymouth Post, April 21, 1977, p. 1, "Around-the-world traveling takes plane, ship, cab, camel/ Palmers: world travelers for 20 years."

New Hope-Plymouth Post, [n.d.], p. 1, "First American tourists in Cuba were Plymouth residents."

Nute, Grace L., "The Diaries of a Swedish-American Farmer: Andrew Peterson," *American Institute of Swedish Arts, Literature and Science, Yearbook,* 105-132 (Minneapolis, 1945). Used with permission.

Qualey, Carlton C., "Diary of a Swedish Immigrant Horticulturist, 1855-1898," *Minnesota History,* 43:63-70 (Summer, 1972). Used with permission.

St. Paul Sunday Pioneer Press, September 30, 1973, p. 25, "Waconia pioneer helped inspire 'The New Land'" (first of two parts by Bill Diehl).

St. Paul Sunday Pioneer Press, October 7, 1973, p. 25, "'New Land' Drama behind Swedish movie" (second of two parts by Diehl).

Sellman, Jerry, "A Guide to Chisago County," a special tourist paper printed by the *Chisago County Press* (Lindstrom).

Smålands-Tidningen, December 28, 1961, "Bellö parish choir director's oldest brother model for Moberg's Karl Oskar. The most remarkable emigrant from Småland a native of Östergötland! 'Red Shines the Cabin' produces discoveries" is the title of the article describing the unifying characteristics of this song. Translated by Susanna Thilquist.

Vetlanda-Posten, April 1, 1961, p. 9, "Småland's Song was written in ten minutes," called attention to the tribute being paid fifty years after the song was first written. Translated by Susanna Thilquist.

Unpublished Sources

Carver County Park Commission minutes. Since the plans of the Waconia Bicentennial Commission Island Committee fit the thematic scheme outlined by the state and federal governments, several members of this committee attended a Park Board meeting at the Carver County Courthouse Annex in Waconia on June 18, 1975. The committee explained its decision to promote a program that would feature learning opportunities for local youth groups. The concept included citizen participation (young adults and other volunteers from church and civic organizations) to provide manpower in a cooperative, countywide effort to develop Coney Island of the West into a primitive camp site. Young people and visitors would then learn about the history of the area through such features as markers along the trails.

The committee agreed that recognition of the historic integrity of the island (local property owners had long ago abandoned it) would also be promoted through a site survey. This effort would then be followed by a feasibility study to determine the value of existing buildings and the role they might play in future land-use decisions.

On August 11, 1975, the completed papers, called the Minnesota Historic Places Survey, and supporting documents, were turned over to Paul Waldron, Carver County Public Works employee. He delivered the survey to the Minnesota Historical Society. Charles W. Nelson, the society's architectural historian, and Doug George, one of its archaeologists, met with Waldron and the Island Committee. On that day—September 22, 1975—Nelson and George completed their on-site research of the island. Nelson subsequently processed the nomination form requirements and presented the report to the State Review Board at a meeting held on January 21, 1976. It was at this time that Coney Island of the West was nominated to the National Register of Historic Places. On August 19, 1976, it became official: the United States Department of Interior accepted the nomination and placed Coney Island of the West on the register.

Related Reading

Coney Island of the West Appraisal Report (Shakopee, 1976). This material was prepared by Bert A. Noterman, I.F.A., and LeRoy F. Houser, A.M.A., on behalf of the Island Committee for the Waconia Bicentennial Commission on April 10, 1976.

Miller-Dunwiddie-Architects, Inc., *Coney Island of the West, A Research and Planning Study* (Minneapolis, November 26, 1979). This report followed recommendations made by the Island Study Committee for the Waconia City Council.

United States Department of Agriculture, Soil Conservation Service, *Inventory & Evaluation for the Carver Soil and Water Conservation District, Coney Island, Lake Waconia,* Waconia, Minnesota. A Coney Island study prepared for the Island Committee of the Waconia Bicentennial Commission on June 13, 1975.

Chapter 1

Barton, H. Arnold, *Letters from the Promised Land: Swedes in America, 1840-1914,* 12, 22, 277, 290 (Minneapolis, 1975).

Hillebrand, Percie V., *The Swedes in America,* 31 (Minneapolis, 1966).

Johansson, Anne-Marie, "Unikt utvandrardokument i Arboga Tor är släkt med Moberg's Karl Oskar" ("Unique Emigrant Document in Arboga Tor is Related to Moberg's Karl Oskar"), *Arboga Tidning/Bärgslagsbladet* (Arboga, Sweden), September 1, 1978, p. 16. Translated by Susanna Thilquist.

Kastrup, Allan, *The Swedish Heritage in America,* 161-163 (St. Paul, 1975).

Magnuson, Norris, "Our Unsung Heroines," *The Standard,* 10 (May 15, 1977).

Moberg, Vilhelm, *The Emigrants* (paperback), 11-13, Popular Library, a unit of C B S Publications, the Consumer Publishing Division of C B S Inc., by arrangement with Simon and Schuster, Inc. The name Åkians was taken from the group's leader Åke Svensson, who lived in Ljuder parish in Konga County about 1780.

Nelson, Vernon H., "The Moravians at Bethlehem," *Life in Early America,* 26-63 (August, 1978).

Olsson, Nils William, *Swedish Passenger Arrivals in New York 1820-1850,* 26, 38, 43 (first book, Stockholm, Sweden 1967).

Scott, Franklin D., *Sweden in the Nation's History,* 352-356 (Minneapolis, 1977).

von Wachenfeldt, Curt, "Background to Peter Cassel's Emigration," *The Swedish Pioneer Historical Quarterly,* 32:96-105 (April, 1981).

Unpublished Sources

McKnight, Roger, "The Journal of F. O. Nilsson: An Early Minnesota Circuit Rider," p. 4, 6, 23. The Reverend Frederick Olaus Nilsson's original journal (translated by Joseph Tanquist) is owned by Bethel Theological Seminary in St. Paul.

Related Reading

Friman, Axel, "Notes on a Wisconsin Pioneer," *The Swedish Pioneer Historical Quarterly,* 13:5-8 (January, 1962).

Friman, Axel, "Early advice to Prospective Emigrants: Carl Friman's Letter to Aftonbladet, 1842," *The Swedish American Historical Quarterly* (formerly *The Swedish Pioneer Historical Quarterly),* 33:79-83 (April, 1982).

Chapter 2

Barton, *Letters,* 53-56. Used with permission.

McKnight, "Andrew Peterson's Emigrant Voyage of 1850," *The Swedish Pioneer Historical Quarterly,* 31:3-11 (January, 1980).

Olsson, Nils William, *Swedish Passenger Arrivals in U.S. Ports (except New York),* 38-42 (second book, St. Paul, 1979). Olsson found it difficult to decipher the records kept by the clerk of customs, but decided the captain's surname was either Lindgren or Lundergren. Olsson's books (published in 1967 and 1979) include vital statistics about most of the passengers – a valuable summary of information used in this study.

Scott, *History,* 351.

Chapter 3

Barton, *Letters,* 23.

Hagstrom, G. Arvid, *History of the Bethlehem Baptist Church,* 9 (Minneapolis, 1946).

Holcombe, Returne I., and William R. Bingham, *Compendium of Carver and Hennepin Counties, Minnesota,* 325 (Chicago, 1915).

Jordan, Philip D., "In the Shade of the Old Apple Tree," *Palimpsest,* 55:68 (May/June, 1974). Jordan noted that in 1849, Neally and Brothers Birds Nest Nursery of Burlington promised they would deliver trees without charge to the levee for those customers wishing to carry their stock home by boat.

Kastrup, *Swedish Heritage,* 239.

Magnuson, *The Standard,* 10 (May, 1977).

Melloh, Ardith K., "Life in Early New Sweden, Iowa," *The Swedish Pioneer Historical Quarterly,* 32:135 (April, 1981).

Olsson, *Passenger Arrivals* (first book), 64.

Proescholdt, Kevin, "The Demography of the New Sweden Settlement in Iowa, 1845-1880," *The Swedish Pioneer Historical Quarterly,* 32:147 (April, 1981).

Setterdahl, Lilly, "Peter Cassel's America," *The Swedish Pioneer Historical Quarterly,* 32:116, 119 (April, 1981).

Unonius, Gustaf, *A Pioneer in Northwest America, 1841-1858,* 2 vols., J. Oscar Backlund, trans., Nils William Olsson, ed. (Minneapolis, 1960) 2:226. This second volume completes the English translation of the memoirs of Gustaf Unonius in which he tells of entering the Episcopal ministry and visiting Swedish settlements in Illinois and Iowa.

Unpublished Sources

Giaquinta, Joyce, manuscript librarian, Iowa Historical Department, Division of the State Historical Society, stated in a letter to Josephine Mihelich, February 8, 1979, that the city directories in Burlington did not list the name of Neally under the business heading of nurseries until 1865. Then the *Iowa State Gazeteer* (page 582) listed Neally Brothers and Bock as partners under the description of nurserymen, seedsmen, and florists.

Swenson, Robert O., copies of the Scandia Baptist Church Membership Records, 490-497, from the Bethel College and Seminary archives in St. Paul. Swenson's copies or collection of unpublished research papers (now at Downer's Grove, Illinois) were duplicated for this study.

Waters, Clyde C., "Genealogy Charts – Peterson, Johnson, Norman, Anderson and Fredien families," unpublished papers in private collection of Virginia Anderson, granddaughter of Per Daniel and Caroline Anderson. Used with permission.

Wettstein, Helen Booth, "Our Linnéa Story," unpublished papers; Linnéa Andrén's letter to cousin Helen Wettstein (granddaughter of the Reverend John Anderson and Andrew Peterson's sister Maria Christina), July 11, 1961, in private collection of Helen Wettstein. Used with permission.

Chapter 4

Blegen, Theodore C., *Minnesota: A History of the State,* 395 (St. Paul, 1963).

Folwell, William Watts, *History of Minnesota*, 1:359 (St. Paul, reprint ed., 1956).

Holcombe and Bingham, *Compendium*, 191, 218, 325.

Melloh, *The Swedish Pioneer Historical Quarterly*, 32:129, 141. Used with permission.

Olsson, *Passenger Arrivals* (second book), 34.

Upham, Warren, *Minnesota Geographic Names: Their Origin and Historical Significance*, 83 (St. Paul, reprint ed., 1969).

United States Manuscript Census Schedules, 1860 Carver County, p. 39, in the Division of Archives and Manuscripts, Minnesota Historical Society.

Waconia Patriot, September 13, 1912, p. 1.

Waconia Patriot, June 12, 1975, p. A4 (Bicentennial Farm Features).

Waconia Patriot, July 17, 1975, p. 2.

Unpublished Sources

Carver County, *The Book of Plats*, 4, Office of the Register of Deeds, Carver County Courthouse, Chaska.

Carver County, *Index Book "A."* See Laketown for names of title holders, property descriptions, entree, and patent dates. This book is located in the office of the Register of Deeds, Carver County Courthouse, Chaska.

Laketown Township, *Record Book "A,"* 1859-1863, p. 19.8; in the Carver County Historical Society, Waconia.

McKnight, "Nilsson Journal," 6-8, 21.

Chapter 5

Hagstrom, *Bethlehem Baptist Church*, 13.

Holcombe and Bingham, *Compendium*, 217, "King Oscar's Settlement"; 232, Methodist Church; 233, the Reverends Nilsson and Palmquist; 244, Gotha Church; 295, Phillip O. Johnson.

Johnson, Emeroy, *A Church is Planted*, 91, 92, 94, 97 (Minneapolis, 1948).

Kastrup, *Swedish Heritage*, 202.

Lofstrom, Ted and Lynne Van Brocklin Spaeth, *Carver County: A Guide to Its Historic and Prehistoric Places*, 33 (St. Paul, 1978).

Magnuson, *The Standard*, 10.

Nelson, Ernest G., "Historical Sketch of the South Isanti Baptist Church," *Centennial Program of the One Hundredth Year Jubilee, 1860-1960* ([Isanti ?], 1960).

Norelius, Eric, *The Swedish Lutheran Congregations and History of the Swedes in America*, 711 (Rock Island, Illinois, 1890). Written in the Swedish language, the translated information referred to in this chapter was the work of Susanna Thilquist.

Norelius, Eric, *Early Life of Eric Norelius 1833-1862*, p. 291 (Rock Island, Illinois, 1934). The journals of Norelius were translated by Emeroy Johnson and published in book form by the Augustana Historical Society.

Sisell, Andrew, *A Missionary's Notes and Experiences on the Red River Valley Field* (Isanti, 1982). This journal was translated and printed in English by the Reverend Ernest G. Nelson.

Tideman, Carl G., *A Brief History of the Scandia Baptist Church, 1855-1930*, p. 32, 40. 51 ([Waconia?], 1930). This memorial tribute was published for the seventy-fifth anniversary of the church in 1930.

United States Census, 1860, Carver County, p. 36.

Wipf, D. S., *Minnetrista Baptist Church, St. Bonifacius, Minnesota*, n.p. ([Delano], 1958). Irene Maas served as the committee chairperson in charge of this publication, printed for the 1958 centennial celebration of the church.

Unpublished Sources

Carver County, *Index Book "A."* See Laketown for list of successive title holders *(map 20: 45)*.

McKnight, "Nilsson Journal," 2, 9-13, 15. McKnight mentioned the name of Virgil A. Olson, who in 1962 presented a vivid account about F. O. Nilsson. Nilsson's work was a testament to the early groundwork for the Baptist church in Minnesota. McKnight followed Olson's brief review with another in-depth analysis and said, "Though not a study of theological views, the present paper is intended, as an outgrowth of Olson's analysis, to present further details illustrating the nature of Nilsson's journal as well as its place in immigrant history."

Swenson, "Membership Records," 490-492.

Chapter 6

Holcombe and Bingham, *Compendium*, 257, Alfred and Taylor August Johnson.

Larson, John W., *Those Army Engineers: A History of the Chicago District, U.S. Army Corps of Engineers*, 174 (Washington, D. C., 1979).

Unpublished Sources

Swenson, "Membership Records," 491 (Elsa's baptism).

Waters, "Genealogy Charts," 2 (Elsa Ingeman).

Chapter 7

Carley, Kenneth, *The Sioux Uprising of 1862* (St. Paul, 2nd ed., 1976).

Folwell, *Minnesota*, vol. 2 (St. Paul, reprint ed., 1956 and 1961). Carley in his book (cited above) wrote that volume 2 of Folwell's history, originally published in 1924, "contains the best account of the Uprising yet written."

Holcombe and Bingham, *Compendium*, 225, Captain Edwin Bell; 258, Company B and Company H; 297, Milton Jadwin.

Minnesota Stats Tidning, January 4, 1877-December 24, 1897 (microfilm copy in Minnesota Historical Society; translated by Susanna Thilquist).

Unpublished Sources

Lundsten, Rhoda, "The Saga of Sunny Hill Farm" (June 1856-July 1956) Chapter 2. These unpublished papers, in booklet form, include Frank Lundsten's welcome address during memorial services in Scandia, held in 1923, and comments made during a pioneer observance held in Delano on February 22, 1938. This information has been combined with reminiscences written by the grandchildren and great-grandchildren of John and Maja Lisa Lundsten.

Servin, Jeanette. Jeanette explained her relationship to Taylor August Johnson and enclosed related information about her family in a letter sent to Josephine Mihelich on November 16, 1982.

Chapter 8

Blegen, *History of the State*, 233.

Holcombe and Bingham, *Compendium*, 253, recruits; 265, Per Daniel Anderson.

Unpublished Sources

Anderson, Per Daniel. Copies of Per Daniel's April 1, 8, 28, 1865, letters to Caroline are currently in the possession of his granddaughter Virginia Anderson. They were translated by Susanna Thilquist.

Laketown Township, *School Records,* [1868-1874]. The names of Nicholas and Elna Swenson's children appear on page 46. In Carver County Historical Society, Waconia.

Interviews

Osborne, Lillie (Larson), January 5, and February 13, 1978, conversations with Josephine Mihelich. Lillie was a dedicated teacher and accomplished artist. She married Albert Instances Osborne, a Baptist minister, raised four children, and toward the end of her life resided at the Colonial Acres Health Care Center in Minneapolis, where she died on May 14, 1982, at the age of 91.

Peltz, William, conversations with Josephine and William Mihelich, which included references to basswood and rope.

Chapter 9

Holcombe and Bingham, *Compendium,* 253, Otto Broberg.

Unpublished Sources

Carver, County, *Will and Decree Record,* Book "B," 47, office of the Register of Deeds, Carver County Courthouse, Chaska.

Lundsten, "Sunny Hill Farm," Chapter 3.

Chapter 10

Holcombe and Bingham, *Compendium,* 307, Frank Lundsten.

Unpublished Sources

Lundsten, "Sunny Hill Farm," genealogy, Chapters 1, 4.

Interviews

Lundsten, Otto. His apprenticeship was confirmed during a telephone conversation with Tracy DuToit Swanson (daughter of Louise and Dana DuToit), Chaska, on May 11, 1982, by Josephine Mihelich. Louise DuToit, then eighty-eight years old, is the daughter-in-law of George DuToit, and the mother of Tracy Swanson.

Chapter 11

Folwell, *Minnesota,* 4:137, 335.

Tideman, *Church History,* 40.

Unpublished Sources

Laketown, *Book "A,"* 86, 112.

Laketown, *School Records* [1868-1874], 46, attendance for 1871; 9, November 4, 1871, meeting and December 21, 1872, land purchase.

Laketown Township, *School District and Estray Book,* 1862, p. 5, Henry Gerdsen, town clerk. In Carver County Historical Society, Waconia.

Interviews

Siewert, Rudolph, April 26, 1982, conversation with Josephine Mihelich. Siewert, former Carver County superintendent of public schools and translator of early school records also provided copies of information from research papers he used for his master's degree in education administration. Original papers in possession of Siewert, Chaska.

Chapter 12

Blegen, *History of the State,* 197.

Centennial Historical Committee, *Maynard Baptist Church, 100 Years—In the Service of Our Lord,* 3 (Montevideo, 1972).

McKnight, "Andrew Peterson's Journals: An Analysis," *The Swedish Pioneer Historical Quarterly,* 28:157, 162 (July, 1977).

Qualey, *Minnesota History,* 43:68.

Tideman, *Church History,* 50.

Unpublished Sources

McKnight, "Nilsson Journal," 17.

Interviews

Anderson, Mrs. Emil, and Mrs. Rodney Weberg, July 1, 1978, conversation with Josephine Mihelich relating to property once owned by Peterson's sons in Chippewa County. Frank and Carl's place is still called Fairview. Mrs. Weberg is the present farm occupant.

Chapter 13

Hagstrom, *Bethlehem Baptist Church,* 12.

Holcombe and Bingham, *Compendium,* 252, Second Minnesota Infantry; 325, condensing plant; 334, Swanson; 241, gristmill.

Peterson, O. T., *First Year Book of the Twin Cities—Aberdeen-Yellowstone Park Trail* (Twin Cities-Aberdeen-Yellowstone Park Trail Association, 1914).

United States Census, 1860, Carver County, 39, 45.

Unpublished Sources

Carver County, *Lands- Book "A,"* 186, Iron Mike, railroad. Office of the Register of Deeds, Carver County Courthouse, Chaska.

Laketown, *School Records.* [1868-1874]. The names of Michael and Margaret Reichenberger's children appear on page 48.

Laketown, *Book "A,"* 86, Iron Mike, township road, March 27, 1862; 8, public highway field notes, February 4, 1865.

Nordberg, Mrs. Rueben (Lucy Ryther), "Autobiographies of Louise and Theodore Nordberg," unpublished personal history as well as collection of papers in Mrs. Rueben (Lucy) Nordberg's possession. Lucy Nordberg was a teacher at the public school in Victoria in the 1930s and was married to Louise and Theodore's son Rueben on June 5, 1935. She was widowed in 1957 and today resides in Park Rapids.

Throdahl, June (Justus). Biographical information about Andrew Justus was compiled by June Throdahl and received by Josephine Mihelich on November 6, 1982. The Lundsten papers, "The Saga of Sunny Hill Farm," page 6, noted that Andrew Justus and his family arrived in the first Packard to have been driven on the lane leading to Lundsten's home.

Interviews

Brethorst family interview (taped) by Josephine Mihelich during a family gathering held September 27, 1979, at the country home of Charlie Maas near Delano.

Buelow, Anna, June 28, 1978, conversation with Josephine Mihelich.

Chapter 14

Holcombe and Bingham, *Compendium,* 250, Joseph Frey, soldier and former owner of John Nelson's farm.

Unpublished Sources

Nelson, John and Benedicta. Personal church papers are from the collection of granddaughter Amy Nelson (Mrs. Earl Lyford of St. Paul) and were translated by Susanna Thilquist.

Chapter 15

Centennial Anniversary of Moravian Church of Lake Auburn, 1858-1958, p. 7 ([Chaska?], 1958).

Holcombe and Bingham, *Compendium,* 287, Henry Gerdsen; 294, John Holtmeier; 324, George Ottinger; 329, Henry Rietz.

Mumford, A. H., *Our Church's Story, Being a History of the Moravian Church for Young People,* 9-12 (London, 1911).

Unpublished Sources

Laketown Book *"A,"* 114, power of attorney.

Interviews

Ottinger, Mrs. Arthur (Esther), March 7, 1981, conversation with Josephine Mihelich.

Related Reading

North American Moravian. This official journal of the Moravian Church in America, published in Bethlehem, Pa., featured the following articles of local and national historical interest:

Dreydoppel, Susan M., "With Their Hands," April, 1983, p. 22. A story about Carver County Moravians Herman Holtmeier and Frederic Schwalbe and their missionary work in Alaska.

Fries, Adelaide L., and Minnie J. Smith, "200 Years at Friedland" (Winston-Salem, N.C.), February, 1975, p. 15-19.

Heath, Marvel R., "Fiftieth Anniversary of Lake Auburn Home," November, 1978, p. 3-5.

Marx, Elizabeth, "We Welcome You," March, 1978, p. 7.

Schattschneider, "John Hus...and Us," July/August, 1979, p. 9-12.

House and Garden, "Sharing a Celebration–July Fourth in Old Salem," 22-29 (July, 1973).

Kuest, Frank, "America's Bethlehem," in *The American Legion Magazine,* 4 (December, 1977).

Nelson, Vernon H., "Life in Early America: The Moravians at Bethlehem," in *Early American Life,* 26-29 (August, 1978).

Ondovisik, Maryann, "Little Town of Christmas," in *Holly Hobbie's Home Times,* 34-37 (Winter, 1979).

Chapter 16

Holcombe and Bingham, *Compendium,* 284, Swan Freed.

Tideman, *Church History,* 33.

United States Census, 1860, Carver County, 41.

Unpublished Sources

Swenson, "Membership Records," 493.

Chapter 17

Alderman, William H., *Development of Horticulture on the Northern Great Plains,* p. 29, 74 (St. Paul, 1962).

Blegen, *History of the State,* 200, 291, 395, 400-403.

Bowen, Ralph H., ed., trans., *A Frontier Family in Minnesota: Letters of Theodore and Sophie Bost,* 284 (Minneapolis, 1981).

Green, Samuel Bowdlear, "Apples to Plant," *Farm, Stock and Home,* 7:360 (September 15, 1891).

Holcombe and Bingham, *Compendium,* 123, first agricultural fair in Minnesota.

Map of Carver County, Minnesota–Dahlgren and Chanhassen Townships, (Minneapolis, 1880); homesteads of Charles Luedloff and Theodore Bost.

Minnesota Horticultural Society, *Annual Report, 1884,* p. 171-174; *1898,* p. 194.

Seymour, E. L. D., *The Wise Garden Encyclopedia,* 624 (New York, 1951).

Waconia Patriot, September 15, 1977, p. 9A.

Weekly Valley Herald (Chaska), September 18, 25 and October 16, 1868.

Chapter 18

Blegen, *History of the State,* 291.

Holcombe and Bingham, *Compendium,* 241, local breweries.

Scott, *History,* 354.

Chapter 19

Unpublished Sources

Peterson, Andrew's letter, dated October, 29, 1897, to his niece, Mrs. Fred (Ruth) Johnson, is now in the Wettstein collection, "Our Linnéa Story."

Peterson, Carl, and the information on his marker at the Kirkwood, Illinois, cemetery is from the papers of Terrell Anderson, great-grandson of John and Maria Christina Anderson.

Wettstein, "Our Linnéa Story"; Linnéa Andrén's letters to Wettstein, August 21, 1961, Cousin Amy and terrible happenings; June 20, 1961, Swedish Academy and Grandmother's death in 1892. Used with permission from Helen Wettstein.

Chapter 20

Hartley, Lucie K., *The Carver Story,* 23 ([California, 1971]). This excellent book covers the lives of families and events in Carver. Additional information is in *Chaska: A Minnesota River City,* by La Vonne E. Barac (vol. 1, the 1800s, and vol. 2, 1900-1950) ([Missouri, 1976 and 1980]); *Cologne: The first 100 years,* by Rosie Fahey, Marcia Tellers, and Lorna Wolter (Chaska, 1981); *Norwood Centennial 1872-1972,* by Conrad R. Haarstad (Glencoe, 1972); *The 125th Anniversary of the City of Young America, Minnesota, 1856-1981* ([Norwood], 1981); and *Watertown Centennial 1856-1956,* by Mr. and Mrs. William Maas, Mr. and Mrs. Walter Vodegel, and Claude C. Teas ([Minneapolis], 1956). These historical works also illustrate with pictures some of the social and economic conditions affecting the pioneers in this story.

Moberg, Vilhelm, *Last Letter Home,* 382 (New York, 1956), English translation copyright (c) 1961-1978 by Gustaf Lannestock. With publisher, Popular Library, permission and Albert Bonniers, Foreign Rights.

Smålands-Tidningen, December 28, 1961, "Former Native of Svinhult in U.S.A. Model for the Emigrants' Karl Oskar"–a photo caption.

Unpublishd Sources

Wettstein, "Our Linnéa Story." The original copy of the last letter home has since been made part of Vilhelm Moberg's permanent manuscript collection which is housed at the Emigrant Institute in Växjö, Sweden. The translation, by Elsa Carlson, a friend of Helen Wettstein, has been included with the letter, newspaper articles, and photographs in the scrapbook called "Our Linnéa Story." Although the Minnesota Historical Society has a copy of this letter today, it was not part of its collection when Moberg was doing his research in the archives.

The envelope addressed to Widéen bears three postmarks: Waconia, April 19, 1898; New York, April 21, 1898; and Laholm, 1898.

Chapter 21

Minnesota Horticulural Society, *Annual Report*, 1898, p. 194, tribute.

Waconia Patriot, Obituaries: October 23, 1908, p. 8, Josephine; June 30, 1921, p. 8, Frank; March 16, 1922, p. 1, Elsa; January 10, 1929, p. 1, George; March 13, 1930, p. 1, John; July 31, 1941, p. 1, Oscar; November 6, 1941, p. 1, Charles; May 27, 1943, p. 1, Emma.

Weekly Valley Herald (Chaska), April 7, 1898, p. 8, Andrew Peterson's obituary.

Chapter 22

Waconia Patriot, May 15, 1975, p. A4, one of several feature stories (from past editions of the *Patriot*) related to visitors, boat excursions, and the history of Coney Island of the West.

Waconia Patriot, August 26, 1904, p. 1, September 2, 1904, p. 1, both on tornado.

Unpublished Sources

Carver County, *Clerk's Book of Records*, School District 17, 1903-1915, p. 17, sold wrecked school; in Carver County Historical Society, Waconia.

Chapter 23

Beijbom, Ulf, and Sten Almquist, "Vilhelm Moberg: In Memoriam," *The Swedish Pioneer Historical Quarterly*, 25:72 (January, 1974). See page 72 for picture of Vilhelm Moberg and the Scandia Baptist Church.

Blegen, *History of the State*, 396-398, cooperatives; 400, community clubs and farming interest.

Folwell, *Minnesota*, 4:334, 337.

Holcombe and Bingham, *Compendium*, 305, Herbert Lohmar; 334, John Swanson.

Meyer, Paul S., *100 Years of Gospel Work* 1855-1955, n.p. ([Waconia?], 1955).

Tideman, *Church History*, 24, discipline.

Waconia Patriot, May 26, 1927, p. 10, November 10, 1927, p. 1, cooperative creamery.

Unpublished Sources

Carver County, *Clerk's Records*, District 17, 1903-1915, p. 14, Estella L. Elke, specifications and cost; 27, January 31, 1927, type of school and cost.

Mulhern, Florence. A personal paper entitled, "The 4-H History of Florence Mulhern" currently exists with research papers compiled for this book. This material had been prepared by Mulhern and includes the signatures of former 4-H members Sarah M. Peterson and her sister Ruth. They verified statements made in this summary of information on June 20, 1981.

Peterson, Milo, "The Community Club as a Factor in Rural Life" (research papers prepared for college).

Interviews

Interviews with John Klatt and William Peltz, August 4, 1977, and November 18, 1977; Albert Schwichtenberg, November 5 and December 27, 1977; and Arnold Westphal, May 19, 1982. Westphal's family operated a creamery near Milwaukee at Hartford, Wisconsin. He also followed a career similar to that of his parents, after graduating in dairying from the University of Wisconsin at Madison.

Related Reading

Benson, Louis, *Trinity Lutheran Church, Watertown, Minnesota, 1858-1983* ([Wayzata], 1983). This book was published with help from a special committee, which updated reports about past activities and gathered all of the photographs used in the church history.

Kruger, Robert L., *East Union Lutheran Church, One-Hundred Twenty-Five Years, 1858-1983* ([Chaska], 1983). Ardis Patterson and Gayla Mattson helped compile the information printed in this book.

Kurger, Robert L., *West Union Lutheran Church, One-Hundred Twenty-Five Years, 1858-1983* ([Chaska], 1983). This project reached its conclusion through the effort of committee members Marion Johnson and Kay Hunt.

Chapter 24

Lundquist, Abrah. "Song of Småland" copyright ©.

Vetlanda Posten, April 1, 1961, "Småland's Song was written in ten minutes – since childhood her heart is in Bellö, says the vivacious author."

May 13, 1961, "Småland is the name of the beloved [or cherished] area."

May 16, 1961, "The Smålands song concert received praise from the press. 'Song of the home area' is worthy of being a folk song."

Smålands Tidningen, December 28, 1961, "A Unifying Song"– a subtitle.

Smålands Tidningen, (?), November 6, 1962, "Småland is in Mourning. Linnéa Andrén is Dead."

Widéen, Harald, The Composer-Ivar Widéen's Published Works; posthumous unpublished material (104 pages), Gothenburg, Sweden, 1936, translated by Susanna Thilquist. The combined effort of Ivar Widéen and Linnéa Andrén, "The Song of Småland," appears in the following musical publications:

Men's Choir, Abrah. Lundquist's Music Publishers, Stockholm.

Men's Quartets (1912), no. 6 in the Quartet Library.

Songs for Men's Voices, library at the Musical Academy in Sweden, 1911-15, 1921-25, arranged by Edv. Akerberg – piano with words (1912).

Music for the Home for Piano, 46, with words. Beautiful Ballads, Folk Songs, Students' Songs, Bellman's Melodies, Songs from Operas, Marches, Hymns and Chorales (1921-25).

Popular Songs for Piano, 8, 9., library at the Musical Academy in Sweden, 1916-20.

Songs for Mixed Choir, 1931-44, no. 21.

The Home Community Choir, no. 1.

The Ladies Choir, no. 42. Songs for training schools and other similar secondary schools, arranged in three and more parts by Herman Berens (Stockholm, 1913).

Swedish Songs, Eggeling's Songbook, no. 35. For school and home, published by Malin Holmstrom-Ingers (1917).

Werther Carlsson, *Choir Songbook for Secondary Schools and Young People's Schools together with an Outline of Music History,* no. 54 (Stockholm, 1925).

Smålands Student Society in Uppsala Songbook, 11 (1936).

Swedish School Quartets, no. 94 (Stockholm, 1950).

The Temperance People's Songbook, no. 70 (Stockholm, 1954).

Abrah. Lundquist's Orchestra Library, no. 118 (1931-44).

To Smålands Singers Association.

Unpublished Sources

Wettstein, "Our Linnéa Story," Linnéa Andrén's letters to Helen Wettstein,

June 20, 1961, the best about "Smålands Sangen"; August 21, 1961, remarks about Halmstad; September 30, 1962, Linnéa's reports of contributions from America in *Göteborg's Handels- och Sjofartstidning.* Used with permission from Helen Wettstein.

Chapter 25

Arboga Tidning/Bärgslagsbladet, September 1, 1978, p. 16, "Unique Emigrant Document in Arboga Tor is Related to Moberg's Karl Oskar."

Chisago County Press, June 7, 1978, p. 3, "Shared History," and August 30, 1978, p. 13, "Waconia diaries share Karl Oskar History."

Minneapolis Tribune, November 20, 1977, "Searching for Sunrise; A Swedish Saga" featured in the *Picture* magazine section of the Sunday paper.

Unpublished Sources

Carver County Historical Society *Certificate of Incorporation,* October 30, 1950, p. 1, Article 2. Although the statement, "to bring about the preservation of buildings, monuments, and markers" was an important corporation priority, this program had not been implemented on the local level. (Wendelin Grimm's farm received National Register credentials through an isolated site survey report prepared by the Minnesota Historical Society prior to 1976.) Records of Articles of Incorporation and Bylaws are located in the Carver County Historical Society, Waconia, and Minnesota Historical Society, St. Paul.

Related Reading

Carver County Herald (Chaska), May 20, 1976, "Historic sites in Carver County: Facing the issues," was the beginning of a series of articles printed about the open forum, survey work, and the Harvest Festival. Other stories appeared in the following editions: May 27, June 3, 17, September 2, October 7, 1976; August 17, October 19, December 21, 1977; January 4, 18, 25, February 15, August 9, and September 13, 30, 1978.

Carver County News (Watertown), May 20, 1976, "Open forum at Waconia," was the beginning of a series about the forum, survey work, and the Harvest Festival. Other articles appeared in the following editions: June 3, 17, September 2, October 7, 1976; September 15, October 27, 1977; January 19, 26, August 10, and September 7, 21, 1978.

Chisholm Free Press, September 15, 1978, "A Swedish journalist finds people on the Range extra special"; September 21, 1978, p. 8, "Swedish festival to be held at historic site."

Johnson, Emeroy and Barbro Roehrdanz, *A Guide to Swedish Minnesota* (Minneapolis, 1980). This comprehensive book about Swedish settlements in Minnesota includes statements about a variety of popular attractions throughout the state.

Kirkeide, Leslie, "Harvest Festival to honor pioneers," *The Farmer,* September 2, 1978, p. 70.

Lofstrom and Spaeth, *Historic and Prehistoric Places.* A map or guide has been featured with information about places included in site survey reports prepared for Carver County. Most of the landmarks have been listed on the National Register of Historic Places—a direct result of the Open Forum held June 9, 1976.

Minneapolis Tribune, June 6, 1976, "Historic sites to be subject of Waconia forum," September 17, 1978, "Festival will celebrate legacy of hardy pioneer from Sweden."

"Minnesota County to honor pioneer farmer in Waconia," *Swedish Council News,* Summer, 1978, No. 3.

Norwood Times, May 20, 1976, "Carver County open forum is June 9." Articles about the forum, survey work, and the festival also appeared in the editions of June 3, 17, August 26, September 8, 1976; September 22, October 27, 1977; January 26, August 10, and September 7, 21, 1978.

Waconia Patriot, May 20, 1976, "Open Forum on historic sites scheduled June 9." This and other articles about the forum, survey work, and the festival appeared in the editions of May 27, June 3, 17, August 26, October 7, 1976; January 27, April 14, September 5, October 27, December 8, 1977; January 5, 19, 26, February 16, March 2, July 20, August 10, 31, and September 21, 1978.

Chapter 26

Profile: Hennepin County, supplement in *Minneapolis Tribune,* January 28, 1979, includes a report about Wendelin Grimm's farm.

Tideman, *Church History,* 36, 38.

Related Reading

ADvocate, December 14, 1981, p. 3, "Christmas; once a more simple time of ingenuity, creativity." This account, printed in a local advertising circular, is the beginning of a series of articles called "Looking Back." They were compiled and written by members of the Carver County Historical Society and concluded July 17, 1982, p. 8, with "Main Street in the 30s."

Waconia Patriot, April 10, 1975, p. A4, "A history of Coney Island (Paradise Island) and Clearwater Lake (Lake Waconia [Waconia Lake]) in Carver County, Minnesota." This story was compiled by newspaper editor Elmer F. Miller from old newspaper accounts as well as college papers written by Donna Bean and Grace Lahr. The series concluded with Frank Sisser's, "Final reflection; Coney Island Today: The skeleton of better days," on November 13, 1975, p. 2. This entire account was also repeated in 1981 as a series in the *ADvocate,* an advertising circular.

INDEX

References to the property map on page 20 are given in this index as follows:

Nilsson, the Reverend Frederick Olaus *(map 20: 41, 47, 47A).*